FINDING RADHA

Finding
Radha

THE QUEST FOR LOVE

Edited by

MALASHRI LAL *and*
NAMITA GOKHALE

PENGUIN BOOKS
An imprint of Penguin Random House

PENGUIN BOOKS

USA | Canada | UK | Ireland | Australia
New Zealand | India | South Africa | China | Singapore

Penguin Books is part of the Penguin Random House group of companies
whose addresses can be found at global.penguinrandomhouse.com

Published by Penguin Random House India Pvt. Ltd
4th Floor, Capital Tower 1, MG Road,
Gurugram 122 002, Haryana, India

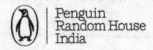

Penguin
Random House
India

First published in Penguin Books by Penguin Random House India 2018

Introduction copyright © Namita Gokhale and Malashri Lal
This anthology copyright © Penguin Random House India 2018
Copyright for the individual essays vests with the respective authors
Pages 249–51 are an extension of the copyright page

The views and opinions expressed in this book are the authors' own and the
facts are as reported by them, which have been verified to the extent possible,
and the publishers are not in any way liable for the same.

While every effort has been made to trace copyright holders and obtain permission,
this has not been possible in all cases; any omissions brought to our attention
will be remedied in future editions.

ISBN 9780143441458

Typeset in Adobe Garamond Pro by Manipal Digital Systems, Manipal

Printed at Repro India Limited

www.penguin.co.in

MIX
Paper from
responsible sources
FSC® C047271

To the memory keepers and all who remember and record the stories of our culture

To the friends and colleagues who have helped and sustained these efforts

To Sudhir Mathur for his unstinting support of the arts and creative spaces

To Aman Nath for, once again, finding the image that mirrored the essence of the book

To Radha, in all her forms and manifestations

CONTENTS

ACKNOWLEDGEMENTS

WE ARE GRATEFUL to the scholars and writers who generously shared their thoughts, published as well as unpublished, and contributed their unique perspectives to this anthology. We thank the copyright holders for their permissions from the diverse sources, which are listed separately. We thank our friends Alok Bhalla and Alka Tyagi, who suggested and helped us track rare sources. We acknowledge and appreciate the inspired and meticulous assistance from Anisha Lalvani and are grateful for the professional expertise of Dr Sufian Ahmad, librarian, Sahitya Akademi, and Debasmita Dutta for her research. Deep gratitude to Manasi Subramaniam for her acute eye in shaping the emerging manuscript, Rachita Raj for her patient editing and Gunjan Ahlawat for bringing the book to life. Thank you again, friends and family, for cheerfully supporting our passion—and sometimes madness—in our quest for Radha.

INTRODUCTION: THE DREAM OF THE AWAKENED

NAMITA GOKHALE

HOW DID RADHA come to me? Perhaps it was when I was roaming the narrow lanes of Vrindavana, in search of these elusive mysteries. Amidst the groves of ancient basil bushes stood a room with a bed in it, designed in the style of a government guest house in a minor mofussil town. It had iron shutters through which I could glimpse a postered bed. It was here that they met, those two, in a timeless nocturne, through the yugas, across the ages.

The attendant priest handed me a bundle of prasad. The packet he gave me contained some sweet crumbling pedas, fragrant tulsi leaves, a folding mirror, some bindis, glass bangles, a bottle of cheap fluorescent-pink nail polish. The last three items constituted a traditional 'suhag ka pitara', a gift symbolizing the auspicious feminine. It was a moment of illumination. The importance of it, the crucial nuance, came to me in a flash. The mirror was a gateway to the recognition of selfhood. The bangles were a form of armour. I don't ever wear bindis, but they represent the awakening of the third—the inner—eye. It was the nail polish that moved me the most, it spoke to me of hopes and yearnings and betrayals, the entire tradition of 'shringara rasa', the evocation of the mood of romantic and erotic love from the *Natyashastra* that is such a deep undercurrent of Indian culture.

We began this quest for Radha some years ago, after Dr Malashri Lal and I had completed our edited anthology *In Search of Sita*. Radha is an all-too-human goddess, a sublime yet sensual emblem of mortal and divine love. She is subversive in that she possesses an autonomy rarely available to feminine deities. She lives by her own rules, and not those of the world. She is the essential Rasika, the aesthete of passion, and her wild heart belongs only to herself.

Like Sita, Radha is also a manifestation of Lakshmi. Radha is the essential Shakti of Krishna, just as Sita is the consort of Rama. Yet their lives span very different arcs. Sita is the sterling emblem of familial duty, who unflinchingly complies with the diktats of her patriarchal and hierarchical world. She is relentlessly questioned and tested, and subjected not once but twice to the 'Agni *pariksha*', the test by fire, driving her to relinquish the harsh obligations of royal conduct and return deep into the womb of the earth mother.

Radha, the bucolic milkmaid, follows the dictates of her heart, of her instincts, of her passion, to seek union with her innermost self. She is her own mistress even in the act of surrender to her beloved. And it is this aspect of her that is worshipped, if not emulated, in shrines, temples and festivals all across India even today.

The enigma of Radha and the example of Sita coexist and are both contained in the apparent paradoxes and composite unity of the Hindu religion. The lack of any textual references to Radha in the Mahabharata, and the only indirect allusions in the *Srimad Bhagavatam*, establish that the rebellious figure of Radha was born of the ahistorical collective consciousness of religion and culture. She was born of the need to establish a direct emotional and mystical relationship, a sensual, tactile, immersive connect, with the sacred. Radha's divine lover, Krishna, was later married to Rukmini, and to Satyabhama, and later in some texts, to Jambavanti. Yet he remained hers, and she his, in the hearts and minds of the devout.

India's great epics and scriptures were born of orality; they have been retold, reinterpreted and reimagined through millennia. Even as the plasticity and porous narrative of oral traditions yielded to the stricter boundaries of textual veracity, the format of palm-leaf manuscripts was amenable to interpolations and imaginative embellishment. These acts of appropriation and interpretation and translation through successive generations, through the centuries, led to the continuous rediscovery of the core stories, and kept them relevant and contemporary across the passage of time. They were birthed anew and belonged to each poet, scribe or bard, each dancer and sculptor, who bestowed them with form and creative reality.

The figure of Radha was first mentioned in the medieval period, in the exquisite *Gita Govinda* of the poet Jayadeva of modern-day Odisha, and in the maha-mantra of Radha and Krishna extolled by Nimbakacharya in the 11th and 12th centuries. This anthology carries many perspectives on how the visualization and iconography of 'Radharani' evolved, through the Chaitanya school of Vaishnavism, and the philosophical and poetic interpretations of the Bhakti movement. These traditions were continued in the late 15th century in the magnificent poetry of Chandidas of Bengal and Vidyapati of Mithila, and later in the verses of the blind seer Surdas.

The essence of the relationship between Radha and Krishna resides in its spontaneous acquiescence to the moment of joyous union, and its disregard for imposed social boundaries in love, sacred or profane. This sense of abandonment, of surrender, would have been, and still is, exhilarating and liberating in a prescriptive and regimented society.

The sensory and the physical are as profound as all the navel-gazing in the cosmos. Our duplicitous and illusory world belongs to the realm of what is described as maya, and we are all entangled in the 'maya *jaal*', in the phantasmagorical web of the virtual and the unreal. The amorous frolics of the divine lovers are described not as Maya but as Leela, as the eternal play of consciousness, the dream of the awakened.

As with depictions of Shiva and Parvati, there is a remarkable gender fluidity in images of Radha and Krishna. She is him as he is she; together they are '*ardha* Radha Venudhara'—the two halves of one self, joined in the ultimate rasa of spiritual rapture. In the complicated inversions that come so easily to Hindu mysticism, Shri Radha is Krishna himself represented in female form. Her relationship with the other milkmaids, the *gopi*s, is one of sisterhood.

The *sakhi*, or female friend and confidante, is an important motif in the tales of Radha and Krishna, celebrating sorority and the dance of love.

Radha consciousness, so deeply rooted in this soil, continues to emerge in the most unexpected ways. Manipur is in the northeast of India, bordering Burma, and has a special connect with the Mahabharata, as the ancient lineage of its royal family supposedly traces it genealogy from the Pandava prince Arjuna and his wife, Chitrangada, who was from these parts. I encountered the Manipuri Raas Leela in the translated memoirs of the great writer Princess Binodini. This is how she describes it.

> During the offering of *Maha Raas* to Lord Govinda, in the episode called *The Disappearance of Krishna*, Tamphasana would wear ritually pure clothes and enter the enclosed circle of the performance hall of Lord Govinda very early on. Later, at the time of Krishna's disappearance, she would sing the role of Krishna. I remember the song even today as it was rehearsed often in our house. It went like this:
>
> *When you can walk no more*
> *Beloved Radha*
> *Place your feet upon my shoulder*
> *My dear Subadani*
>
> This is how I remember it. How sweetly my frail sister sang it! I remember how, when she sang, my father would hasten from his royal seat, and weep as he offered his turban and prostrated himself before the Brahmin dance teacher. In those days it was not the custom to enter the dance circle in the performance hall to offer scarves or money. It was especially prohibited at the palace. If anybody offered anything, it could only be to Lord Govinda.[1]

Vaishnavism came to Manipur around 1470, and the 17th-century monarch Rajarshi Bhagya Chandra established the practice of ritual

Raas Leela, incorporating the Meitei interpretation of Vaishnavism into the spiritual force of a dance form in the tender Madhura Raas and the devotional Bhakti Raas.

Be it the continuity of dance traditions in Manipur or the ever-popular devotional songs of Meera Bai, interpreted through cinema, Radha lives on in everyday life around us. The emotions invested in her are intense and intuitive.

Then there is the intriguing figure of self-admitted spiritual guru Radhe Maa, whose videos from various *jagrans* have gone viral on the Internet. Radhe Maa was born Sukhvinder Kaur to a Sikh family in the Gurdaspur district of Punjab. Initiated at the age of twenty-three by the Paramhans Dera in Hoshiarpur to become 'Radhe Maa', she gained an influential disciple early on, whose family owned a chain of successful sweet shops. Her clothes, lipstick, the furniture, carpets and curtains, even the ceilings in her bungalow in Borivili, Mumbai, are all painted red, as are the lifts in the building. Her life as a self-proclaimed god-woman and cult leader has been mired in controversy and litigation. Her website and Facebook account reveal a standard sanctimonious tone interspersed with whacky photographs. She looks like a downmarket model, with good skin and an admirable figure for her fifty-plus age group. A 'hot avatar', she poses in red miniskirts and boots. She has an eye for the news, and there are photographs of her in a red bikini in circulation. The Akhil Bharatiya Akhara Parishad, the apex body of Hindu sadhus, has mentioned her on their list of fourteen 'Fake Spiritual Leaders'.

What does Radhe Maa of Borivili have to do with her namesake Radha, the beloved of Krishna, and their pastoral romance? I pondered this, and I do not know. It is one of the mysteries of Hinduism, where everything becomes the opposite of what it once was.

The ignominies of popular culture and social media natter continue to embarrass my online research. An evocative thread describes Radha 'becoming like a side character of a movie, disappearing after the interval'.

So let me return to stories of long ago, and a tale I encountered in a now-forgotten book, of how Radha, as an aged woman, travelled to Dwarka to meet Krishna. She was old and tired, and the journey took its toll on her. When they met, the intervening years fell away, and their hearts beat as one. She feasted her eyes, and her spirit, on the divine presence of Krishna, though no words were exchanged between them. No one in the splendorous city of Dwarka, with its spired roofs and silver domes, knew who the wrinkled woman was, but she was given shelter and a place to stay.

One day she set off for the forest. She and Krishna were still one, as they always had been. He followed her and they met, once again, in the dark night, amidst the scented jasmine bushes. Radha's time was near, and she was about to leave her body.

He asked what she wished of him. 'Play the flute for me,' she said. And so Krishna coaxed a divine melody from his wooden flute and dedicated the raga to Radha, the milkmaid of Gokul. As she listened to him, her soul left her body and merged into his. His flute fell silent. Infinitely saddened, yet secure in her presence within him, he broke the flute into two and threw it away. He never played the flute again, but the melody to Radha remained ever in his heart.

INTRODUCTION: RADHA THROUGH MANY EYES

MALASHRI LAL

Krishna-pranadhidevi cha
She is the presiding deity of Krishna's life

GROWING UP IN Jaipur, the imposing Govind Devji temple in the City Palace was a constant presence in my cultural thinking. The story of its origin pointed towards the inextricable links between religion and society, history and myth, oral and scripted expressions, and that emblem of a protean culture in India has continued to shape my research and writing. When Namita Gokhale and I framed the concept note for our book *Finding Radha: The Quest for Love*, about three years ago, the composite Indian ethos was foremost in our minds. Like our previous book together, *In Search of Sita: Revisiting Mythology*, the fascination with our inherited and malleable legends came to rest on another less-understood figure, Radha. In my imagination, embellished by folklore, Lord Krishna at Govind Devji began to speak of how he was shaped by an assiduous sculptor Bajranabh, who just couldn't get His image right, till an elderly woman, who was watching the sculptor labouring over his third attempt at the statue, suddenly pulled down her *ghunghat* and whispered shyly, 'That is Him'.

Was this woman the generic Radha, the eternal partner of Krishna through the ages and many tales? She knows that Krishna is mercurial and hard to capture, but she rests secure in the knowledge that He cannot remain independent of her love. From Puranic literature to contemporary times, writers, painters, musicians and dancers have interpreted the legend of Radha–Krishna in multiple configurations, and through a range of philosophies that straddle earthly realism as well as ephemeral abstractions. But Radha, she eludes the grasp, preferring to stay mysteriously out of reach, making possible another attempt and yet another. We found innumerable publications on the divine Krishna, but almost no centrality was given to Radha in the telling of this timeless romance except in three books, John S. Hawley and Donna M. Wulff's *The Divine Consort: Radha and the Goddesses of India* (1982); Heidi R.M. Pauwels's *The Goddess as Role Model: Sita and Radha in Scripture and on Screen* (2008); and Harsha V. Dehejia's *Radha: From Gopi to Goddess* (2014). Elsewhere, we found insightful chapters within books, but Radharani was one among other divinity figures, not quite commanding a pedestal of her own. Hence our book, where we follow Radha's perspective in texts of literary and cultural value and encourage scholars and writers to present reconstructions of Radha's story. Krishna's charm and dalliance, wisdom and sagacity, are revealed through Radha's eyes, and her words, poignant and passionate, flow with those of the *gopi*s, who are collective participants in the cosmic play of their beloved God.

The Origins of Radha

Almost nothing is known of the origins of the beautiful and nurturing Radha, except in the folklore of Barsana (in the Mathura district of modern-day Uttar Pradesh), said to be her birthplace. Since it is believed that the original temple of 5000 years ago was lost and later reconstructed as Radharani Mandir by Narayan Bhatt, one of the disciples of Chaitanya Mahaprabhu, we value the stories accordingly as devotional offerings. Radha, or 'Shri Laadli Laal' as she is called (meaning 'the most loved one'), resides in an elaborate temple on Brahma Parvat; a smaller temple in the palace courtyard commemorates the family—father Vrishabhanu Maharaj, mother, Kirtida, their daughter, Sri Radharani, and son, Shridama.

Designated areas recall episodes of Radha–Krishna's legend—
Maan Mandir for withdrawal in a sulk, Mor Kutir for the dance of
reconciliation and, interestingly, a pond called Pili Pokhar, where
Yashoda Maiya is thought to have applied turmeric paste to Shri
Radha's hands, accepting her as Krishna's bride.

Literary evidence is far less specific about the physical existence of
Radha. Devdutt Pattanaik says in his essay in this book, 'The earliest
tales of Krishna, found in the Mahabharata, compiled between 300 BC
and 300 AD, only refer to, but do not describe, his [Krishna's] early life
in the village of cowherds. Later, around 400 AD, the *Harivamsa* was
added as an appendix to the Mahabharata. This described in detail
Krishna's life in Gokul, including his dalliances with milkmaids. But
there was no mention of Radha or any particular milkmaid [. . .] The
women were a collective with whom Krishna danced and sported. The
mood was joyful and carnival-like.'

There was clearly a gap between the Radha of folk and classical
imagination, but here, too, scholars may take different positions.
According to Mandakranta Bose, 'The *Vayu, Matsya* and *Varaha
Puranas* mention Radha but it is in the *Devi Bhagavata, Brahma
Vaivarta* and *Padma Purana* that she is described at length . . .
Her elevation is complete when at one point she is identified with
Lakshmi.' Furthermore, Andrew Schelling has recovered the Sanskrit
poems of Vidya, a hardly remembered woman poet, possibly of the
7th century, in which Radha is mentioned by name.

Poised at the cusp of the human and the divine, Radha, this
beauteous girl-woman is said to be an elder relative to whom the
mischievous baby Krishna is entrusted. The games children play in
innocence and whimsy turn gradually into a love game transcending
the taboos of earthly rules. Was Radha a married woman breaking
out of marital restrictions, or, like Meera, Andal and Lal Ded, was
she a mystical seeker of a perfect relationship?

RADHA THE LOVER

As several of our authors in this book have pointed out, the dominant
image of Radha derives from Jayadeva. According to Jawhar Sircar,

'His immortal *Gita Govinda*, composed in the 12th century, set new trends like the *ashtapadi*, or "groups-of-eight lyrical couplets". He could portray divine love with such finesse that he became the fountain of inspiration for countless generations of poets, singers and dancers since then. Though Jayadeva mixed his Sanskrit with Apabhramsa, an Eastern sublanguage, Brahmanical tradition not only accepted him and his Radha–Krishna, but several learned Sanskrit commentaries [. . .] were actually written on Jayadeva's work.'

Interestingly, so little is known about this magnificent writer that people from Odisha and Bengal continue to quarrel about Jayadeva's birthplace, about whether it is Kenduli Sasan in Odisha, or the village Kenduli in Birbhum, West Bengal—the weightage being in favour of Odisha because its dance and music traditions replicate the classic text. Folklore is never far from classicism and it is believed that Jayadeva thought of his dancer wife, Padmavati, when he described the erotic rasas and the several moods of enjoyment and ecstasy. It is said that as he reached the end of the poem where Radha is first angry, then repentant about her peeve with Krishna, words failed him in ascribing any contrite action to Krishna. Jayadeva abandoned the script and went for a ritual bath, during which interregnum the Lord himself silently appeared and wrote the famous verse *'dehi padapallavam udaram'* (Sri Krishna bows down his head at the feet of Sri Radha) into the manuscript.

Every nuance in romantic love is mentioned in this remarkable, though brief, poem. Opening with a dedication to Saraswati and Lakshmi, Jayadeva sets forth on his journey through the mythical land of Radha–Krishna's mutual, idealized love. The forest of Tamala trees offers refuge as well as challenge to the lovers' trysts, for Radha is a *parkiya*—married to another—but she and the women of Braj are irresistibly drawn to the blue God and his flute. His attention flows to all, though especially to Radha, who shows a variety of emotions reflecting the rasas of Indian dramaturgy. Modesty and sexual desire turn to jealousy and anger when Radha finds out about Krishna's dalliance with another gopi, peeve turns to repentance when she expresses unconditional surrender in her love towards her God.

Responding to the enunciation of such rapture, Pavan K. Varma says, 'All lovers could not but reflect in their own personality some part (*ansh*) of the divine love between the two; conversely, the two incorporated in themselves the personality of all lovers. The canvas of their love was seamless, a painting which amplified and mutated itself in a myriad of reflections.' This leads to the further issue of whether Radha's love is bounded by earthly conditions or whether it transcends them to reach another supernal realm. Literary texts provide several details about Radha's married life—the husband, Ayan, could be caring, as in some versions; the mother-in-law and the community could be cursing her for her adultery, a situation imaginatively elaborated upon by Debotri Dhar in her short story 'A Flute Called Radha'; or she could boldly abandon her home as in Ramakanta Rath's *Sri Radha*:

> I have come out of my house,
> dressed for our night of love.
> I have left my last breath so far behind
> I can't go back to it—

Jayadeva's poem influenced a lineage of writing about Radha's unswerving love, sometimes earthly and sometimes transcendent, often reflecting the social conditions of the times. Makarand Paranjape's essay tracks 'the rise and fall of Radha' in sacred literature showing that 'from the 13th to the 17th centuries what the Radha–Krishna relationship represented was love that was simultaneously intensely erotic and devotional'. His extended argument takes the reader through the prime period of Chaitanya Mahaprabhu personally experiencing the exalted state of 'Radha Bhava' (becoming Radha), the tradition of the Bhakti poets who composed delicate verses on Radha's ephemeral expressions of love, and the development of allegorical interpretations that sanitized the embodiment of sexuality. In fact, Paranjape creates a delightful hypothetical conversation between Radha and Mahatma Gandhi on the meaning of love, sexuality and desire.

RADHA THE ECOLOGIST

The twelve cantos of the *Gita Govinda* continue to be adapted into visual compositions and performative arts, gathering the local vocabulary. The eternal love of Radha–Krishna can be enacted only when Nature is in balance, as evident in the descriptions of Barsana, Mathura and Vrindavana.

Dr Kapila Vatsyayan's substantial corpus of writing traces four centuries of the pictorial journey of *Gita Govinda*. Of the eight monographs that present her incisive commentary, we are privileged to reprint her work on the *Darbhanga Gita Govinda*, which introduces the entire tradition of pictorial representation in Rajasthani miniatures and captures the ecological harmony that surrounds the evocations of Radha's love. 'The similes and metaphors of the poem are transformed into natural landscape—flora, fauna, birds and animals. On the surface all of this appears to be an aggregate of decorative stock motifs, underneath it is the transfiguration of the crucial similes and metaphors of the poem.' In various sets of paintings, Dr Vatsyayan describes the significance of the customary 'arched bower with dangling garlands' used in the Rasikapriya and Rasamanjari portfolios and many others. She looks especially for the symbology surrounding the lovers: 'The reference to the doe-eyed Radha also gives rise to the pictorial motif of the doe so frequently mentioned in the *Gita Govinda*. Cuckoos, bees and peacocks sing, hum and dance throughout the *Gita Govinda*. The Mewari artist provides the pictorial counterpart by painting them along with the *chakora* and the *khanjan* (wagtails) in most paintings of this phase . . .'

The analogy between human and non-human life forms gives intriguing primacy to some neglected creatures such as the *bhramar*, or bees. Medieval literature on Radha carries references to the 'bhramar *geet*', or the 'song of the bees', especially in Nanda Das's poem 'Uddhav's Message', which recounts a very moving episode. Krishna left his *leela sthall* of Vrindavana abruptly, without ever giving a reason to his playmates. Radha and the gopis await his return, certain of their bond of passion, but years go by. The all-knowing Krishna understands their puzzlement and sends Uddhav with a message that He, Lord Krishna, is permanently united with each of them, and hence he resides in their souls. The gopis refuse to accept such a false consolation about Krishna's absence and insist that Uddhav give them a better answer. When his repetitions annoy them thoroughly the gopis call him a buzzing bee, a bhramar, that sings noisily, turning in endless circles. Finally, Uddhav realizes the infinite depth of their trust in Krishna and sees such supreme devotion from untutored village belles as superior to courtly knowledge.

RADHA AND THE GENDER QUESTION

When a woman's sexual desire is transformed into eternal spiritual longing and submission, the gender question could be problematic. Can modern readings of Radha configure the story in ways that show power equilibrium without distorting mythical narratology? Alka Pande's essay 'Becoming Radha' brings theoretical and visual information on Krishna and Radha's 'cross-dressing', quite literally for reasons of play but also as a cultural signifier of gender parity. Pande says, 'According to legend, the women of Gokul could not bear the mischievousness of Krishna and decided to take revenge by dressing him as a woman. The popular lyrics of the thumri "Nar Ko Nari Banao" (Make the Lad a Lass) illustrate this. To dress him up as a woman, they make Krishna wear ghaghra and choli. His hands are made red with *alta*, but instead of getting miffed with the gopis, Krishna goes with the flow and partakes in the pleasure. He eagerly demands jewellery and asks for *shringara*. In Indian literature the sixteen traditional adornments of a woman do not merely enhance her beauty—they are also an *arpana* (offering) for her beloved. This is an important aspect of shringara rasa. The retribution turns into a play, or *leela*, between the gopis and Krishna.'

Radha in her turn:

She wears his peacock feather;
She sports his yellow garment,
He wraps himself in her beautiful sari

How charming the very sight of it . . .
The daughter of Vrishabhanu [Radha] turns [into] Nanda's son
[Krishna], and Nanda's son, Vrishabhanu's girl.

Alka Pande presents several examples of the exchange of attire, which visually conveys a strong message of sexual interplay but also of the psychological transference of attributes designated as masculine and feminine. Indic traditions contain the imaging of the *Ardhanariswara* (God as half woman and half man), generally picturized as Shiva and Parvati, the ideal marital pair. Modified into Radha–Krishna, the cross-dressing denotes empathy for the 'other', though Radha finally tells Krishna that he may dress as a woman but he will never experience *viraha* as a woman, which is the deep anguish of parting from the beloved.

Another aspect of the gender question would dwell upon the abjection of Radha after Krishna leaves Vrindavana. We know very little of her childhood, we know nothing of her ageing; Radha enters the mythical imagination as a nubile woman and exits from the pages with the departure of Krishna for Dwarka. Contemporary writers enter this terrain with innovations that are thoughtful. Dharamvir Bharati's *Kanupriya* (translated by Alok Bhalla) can sound cynical with regard to the meaninglessness of words, empty words; Tarashankar's 'Raikamal' (translated by Aruna Chakravarti) might subvert conventional marriage; while Bulbul Sharma may devise Radha's alluring subterfuges to escape a censorious society—all of this iterating the relevance of Radha in our times.

RADHA IN MUSICAL RENDERINGS

Under a canopy of dark clouds one lazy afternoon, the young Rabindranath Tagore wrote the alliterative lines, '*Gahan kusum kunja majhe*' (in the dense flowering woods), the first lyric penned in *Bhanusingher Padavali*, songs about the passionate love of Radha and Krishna, in imitation of the immensely popular poets Vidyapati and Chandidas. The collection started as a prank, with Rabindranath publishing his series in 1877 in a Calcutta-based magazine named

Bharati. He was delighted when word spread about the 'discovery' of a lost Vaishnava poet whose language was a mellifluous blend of Maithili and Bengali. Rabindranath, relishing the gag, wrote a fictional biography of Bhanusingh in 1884, nudging the critics in the direction of the invented language 'Brajabuli' and leaving clues for a comparison with Vidyapati. Though the prank was uncovered, bringing some embarrassment to the perpetrator and his admirers, the *Padavali* earned justifiable popularity for its lyrics and its easy adaptation to dance forms. Lalit Kumar's commentary and translation of *Bhanusingher Padavali* brings attention to Tagore's poetic persona who warns Radha of the pain of separation that awaits her; Bhanu remonstrates, 'Go wait for him in the last shreds / of your innocence, crazy girl / until grief comes for you.' Yet, Radha, though anticipating sorrow, revels in the ardour of her relationship and nature's blessing of their union.

Not far from Tagore, Kazi Nazrul Islam was born in 1899 in Churulia, a village in the Burdwan district of West Bengal, and received religious education. As a young man he was a muezzin at the local mosque. Nazrul was fascinated by the character of Radha and deeply empathized with a woman's inner life of hesitantly expressed desire. His famous song 'Tumi Jodi Radha Hotey Shyam' (Shyam! If Only You Were Radha) speculates about exchanging the emotions typically attributed to men and women. Hence, as Reba Som discusses the oeuvre of Nazrul's songs on Radha, 'Many of the songs were unabashed expressions of earthly love, conveying love and longing, dejection and despair.' Nazrul, a revolutionary in politics and an extraordinary composer of lyrics, went on to become the national poet of Bangladesh. Reba translates a selection of songs that illustrate 'Nazrul's sensitive handling of woman's emotions through the idiom of the Radha–Krishna romance, lyrically composed in a woman's voice'. Here is a sample:

Who is he, that Beautiful One?
I find myself resounding in the rhythm of his anklet
In the melody of his flute
In the pain of parting on the Jamuna front

I find myself as blossoms in his songs
In the distant unseen
Who is he, that Beautiful One?

Time has only heightened the fascination with Radha's unconditional, 'illicit' romance although Indian society has witnessed such vast changes in social and sexual mores. Some years after Tagore and Nazrul, the post-Independence generation in India has become increasingly moulded by the impact of television and cinema. In the past two decades the interest in mythology has surfaced and strengthened, perhaps as a counterpoint to colonial education, or by way of identity formation within a local milieu. As Namita and I had mentioned in our introductory chapters to *In Search of Sita*, India enjoys a living mythology where interpretations, innovations and interpolations are encouraged. In *Finding Radha*, a similar energy of interpretive 'newness' is tracked in Bollywood cinema in the essay by Alka Kurian, in which adaptations of Radha's legend through plot and music are foregrounded. From *Mughal-e-Azam*'s haunting 'Mohe Panghat Pe Nandlal Chhed Gayo Re' to 'Bol Radha Bol Sangam Hoga Ki Nahi' in *Sangam*, to 'Radha Kaise Na Jale' in *Lagaan*, the enchanting list is fairly long but also presents an unveiling of societal values when these films were popular. Thus, Radha's synchronicity with the times is established. However, when Sonakshi Sinha delivers an 'item number' for the song 'Radha Nachegi' in the 2015 film *Tevar*, the transformation of Radha is quite radical.

Radha's Legacy

The inheritance from Radha takes several directions, as our book will show. To speak of Krishna is to evoke a rooted tradition of religious and cultural ethnography, to speak of Radha is to enter into the interstices of such narratives.

For one, the religious devotion to Radha remains strong through temple practices and the sampradayas with large followings. Shri Shrivatsa Goswami, acharya of the Radha Raman Temple in Vrindavana, writes his essay from the viewpoint of the Chaitanya sampradaya, which sees the ascetic Chaitanya as 'the complete avatar of both Radha and Krishna'. According to Acharyaji, 'As "quintessence of all essences" Sri Radha is the ultimate answer to the human quest—philosophical, theological, existential.' In his highly modern outlook, the love based on 'equality coupled with intensity makes possible a level of rasa unknown elsewhere'. Visiting Vrindavana, as several of our contributors did, the sound of 'Radhe Radhe' brings resonances of what she stood for—dignity and devotion. Film-maker Madhureeta Anand looked for the legacy of Radha among the widows of Vrindavana, many of whom now receive help from philanthropic organizations. Would the inmates here value Radha, would they be 'celebrating the woman who was a wife, a mother and the lover of Krishna? A woman who clearly had it all and celebrated it with no attachment and no apologies?' asks Anand. She was struck by the unswerving faith of the aged, abandoned widows who lived with the security of their daily routine of worship. 'Radha bhava' was their inheritance, and yet, to idealize this existence on charity is questionable. Some decades before Madhureeta, the late Indira Goswami, lovingly known as 'Mamoni Baideo' in Assam, spent two years amidst the widows of the Radhaswami sect in Vrindavana, entering their fold as a compassionate member but also as a researcher. The novel that ensued from this experience, *Neel Kanthi Braja* (excerpted here in a translation by Gayatri Bhattacharyya), is an amazing narrative combining fact and fiction, autobiography and reflection. Saudamini, the protagonist, is a thinly disguised mask of the author. Despite having a supportive community at most times, Saudamini anxiously probes into the implications of widowhood and takes dangerous risks. In such a context, the legacy of Radha questions the systems of a temple economy. The inquiry goes beyond India in Yudit Greenberg's essay comparing the *Gita Govinda* and *Shir Ha-Shirim* (Song of Songs), comprising one of the Hebrew Bible's twenty-four books portraying the sensuous love between a shepherdess and a shepherd in the land of Israel.

A second kind of legacy lies in secular study circles, to seek Radha's place in Indic traditions. As queried by Meghnad Desai,

'Why was it necessary to invent or create Radha as Krishna's consort? My conjecture is that powerful as he was in battle and diplomacy, not to mention as the person who recites the Geeta to Arjuna, Krishna was lacking something. Rama had Sita. Vishnu had Lakshmi. Shiva had Parvati. But who did Krishna have? 16,108 women would hardly qualify as significant in his life. Krishna needed one woman, one he cared about over all others.' Furthermore, is there a sacred geography attached to Radha–Krishna? Renuka Narayanan opens up the less-researched subject of Radha in the literature of south India: 'In my view, a foundational reason for south India's glad receptivity to Radha is the wistful figure of the girl saint Andal, who is believed to have lived in the Tamil region in the 8th or 9th century, well before Jayadeva in the 12th century and Meera Bai in the 16th century. Andal was found as a baby girl mysteriously left on the ground like Sita, by a priest who brought her up as his daughter. Andal saw Krishna as her husband and is believed to have "merged" into the massive idol of Vishnu at Sri Rangam, the southern centre of Vaishnavism. Her songs remain hugely popular in 21st-century India. Andal, who sang of herself as a gopi, was a great influence on the luminous 10th-century founder of Srivaishnavism, Sri Ramanuja.' Narayanan also speaks of the modern saints, Swami Haridhos Giri of Tiruvannamalai, Tamil Nadu, and Vittaldas Maharaj in Tirupati, Andhra Pradesh.

A third legacy resides in the evolution of spiritual interpretations. Among those who have written on this subject, Shubha Vilas, mentioning the Gaudiya Vaishnava tradition says, 'The beloved consorts of Lord Krishna are of three kinds: the goddesses of fortune, the queens and, foremost of all, the milkmaids of Vraja. These consorts all proceed from Radhika. Just as the fountainhead, Lord Krishna, is the cause of all incarnations, Shri Radha is the cause of all these consorts. The goddesses of fortune are partial manifestations of Shrimati Radhika, and the queens are reflections of her image.' In many ways, the exposition on Radha comes full circle in the belief that she and her Lord are One. In the section 'Songs of Radha', Jayadeva's lines resonate timelessly:

Krishna, without you Radha,
Is scorched by love, a flame that burns
As, with every sighing breath, she yearns.

—From *Gita Govinda: Love Songs of
Radha and Krishna, by Jayadeva*, translated by Lee Siegel

Transiting through the ages, gathering tributes from Surdas, Chaitanya, Vidyapati, Balarama Das and innumerable others, Radha keeps appearing in the cycle of mythology, articulating an infinite, cosmic, inseparable togetherness with Krishna. In Ramakanta Rath's words:

*You are the fragrance of rocks,
the lamentation of each flower [. . .]
the fantastic time that's half-day and half-night,
the eternity of the sea's brief silence . . .*

OTHER BOOKS ON RADHA AND OUR EMPHASIS

We deeply appreciate the works of scholarship on Radha that have preceded our book *Finding Radha: The Quest for Love*. While gaining immensely from these publications, we have tried to present largely fresh material, making the elusive goddess Radha accessible in her many manifestations. Our work will naturally invite a correlation with Heidi Pauwels's excellent work *The Goddess as Role Model: Sita and Radha in Scripture and on Screen* (2008). Indeed, these mythical women are a study in contrast: Sita the loyal wife, Radha the eternal paramour. Pauwels's scholarly introduction explores historical narratives on 'love'; among the chapters are included her superb expositions on TV and film. To avoid an overlap, we have emphasized the power of storytelling and invited scholars to delve into Indic traditions and creative writers to imagine their Radha. Another book of high value is by John Stratton Hawley and Donna Marie Wulff (editors), *The Divine Consort: Radha and the Goddesses of India* (1987), in which the symbols and rituals that are inherent to 'devi' give rise to insightful essays on ancient figures as well as new icons such as Santoshi Maa. The sections on Radha have helped us in formulating our thoughts, specifically in relation to secular and religious debates, and we have extracted some sections from Acharya Shrivatsa Goswami's article. Harsha V. Dehejia (editor), with *Radha: From Gopi to Goddess* (2014), comes nearest to our endeavour, and we are grateful for the permission to reprint two essays from this admirable collection discussing Radha as 'both *kamini* and *ramani*, desirable and beautiful [. . .] both a gopi and a nayika'. Here, too, our corpus is somewhat different. We include creative interpretations, translations and a few essays that enter the religious, mythic, historical, social and cultural dimensions around the figures of Radha and Krishna.

We are grateful to all our contributors for sharing this journey of discovery and self-discovery, because in *Finding Radha* we find ourselves. Raised in a rustic village yet consort to the Lord of the Universe, Radha touches the heart of every Indian who recognizes the integrity of unquestioning love and the power of worship—across regions, across languages, across time. The Raas Leela continues.

1

A MILKMAID CALLED RADHA

DEVDUTT PATTANAIK

IT IS IMPOSSIBLE to think of Krishna without thinking of Radha. Theirs is an eternal love story. The stuff of romantic songs. And, yet, some of the biggest Krishna temples in India do not enshrine the image of Radha. In Puri, Odisha, Krishna is enshrined with his sister, Subhadra, and his brother, Balarama. In Udupi, Karnataka, and Guruvayoor, Kerala, and Nathdwara, Rajasthan, Krishna stands alone as a cowherd boy. In Pandharpur, Maharashtra, and Dwarka, Gujarat, he stands alone with the temple of his wife, Rukmini, nearby. Even the most sacred book of Krishna, the *Bhagavata Purana*, does not mention Radha. To understand this, we have to look at the historical development of Krishna worship in India.

It is difficult for many people to accept that religious ideas have a history of their own. The earliest tales of Krishna, found in the Mahabharata, compiled between 300 BC and 300 AD, only refer to, but do not describe, his early life in the village of cowherds. Later, around 400 AD, the *Harivamsa* was added as an appendix to the Mahabharata. This described in detail Krishna's life in Gokul, including his dalliances with milkmaids. But there was no mention

1

of Radha or any particular milkmaid. The women were a collective with whom Krishna danced and sported. The mood was joyful and carnival-like. In the *Bhagavata Purana*, compiled around the 10th century in south India, where the idea of devotion to God visualized as Krishna was elaborated, Krishna disappears when the milkmaids become possessive and seek exclusive attention. The idea that God (Krishna) loves all with equal intensity was visually expressed by making the women dance in a circle, each one equidistant from Krishna, who stood playing the flute in the centre.

Around this time Prakrit literature began referring to one Radha who was portrayed as Krishna's favourite. In Hala's *Gatha Saptasati*, Krishna removes a dust particle, kicked up by cows, from Radha's eye, thus declaring her exalted position in his heart and humbling the other women. In these songs Krishna is not divine; he is a simple cowherd, a hero of the village folk. The songs lack sensual passion and religious ecstasy. Radha is never wife, and the dominant emotion is one of longing, following separation, an emotion that eventually characterizes the Radha–Krishna relationship.

In the 5th century, the Tamil epic *Silappadikaram* refers to one Nal-Pinnai who was the beloved of Mal (the local name for Krishna). Scholars believe that she represents an early form of Radha. This idea of a favourite milkmaid gradually spread to the north and reached its climax with the composition of the *Gita Govinda*, a Sanskrit song written by Jayadeva in the 12th century AD, in which the passion of the cowherd god and his beloved milkmaid was celebrated in a language and style that took all of India by storm.

Jayadeva was born in a village near Puri, Odisha, which is renowned for the grand temple complex of Jagannath, lord of the world, a local form of Krishna. Research has shown that he was involved with Padmavati, a temple dancer, or devadasi, and perhaps even married her. His work was inspired by both his personal experience and his religious beliefs. Each of Jayadeva's songs is composed of eight couplets, known as *ashtapadi*s. Twenty-four ashtapadis make a chapter and twelve chapters make up the entire work. In it Krishna is identified as the supreme divine being—a radical shift from the earlier scriptures where Krishna is one of the many incarnations of

Vishnu. The book uses extremely ornamented language to describe in intimate detail Radha's passion. As one moves from verse to verse, one is transported from the physical realm into the spiritual realm. The erotic longing becomes the cry of the soul for union with the divine. Such an approach was revolutionary; it fired the imagination of the priests and dancers who made it a part of the temple ritual. Being a major Vaishnava religious centre, hundreds of pilgrims from all over India poured into Puri. Day and night, they heard the priests sing Jayadeva's song of Radha's love for Krishna, with the devadasis depicting her yearning for her beloved in graceful dance steps. Before long the visitors were mouthing the lyrics and taking it back to their villages. In less than a century, the *Gita Govinda* transformed from a temporal parochial literary work into a sacred pan-Indian scripture. It completely revitalized Vaishnavism in the subcontinent and catalysed the rise of the Bhakti (devotional) movement in India.

Before Jayadeva, love and eroticism revolved around Kama, the god of lust, and his consort, Rati, goddess of erotics, who were eulogized by poets such as Kalidasa and scholars such as Vatsyayana. With the rise of the monastic orders of Buddhism and Jainism, Kama was demonized into Mara, who had to be conquered by those seeking enlightenment. In the Puranas, stories were told of how Kama was burnt alive when Shiva, the supreme ascetic, opened his third eye. All things sensual came to be seen as fetters that blocked one's spiritual growth. But Jayadeva changed all that. Through his song he made sensuality and romantic emotion the vehicle of the highest level of spirituality. His Krishna was a reformed Kama. His Radha was a reformed Rati. He turned *kama* (lust) into *prema* (romance). Krishna's love for Radha and Radha's love for Krishna were expressed in physical terms but they communicated a profound mystical experience.

The centuries before the *Gita Govinda* had seen the collapse of Buddhist orders and an increased stranglehold of Brahminism based on caste hierarchy and ritualism. God was visualized either as an ascetic (Shiva) or a king (Vishnu). With the arrival of Islam from the 8th century AD onwards, the exalted status given to ascetics and kings took a beating. Cities were razed to the ground. Poets and artists took shelter in the rural hinterland and there discovered the simple ideologies of the village folk based on love and devotion. It is in this environment that poets such as Jayadeva were inspired to shape God as a simple cowherd, accessible through the simplest of emotions, stripped of complex scholarly erudition.

Inspired by Jayadeva, in the 14th and 15th centuries, poets such as Vidyapati and Chandidas further elaborated the relationship of Radha and Krishna. It was always described as a turbulent shift between separation and union, jealousy and surrender. In a rather bold move, these poets saw Radha as a married woman who broke all social norms to be with Krishna. Some folk narratives of this period suggested that she was Krishna's aunt, married to his maternal uncle. Some said she was older, a mature woman, while he was a boy. Even in the *Gita Govinda*, Radha's union with Krishna always takes place in secret. There is constant reference to the threat of social disgrace. By making the relationship illicit and clandestine, the poets heightened the emotional quotient of the relationship. It was seen as true love that transcended custom and law. Devotees came to realize that Radha was the symbol of all those who were 'married' to social responsibilities, seeking liberation and union with their true love—God—who is Krishna.

Many found the use of these extramarital and incestuous metaphors rather scandalous. They moved towards a different theology in which Radha and Krishna were two halves of the whole. She was the material world, he was the spiritual soul. She was the supreme woman, he was the supreme man. They were Goddess and God whose union gave birth to the universe. The world was seen as Radha, born of Krishna's delight. She was Krishna's *shakti*, or power, one who could never be separated from him. This was the *svakiya* (belonging to Krishna) tradition, which distinguished itself from the *parakiya* (belonging to another) tradition. These were expressed in scriptures such as the *Brahma Vaivarta Purana*.

Despite this, across India, Radha is always Krishna's beloved, never his wife. His wives are Rukmini and Satyabhama. Radha's relationship is different in nature in comparison to Sita's relationship with Ram. While Ram is the model husband and Sita is the model wife, Krishna and Radha represent the great lovers who were destined never to unite. Perhaps that is why, except in religious orders of the Gangetic plains that follow the svakiya tradition, Radha is never enshrined in a temple.

Scriptures say that worldly responsibilities force Krishna to leave the village of cowherds and go to Mathura and thence to Dwarka and Kurukshetra. He has to sacrifice the land of pleasure, *vilasa bhumi*, for the land of duty, *karma bhumi*. He has to rescue a world that was descending into anarchy—where women such as Draupadi are being gambled away by their husbands. Radha has to be given up. After leaving her, Krishna never plays the flute, for Radha was his inspiration. The later Krishna never danced or made music. He is no more the cowherd; he was the charioteer riding into battle.

In time, Radha became a goddess in her own right. Without her, Krishna was incomplete. She was the medium through which Krishna could be realized. Metaphysically, Radha came to represent the truth of our soul, the unexpressed, unrequited longings of our heart, suppressed by social realities, which cry out to Krishna. Krishna acknowledges this truth of our being that society denies, each time he dances with Radha at night, outside the village, in secret.

2

IN SEARCH OF THE HISTORICAL RADHA

JAWHAR SIRCAR

WE CANNOT EVER imagine Krishna without Radha, but not many, perhaps, know that she actually entered the life and legend of Krishna rather late. An even-lesser-known fact is that Krishna himself took his own time to blossom into a dominant figure in Indian mythology. Contrary to what most people are told, Krishna was certainly not visible in the Vedic period—when all that was or is 'holy, good and great in India' is claimed to have appeared. His first mention—just a wisp of it—appears well after the Rig Veda had been completed. It is in the *Chhandogya Upanishad* of the 8th or 7th century BC that we get one 'Krishna, son of Devaki': *Krisnaya-devakiputraya*. However sparse, this single mention of Krishna indicates that some legends about him were possibly in circulation somewhere in the post-Vedic period.

This is about the time when the speakers of an Indo-Aryan language were coming to terms with the indigenous people of India—whom they had earlier reviled, rather intensely. Over the next few centuries we get to hear of him, in bits and pieces, in other texts such as the *Taittiriya Aranyaka*, the Jain sacred tales, Panini's *Ashtadhyayi*,

6

and so on. Vasudeva—as a divine character who is distinct from yet allied to Krishna—makes his first physical appearance a century or so before the Christian Era or the Current Era commenced. On one side of a silver coin of Agotheles the Greek we get an image of Vasudeva–Krishna. We must remember that, during this period, Vasudeva was an independent, established deity, while Krishna was a rather amorphous, upcoming deity on whom there was neither any literature nor any icon, till then. Pierre Amiet and his fellow scholars declare, rather decisively: 'There is no evidence of Krishna (or Radha) in sculpture or coinage or inscription before the Current Era began.'[1]

The first clear image of Krishna appears in the Ekanamsa Group of sculptures of 2nd century AD in Gaya, Bihar,[2] where he appears to have broken free from Vasudeva. But he is still yoked with Balarama, whose images, incidentally, are quite visible in the preceding three centuries. This Kushan-period sculpture of Ekanamsa positions Krishna next to Balarama, with a female who is identified as 'Subhadra', their sister. The first sacred text that mentions Krishna is the *Harivamsa* of the 3rd or 4th century, which collated the hitherto-nebulous or patchy tales about Krishna into one authoritative omnibus. It is around this time that the Mahabharata and the Ramayana had reached the final stage of composition after almost five centuries 'in the making'—busy absorbing and sewing together different, colourful tales from all over the Indo-Gangetic plains and beyond. Yet, though both the *Harivamsa* and the Mahabharata extol the 'mature and godly Krishna', we do not come across any corroborative sculpture or other arts. These are all on Bala-Krishna, as are the large number of sculptural or terracotta representations of Krishna that appear in the next 600 years. Gupta and post-Gupta art depict Krishna as a baby or a child, not as a youth or adult—which thus precludes Radha's arrival altogether.

To reach Radha, we need to cross another six long centuries, to reach the 9th-century sacred text, the *Bhagavata Purana*. But before we come to the first Radha-like young woman in Brahmanical literature, we must mention a secular text that mentions Radha. The *Gatha Saptasati* is a collection of 700 verses composed in Prakrit by a king named Hala. We know that he belonged to the upper Deccan but we do not know the time frame for the same. This could have been in the 2nd century AD, which means this book preceded the final version of the Mahabharata and the *Harivamsa*. Or it could have been composed some three or four centuries later—no one knows. We are taken aback at the explicit reference—pada 225 of the first chapter, that says, 'O Krishna, by the puff of breath from your mouth, as you blow the dust from Radha's face, you take away the glories of other milkmaids.'[3] Not only this, we come across a verse in another work, Banabhatta's *Harshacharita*, which describes how 'the breasts of Radha made Krishna dance in the courtyard, and people were amazed'. It is clear that the myth of Radha and Krishna—including his loves, or *leelas*—was surely known to a section of the masses of India, by the middle of the first millennium of the Current Era. The moot point here is, however, that Radha was still not 'recognized' by Brahmanical religion, even though we find Radha in Jain commentaries. In the 7th century, we see a mention in Bhatta Narayana's *Venisamhara*. Another Jain scholar Anandavardhana also mentions her in his famous *Dhvanyaloka* , which preceded the first Hindu sacred text to refer to her, that too, rather indirectly—the *Bhagavata Purana*.

This Purana speaks of an unnamed lady, who is so much like Radha, but she is not called Radha—she actually remains without a name. In his well-researched work, Sumanta Banerjee[4] states that she has been called Anyaradhita, or the 'conciliated one'—which is an appellation, not a proper noun. And she is conciliated by a Krishna-like cowherd called Mayon who frolics with several *gopi*s and disappears, occasionally, with one of them. The *Bhagavata Purana*, however, mentions that she is usually singled out for special favours. Because the cowherd (not Krishna, by name) is divine, this was his way of teaching humility to all the gopis, and even the special gopi was taught her share, by being abandoned, time and again. Book 10, Chapter 30, Verses 36–38 of this Purana describes it all. This solitary word, 'Anyaradhita', is taken by scholars to be the origin of the proper name 'Radha', but as we have seen, the name Radha was already known. We see how much time it takes a folk deity (or a popular tale or rhyme) to reach the next, higher, level—of finding some mention in a sacred text.

Of course, 'conciliation' of Radha does form an integral part of the Radha–Krishna love story and, however 'humiliating' this act may have appeared to patriarchy, the common people enjoyed it. They could, obviously, identify themselves with the repeated episodes of 'conciliation' of the woman—irrespective of the religiously sanctioned prescription of gender domination. These are the subtextual inferences of societal behaviour that copybook historians usually shy away from—as they are more comfortable with indexed hard references to quote from. In any case, it is interesting to note that Brahmanism finally 'legitimized' the character through a new Sanskrit Purana. It is worth noting that this bold Purana was composed in deep Tamil country and not in Braj or Mathura, and that also, by this time, all the eighteen *Maha-Puranas* had either been completed or had reached a stage of maturity. They were all focused on male deities—Vishnu, Shiva, Brahma, Krishna, Agni, Vayu—and the major exception was the *Markandeya Purana* of the 7th or 8th century, which had 'legitimized' Durga. But the Devi Mahatmya episode did not feature in the main body of the *Markandeya Purana*—it came in through an appendix. We also need to be clear that though the *Bhagavata Purana* surely introduced a Radha-like character, who hailed from the community of herders and milkmen, and it also described in detail the divine dance, the Raas Leela, it is actually a long eulogy of Krishna. 'Thou art Brahman, the ancient One, the immortal One, free from all qualities and miseries. Thou art all-bliss . . . the Lord of the Self, Atmesvara . . . who is to be adored' (VIII.12.7).

The fact that this Sanskrit Purana was written by Tamil scholars hints at the existence of a tradition where romance and unorthodox dalliances were accepted. We need to appreciate that Tamil poetry, notably, Sangam literature, was quite familiar with the spirit of *puranchi*—which was not just lovemaking but a sublime experience. The romance described in the *Bhagavata Purana* was thus in the best traditions of Tamil poetry, especially the *aham* variety. Let us recall the story of Andal to understand how deep was the yearning for the lord in Tamil Vaishnavism, the Alvar tradition. Andal could just not live without him and thus merged herself physically into his idol. It is, therefore, not surprising that Sanskrit writers in the Tamil country were more comfortable with a long poetic tradition that celebrated a spirited gopi, called Nappinnai in Tamil lore, who drew Mayon into her dance and was thus his favourite.[5] It was not only in south India but also in eastern India that we get indications of Radha. In the same 9th century we are intrigued to observe a partner positioned next to a sculpture of Krishna in Paharpur in Pala-ruled Bengal. As we have seen, Jain tradition was more open to Radha, while Brahmanical literature was still reticent or ambiguous about her. Jain scholars like Somadeva Suri and Vikramabhatta, who wrote between the 9th and the 12th centuries, continue mentioning Radha.

The real credit for bringing Radha into the mainstream of devotional poetry, however, goes to Jayadeva in eastern India. His immortal *Gita Govinda*, composed in the 12th century, set new trends like the *ashtapadi*, or 'groups-of-eight lyrical couplets'. He could portray divine love with such finesse that he became the fountain of inspiration for countless generations of poets, singers and dancers since then. Though Jayadeva mixed his Sanskrit with Apabhramsa, an Eastern sublanguage, Brahmanical tradition not only accepted him and his Radha–Krishna, but several learned Sanskrit commentaries like Kumbha's *Rasikapriya*, Shankara Mishra's *Rasamanjari* and Tirumala Deva Raya's *Sruti Ranjana* were actually written based on Jayadeva's work. We also have to mention two other later-15th-century poets, Chandidas of Bengal and Vidyapati of Mithila, who elaborated the path-breaking work of Odisha's Jayadeva very picturesquely. The trio's poetry could finally establish the Radha–Krishna legend beyond any challenge. We must not forget to mention that it was Vidyapati who was able to successfully express, for the first time, the subtle nuances that personify the feelings of a woman, which earlier male poets had missed. However, the pinnacle was reached a century later by Surdas—who broke totally free from Sanskrit tradition. By composing in simple and lyrical Braj Bhasha, Surdas touched the common man as none else could dream of. However, Surdas was an *ashtachap* poet and a follower of Vallabhacharya, who did not agree with the questionable marital status that the Radha–Krishna romance represented—so Surdas overcame the distinctly uncomfortable affair by promptly 'getting them married'. Despite this, Surdas's language and emotions were so intense and his style so utterly masterly that he could describe Radha's pangs as a *virahini* as vividly as a passionate, forlorn lover.

We have reached the 16th century now, which is when one can safely aver that Radha and Krishna became an inseparable and accepted part of the Indian tradition. This is also the time when Mughal miniature paintings appeared and started circulating the finest polychromatic paper images all over India. The Rajput schools and other schools of miniature painting introduced the much-needed visual component to the story of Radha and Krishna. The Bhakti movement was another factor that significantly propelled the romantic tale, with Chaitanya beautifully portraying Radha as the metaphor for yearning 'to be one with the Lord'. Along with literature, visual arts and religion came the powerful and immensely popular medium of mass communication—the performing arts. Radha and Krishna were, thus, united forever. We can conclude this brief account of how Krishna arrived nearly one-and-a-half millenniums after the Vedas were first composed, while Radha took another thirteen centuries more, to make it to the top billing position. A bit of history and a minimal sense of sequencing dates and events will easily belie oft-believed, oft-repeated notions of how deities like Radha–Krishna have always been a part of our history and culture since time immemorial—without dates—i.e. *sanatan*, or eternal. We are not demeaning them—we are only clarifying facts, so that those who know less may not hijack them for their own agenda.

3

RADHA AND THE COMPLETION
OF KRISHNA

MEGHNAD DESAI

OF ALL THE characters, human or otherwise, in Indian lore, none is as natural and as concocted as Radha. She does not have the status of someone with divine—or at least seigneurial—sanction. She is not in Vyasa's Mahabharata or *Harivamsa* or even in the later *Bhagavata* dated around the 8th century.[1] Indeed, she is in no classical story. Krishna is described in those earlier stories as playing with innumerable *gopi*s. He marries eight principal queens and 16,100 minor queens. But his name is not associated with any of the 16,108 women. We do not talk of Krishna–Rukmini or Krishna–Satyabhama. We speak only of Radha–Krishna.

Radha, directly by her name, does not appear in Sanskrit literature till after the 1st century AD. She is created by the imagination of an all too human and mortal poet Jayadeva. Thus, no one can project her truthfully as belonging to the Dwapara Yuga, which ended with the Mahabharata war and heralded the beginning of the Kali Yuga. Krishna may have existed as a historical personality, or not. Swami Vivekananda expressed some doubts about the historicity of Krishna. Kosambi says that the Greeks visiting India around the beginning of the Common Era report the worship of someone resembling Krishna who, for them, was like Hercules. Krishna worship seems to catch on in the early centuries of the Common Era. (I discuss these matters in my book *Who Wrote the Bhagavadgita?*, HarperCollins India, 2015.)

But even if we dismiss all these ideas as mistaken, not to say, blasphemous, and assert that Krishna is as written about in the classics and so pre–Kali Yuga, we have to confess to the later import of Radha as his consort.[2]

Why was it necessary to invent or create Radha? Why did she appear so late in the day as an afterthought? But more important than all that, how come, appearing a thousand years after the Mahabharata, she usurps the position of Krishna's favourite consort? She is generally described as a betrothed—if not married—woman. There is no secret about the passionate lovemaking that the youthful Krishna and this older woman indulge in by the banks of the river in Gokul. She disappears from the later story of Krishna, never to be mentioned again. He leaves her behind but with no recorded farewell meeting. It is as if she does not matter to him. And, yet, it is Radha–Krishna which is the celebrated pair.

Why is this so? Was it not thought of as objectionable that an older (albeit young and attractive) woman was abandoning her husband and indulging in amorous play with a young boy? Were the parents not worried that Radha and Krishna were behaving in a manner that was not a good example to set for their daughters and sons? Even if they were broad-minded and dismissed the behaviour as youthful fancy, why elevate the woman who was indulging in such acts to the status of a divine person or at least the favourite partner of a divine person? Or was it believed that as a god Krishna can break all rules of human decorum? He is to be worshipped, not imitated. The generosity of spirit shown with regard to Radha and Krishna despite their 'immoral' behaviour is refreshing.

There are more subversive aspects to Radha. She is an afterthought, but she also emerges from the periphery of Bharatvarsha rather than the centre of Brahmanical culture. K.M. Munshi—a distinguished Gujarati novelist, the founder of Bharatiya Vidya Bhavan, a prominent member of the Constituent Assembly and a minister in Nehru's cabinet—wrote a seven-volume historical novel about Krishna: *Krishnavatar*. He prefaces his chapter on Radha by saying that Radha is a popular creation. She appears first in Tamil and Prakrit sources. *Silappadikaram*, according to him, has a reference to one Nappinnai as Krishna's wife, who is much like Radha. In the *Gatha Saptasati*, written in the 2nd century AD, there is a mention of Radha. From then onwards, Radha, according to Munshi, is frequently mentioned in the erotic poetry of Prakrit authors. There is also a mention in the stone pillars of the 10th-century King Munj of Malwa (973–994). Miller, in her translation, cited above, confirms the name 'Nappinnai', which comes from the south Indian recession of *Harivamsa*, as Krishna's wife.[3]

The climax comes, of course, in Jayadeva's *Gita Govinda*. Jayadeva was the court poet of Maharaja Lakshman Sen (1179–1203). It became a classic within a century and Radha–Krishna worship spread. Vidyapati and Chaitanya also wrote Radha into their poems.

Munshi's own characterization of Radha is interesting. She appears in two chapters in the first volume, which covers Krishna's childhood. She is said to be betrothed to Ayan who is away from Gokul, fighting as a soldier in Kamsa's army. Munshi gives Radha's father's name as Vrishabhanu, and describes Radha as having lost her mother at a young age, growing up with her grandmother before coming to Vrindavana to stay with her father. She finds the child Krishna fascinating, as he does her. In a later chapter, Krishna shocks his parents by expressing a desire to marry Radha. He is dissuaded by Sandipani and his parents, who tell him that he has been created for a divine mission; Radha disappears from the story.

The brief encounter between Radha and Krishna takes place in Munshi's story within Radha's home, where Krishna's family has recently arrived as their village is threatened by wolves. In the morning, Radha wakes Krishna up and they go bathing. There is much playing. Radha is infatuated with the boy Krishna and his playing of the flute.[4]

The puzzle remains. Why was it necessary to invent or create Radha as Krishna's consort? My conjecture is that powerful as he was in battle and diplomacy, not to mention as the person who recites the Geeta to Arjuna, Krishna was lacking something. Rama had Sita. Vishnu had Lakshmi. Shiva had Parvati. But who did Krishna have? 16,108 women would hardly qualify as significant in his life. Krishna needed one woman, one he cared about over all others. One who could pine for him and make him miserable if she were to neglect him. Jayadeva's Radha is sad but proud. She will not go to Krishna where he may be playing with the many gopis. She sends her friend to fetch Krishna, who finally arrives to complete their Union. Without Radha, Krishna is incomplete and hence not fully divine. Radha completes Krishna.

It is her radiant presence for a short but intense period in Krishna's life that determines her identity. She does not appear later in his life as he goes on to accomplish many things. She is not a trophy he can show off. She is ephemeral but luminous—a dazzling, beautiful and erotic presence in his life. In her he finds fulfilment and in no other.

All this is imagined by his devotees. They attribute these qualities to Radha. They want to associate Krishna to a unique woman. He cannot have her for himself because she is married. The devotee cannot have God for herself. Krishna is willing to spend intense moments with Radha knowing full well that these moments are precious and limited. So the brief time together has to be enjoyed with great intensity. This is what the devotee will do. S/he will contemplate Radha and Krishna for a short while but intensely. The longing Radha and Krishna had for each other is what they have for their favourite pair. Radha and Krishna together steal a few moments and achieve a happy, perfect Union. That is all the devotee can hope for.

The significance of Radha's emergence from the periphery of Hinduism rather than in its core mythology is also worth analysing. My conjecture is that the spread of Bhakti is at the heart of this. The Bhakti movement originates in south India and goes north. Buddhism had inaugurated the cult of a personalized God. The multiple gods in the Rig Veda and later get truncated within Hinduism into a few Gods—Shiva, Vishnu and Kali in their multiple manifestations. Bhakti was all about a personal God whom the devotee could associate with in a human relationship. She could chide, love, get angry with and envelop the God in her devotional feelings, as indeed Radha does with Krishna. Shiva is humanized by Parvati though otherwise he can be destructive. Krishna is made human by Radha. Until the advent of Bhakti, Krishna does not need Radha. It is as a personal God during the rise and growth of the Bhakti movement that Radha comes to the rescue of Krishna and completes him as a God whom people can love.

Radha was created by the people to make Krishna a more lovable God than he would have been without her.

4

GITA GOVINDA: ILLUSTRATED MANUSCRIPTS FROM RAJASTHAN

KAPILA VATSYAYAN

ALTHOUGH MUCH HAS been written on the emergence and development of the diverse schools of Rajasthani painting and the characteristics which distinguish one school from the other, the role of the *Gita Govinda* in shaping the pictorial styles has not been as clearly defined. A perusal of the *Gita Govinda*–illustrated manuscripts from Rajasthan offers convincing proof of the unique impact of this work on the arts of Rajasthan, particularly music and painting. From the third quarter of the 16th century to the first quarter of the 20th century, at least twenty complete sets must have been executed. Many more may come to light if the unpublished collections of the several private and public libraries are carefully examined. Even from the illustrated manuscripts studied by the author, it should now be possible to place these manuscripts in a chronological order with a rough identification of provenance and sub-school.

The first *Gita Govinda*–illustrated manuscripts begin to appear in the late 15th or early 16th century. The illustration of the manuscript discovered by Mazmudar is the earliest belonging to a period roughly from 1485 AD to 1525 AD. The illustrations are restricted to the ten avatars[1] and stylistically they are a close parallel to the Jain miniatures of the period. Possibly, the manuscript was executed in Gujarat. Their abstract quality without human figurative drawing is a distinguishing feature.

Thereafter appears the set of the *Gita Govinda* illustrations executed in the *Caurapancasika* style, possibly belonging to the period 1525–75 AD. A few folios are in the collections of the Prince of Wales Museum, Mumbai. Judging from these folios, it would appear that the set contained nearly 150 folios and that an attempt was being made to illustrate each verse.[2] For the first time in these paintings appear cuckoos, birds and animals, which can be directly related to the verbal imagery of the poem. Unlike the illustrated manuscripts of the Ramayana and the Mahabharata, the artist is obliged to discard the straight sequential narrative of events; he adopts, instead, another technique of transforming the verbal imagery and phraseology into pictorial motifs. A detailed reappraisal of this set is essential because it is the commencement of a new pictorial vision which is clearly different from the narrative approach of Indian relief sculpture. The content of the *Gita Govinda*, thematically, is thin; its strength and power lie in the dramatization of the inner emotional states through a rich and multilayered structure of similes and metaphors. Also, here, the drama of human emotions takes place through the narration, reminiscence and fantasy of two characters: the third (i.e. the *sakhi*) is the bridge between the two. The painter of the *Gita Govinda* in the *Caurapancasika* style presents a pictorial counterpart by dividing his surface through central trees, arches and bowers. This enables him to demarcate areas and also provide continuity. The change from the geometrical segments of the Jain painting is unambiguous: the difference between this treatment of flat surface and the multiple planes of Mughal painting is also clear. This compositional structure of the paintings of the set marks the beginning of a pictorial vision which is quite distinct from that followed in the *Bhagavata Purana* and *Caurapancasika* paintings in the same style. This is in no small measure accounted for by the demands made on the painter by the text he was handling.

Almost contemporary are three other sets which were certainly executed in north Gujarat and Kankroli, Rajasthan. Scholars have so far placed them in the last decade of the 16th century and the first decade of the 17th century. The first is the pocket *Gita Govinda* with fifty illustrations in the B.J. Institute of Indology, Ahmedabad. The paintings are executed in what has been termed as a folk idiom.[3] Although there is some element of truth in this, a comparison of the paintings of this set with those of the illustrations of the *Gita Govinda* in the *Caurapancasika* style makes it clear that these are not totally unrelated happenings in the different regions of India. The fundamental principle governing spatial composition is variations of a similar if not identical pictorial vision.

More important are the other two sets with more than 150 paintings in each set. The first is a set of 150 paintings in the Kankroli Palace.[4] Stylistically, these paintings recall the leaves from the *Dashamaskanda* paintings, and there are few similarities with the *Caurapancasika*-style *Gita Govinda* of the Prince of Wales Collections. The painter of this set divides the flat surfaces into different zones through trees and foliage and arranges groups of figures within the arches formed by the branches. The figurative drawing and the costuming, however, have strong affinities with the paintings of the *Dashamaskanda* of the Jodhpur Library.[5] The figures of the asuras Madhu, Mura and Naraka are close to those which we see in the *Laghu Samgrahani Sutra* dated 1583 AD.[6] The paintings were possibly executed in the last decade of the 16th century. The 150 illustrations of another set of *Gita Govinda* of the N.C. Mehta Collections[7] are an important landmark. They follow the same format but there is evidence here of more than one artist executing the paintings. Some have close affinities with the *Balagopala-Stuti* paintings, others with the Kankroli *Gita Govinda*, and yet others are reminiscent of figures seen in the *Gita Govinda* in the *Caurapancasika* style. This is clear from the treatment of the Kama figure. Important is the use of a central tree as a divider and the appearance of large bees and cuckoos. The asura figures of Mura, Naraka, etc., disappear, although the stylization of some avatars, particularly the Narasimha, recalls similar delineation in the Jain schools. Despite the late N.C. Mehta's detailed article in JISOA (Vol. 1945), a reappraisal of this set of illustrations is necessary.[8]

To these three sets of the period (1590–1610), we have to add now the eighteen folios acquired by the Maharaja Sawai Man Singh II City Palace Museum, Jaipur.[9] The set must have had about 140 paintings and they were also executed somewhere in north Gujarat. The eighteen folios now extant bear testimony to the diligence with which the *Gita Govinda* was being painted. There is a verse-to-verse and line-to-line relationship between the verse and the pictorial transfiguration. The format is similar. A horizontal flat surface is spatially divided through trees, branches and foliage, and the figurative drawing is encased within them. However, the branches of the trees do not become an arch or a bower as in the *Caurapancasika* group. Stylistic affinities between this set and the Kankroli set are many, particularly in respect of figurative drawing. The figures of Mura, Madhu and Naraka are almost repeats of what we see in the *Laghu Samgrahani* in 1583 AD, and the *Dashamaskanda* paintings of the Jodhpur Library and the National Museum and the Jagdish Mittal Collections, all attributed to the first decade of the 17th century.[10] A comparison of these illustrations with those of the Kankroli and N.C. Mehta *Gita Govinda* on the one hand and the *Dashamaskanda* paintings on the other would place these paintings somewhere between 1590 and 1600 AD and not later. A detailed analysis of the folios has been undertaken elsewhere.

The most significant set of illustrations, however, comes from a manuscript dated 1594 AD from Jaur in Rajasthan, now called the Jaur *Gita Govinda*, in the collections of the National Museum.[11] Stylistically, these illustrations have nothing in common with all the sets mentioned above. The illustrations support a Bagari text and are executed in a free style close to the *Panchatantra* paintings in the Bharat Kala Bhavan. In each folio, there are specific compartments and there is no attempt to provide continuity and overlapping areas through trees and foliage. The farther eye continues and there is a charming vivaciousness in the figurative drawing. The painter achieves a new sense of movement in these paintings although adhering to the stylistic features of the Palam *Maha-Purana* and other Jain illustrations. A detailed analysis of this set has been undertaken in a separate monograph.[12]

These sets thus constitute what we may term as the first phase of the illustrations of the *Gita Govinda* from north Gujarat and Rajasthan. Within the phase, there can be a further division of the paintings into (i) those which follow the western Indian idiom of the *Balagopala-Stuti Panchatantra* paintings, i.e. the Jaur *Gita Govinda*, (ii) those which have affinities with the *Dashamaskanda*, the Kankroli and the Maharaja Sawai Man Singh II City Palace Museum, Jaipur, sets, and (iii) those which belong to the *Caurapancasika* school and a mixture, i.e. the Prince of Wales *Gita Govinda* and the N.C. Mehta *Gita Govinda*.

The second phase begins sometime in 1640 AD, after the execution of the Bhandarkar Collection *Bhagavata Purana* by Sahibidin. This is the beginning of the Mewar School proper. Four sets of this period are known. Two are dated 1629 AD by Andrew Topsfield. Scattered folios are extant in the Jodhpur Collections.[13] The text is in Rajasthani. Two others with a Sanskrit text are in the Kumar Sangram Singh Collection and thirty-seven illustrations from a manuscript in the Saraswati Bhandar, Rajasthan (Oriental Institute). These support a Sanskrit text and are in a different format. We would place these around 1640–60 AD. In the first two, there is a mechanical compartmentalization. In the next two, there is a development, both thematic and stylistic. The flat surface division is replaced by the use of different planes. Instead of repeating the same character through different figures in diverse spatial areas, a single emotive situation is sought to be depicted. At best there are two divisions and the narrators of the different *sarga*s (section of a poem) (whether Jayadeva, sakhi, Krishna or Radha) are omitted. The painter focuses attention on the dominant mood of the entire *prabandha* (section) and composes his painting as a whole and not as a narrative of diverse emotions. This is a marked change from the first phase where the painter was trying to transform the sequential narrative depiction of relief sculpture into a lyrical dramatic situation by using trees as dividers or encasing figures in different geometrical compartments. In the second phase a single tree or a glade serves as the divider, and often even this is dispensed with. The Saraswati Bhandar manuscript is remarkable for its chiselled figurative drawing and its sophisticated draughtsmanship and tonalities of colours. In comparison, the paintings of the Kumar Sangram Singh Collection *Gita Govinda* are grosser. In the Jodhpur and Bharat Kala Bhavan *Gita Govinda* paintings, there are both compartments and bowers but they are not used significantly. The most important difference is in the Kama figure who appears in a female form.

The third phase of the Rajasthani paintings based on the *Gita Govinda* belongs to the last quarter of the 17th century and the first quarter of the 18th century. Although critics have dismissed this phase as decadent and lacking in refinement, these paintings in a larger format herald a new phase in Mewari painting which reflects a deep understanding of the text. Indeed, it is the logical culmination of what begins with the *Caurapancasika Gita Govinda*. The division of the pictorial surface into different areas and the attempt to portray variations of the mood of this group of paintings as also to delineate a single situation of the second phase coalesce into a distinctive late 17th-century school. The arches of the first phase become bowers representing consecrated celestial space and the trees represent terrestrial space. There is a rich and diverse play of planes, a sense of linear perspective and an intense preoccupation with the transfiguration of the poetic image into a pictorial one. The similes and metaphors of the poem are transformed into natural landscape—flora, fauna, birds and animals. On the surface, all this appears to be an aggregate of decorative conventional stock motifs. Underneath it is the pictorial transfiguration of the crucial similes and metaphors of the poem. The portrayal is no longer limited to the theme and the action of the story; it is a pictorial recreation of the text. Evidently, although Kumbha and Mananka's commentaries must have popularized the *Gita Govinda* by the end of the 15th and the early part of the 16th centuries, it took some more decades before the full erotic and mystical import of the poem was fully understood. This could well have been the result of the development of the several Vaishnava cults in Vrindavana and ultimately in Nathdwara. The Vallabha sampradaya and the Nimbarka school gave a fresh impetus to the *Gita Govinda*. From a poem of *shringara*, the nayaka and nayika-*bheda*, it was elevated to a doctrine of the *madhura* bhakti school. A perusal of the paintings of this third phase makes it clear that the literary lyrical beauty of the poem is superimposed by another level of deification of the characters of the poem. Many stylistic developments were inevitable. No longer could the painter restrict himself to aesthetical typology based on the nayaka and nayika-bheda of the *alamkara* shastra; nor could he be satisfied with the portrayal of single situations. A constant reminder of the poem to be sung before the Lord was necessary. It was also necessary to elevate the human drama of the two lovers to the divine agony of the godhood and the human soul (*paramatma* and *jivatma*). The refrains of the musical composition became logically the repetitive motifs of the specific sargas; they provide the thematic and pictorial unity to specific groups of paintings within a set. This is the outstanding feature of the Mewari set of this period, especially those in the collection of the Udaipur State Museum, Udaipur. Others follow the method even if they do not achieve the same level of excellence. The paintings of each prabandha are held together with a single repetitive pictorial motif in one part of the painting. The second part presents the actual emotive state described in verse after verse. The paintings are to be viewed sequentially together and not in isolation. Seen thus, poetry and music sing through them, although at first glance they appear repetitive. Alongside is the necessity to communicate the transcendental nature of this drama of human emotions. Pictorially, the artist develops the thin arches of the branches of the *Caurapancasika* group, and this leads to the emergence of an arched bower almost like a semicircular wreath: the divine pair singly and together appear either within or against the background of this arched bower. A set of *Gita Govinda* paintings with leaves dispersed in different parts of the world[13a] is a typical example.

All these sets depict this arched bower with dangling garlands. The image of the wild-flower-garlanded Krishna, the image of Radha and Krishna separated and united, undoubtedly provided the stimulus for this pictorial motif. Understandably, it is freely used thereafter in the paintings of the *Rasikapriya* and *Rasamanjari* and many others. The reference to the doe-eyed Radha also gives rise to the pictorial motif of the doe so frequently mentioned in the *Gita Govinda*.

Cuckoos, bees and peacocks sing, hum and dance throughout the *Gita Govinda*. The Mewari artist provides the pictorial counterpart by painting them along with the *chakora* and the *khanjan* (wagtails) in most paintings of this phase of Mewari paintings. Nowhere are these purely decorative, as remarked by some critics. Equally significant is the emergence, during the second and third phases of Mewari painting, of the pictorial motif of overcast clouds and a row of cranes. On the surface, this is pretty and decorative, symbolic of clouds and rain. The description of birds flying in the clouds carrying messages of love has great antiquity in Indian poetry. However, it was only Jayadeva who compared the white garland on Krishna's dark body to the white cranes on the dark clouds. The renewed popularity of the poetic motif in Indian paintings is once again inspired by the imagery of the eleventh prabandha of the *Gita Govinda* beginning with '*Rati sukha sare*' and the line '*urasi murare . . .*', '*balaka . . .*', etc. (V.11, 6).

One could go on adding to this list of pictorial motifs inspired by the *Gita Govinda* in Mewari painting, but perhaps one last reference to Kama and Ratipati will suffice. The *Gita Govinda* in the *Caurapancasika* style and the N.C. Mehta *Gita Govinda*, the Kankroli *Gita Govinda* and City Palace, Jaipur, all portray Kama. He is seen in pyjamas and kurta (*chakadara jama*) holding a bow and arrow. In some the turban is typical of the *Caurapancasika* group and in others he wears a tiara. In the paintings of the second phase, he is seen as a woman. Only in the paintings of the third phase of Mewari painting does the Kama figure undergo a radical transformation. He is no longer sketched as large; he is diminutive, almost symbolic, and is seldom at the same level as that of Krishna and Radha. He now hides in trees and bushes, appears from nowhere and disappears into lush foliage. Wherever the text refers to him as Ratipati, he is accompanied by Rati, his consort. The development of this motif is a further refinement of what is witnessed in the first two phases. The detailed folio-to-folio analysis of four sets belonging to this phase has been attempted elsewhere.[14] From that analysis it was evident that the sets must have been executed possibly by three artists extending over a period of at least fifty years. This is also borne out by the quality of refinement and sophistication, and the lack of it. Also, by the middle of the 18th century, the superscription text is often a Rajasthani version and not the original Sanskrit. This also accounts for pictorial variations within the same style.

Contemporary but distinct is the emergence of the refined Bundi style. The *Gita Govinda* inspires a remarkable set of 150 drawings now in the Bharat Kala Bhavan collection. The creative genius of the artist makes full use of the poetic and pictorial motifs and creates a stunning series of drawings to match the poetry. These paintings provide the wide range of interpretative possibilities based on the same text and within the framework of the pictorial vocabulary of a specific style. This set should be attributed to the end of the 17th century. It is a close parallel to the set of Bundi drawings in the National Museum collection. A fuller analysis of each of these drawings is contained in an independent monograph.[15]

To this phase of Rajasthani painting also belongs the set of *Gita Govinda* paintings executed in the Malwa idiom, now in the private collections of Maharaja Bhawani Singh. They represent yet another example of illustrating the *Gita Govinda* through a distinctive pictorial style.

Finally, there is the last phase belonging to the latter half of the 18th century and the first half of the 19th century. Again, within the period, many sub-schools and styles develop. The *Gita Govinda* sets of this period can also be viewed as the last phase of Mewari painting; today they are termed as the paintings of the Jaipur Amber School. Similar sets appear in Jodhpur, Darbhanga and Mithila. Nearly seven such sets of illustrated manuscripts have come to light. The City Palace Museum, Jaipur, has three illustrated sets (Nos. 2163, 2165 and 2172). The Darbhanga Sanskrit University library has another three and the Jodhpur State Archives has one such set. While it is difficult to establish an exact chronology of these sets of paintings, a study of the 150 paintings of these sets would lead to the conclusion that the set of illustrations (presently in Darbhanga) is perhaps the earliest amongst this group. Twenty-seven paintings accompany a text written on sixty-six folios (122 pages). In most cases one painting illustrates prabandha: only one prabandha (No. 22) has two. There is an introductory and a concluding painting. The City Palace Museum set of paintings (No. 2165) evidently belongs to a slightly later period (early 19th century) and the second set is perhaps still later (No. 2163), around 1830–35. Two other sets in Darbhanga are in pocket-size, with diminutive paintings. These belong to the late 19th century along with a few folios acquired by the National Museum recently. Contemporary is a set in the City Palace Museum (No. 2172) in a larger format and another in Darbhanga. Both these sets, although accompanying the *Gita Govinda* text, are, in fact, raga and ragini paintings attributed to each of the prabandhas of the *Gita Govinda*. The illustrations in the Jodhpur Archives also illustrate only the avatars. Amongst the Rajasthani paintings of *Ragas* and *Raginis* of diverse sub-schools, few are related to the text of the *Gita Govinda*.

It was necessary to introduce the Darbhanga set against the background of the *Gita Govinda* paintings in north Gujarat and Rajasthan from the 16th century onwards, particularly Mewar, because only then can the nature of the developments which take place in this last phase of Rajasthani paintings be traced. While the text of the *Gita Govinda* remains constant, the interpretations are directly governed by earlier pictorial styles. While the sets of the first, second and third phases manifest the artists' desire to interpret the theme, the emotion or the phraseology creatively and imaginatively, the artists of the fourth phase are overpowered by the pictorial interpretations of their predecessors. The motifs which transfigured the verbal imagery into the pictorial become stereotyped conventions and lose some of their freshness and vitality. Many pictorial devices which were necessitated by the artists' desire to comprehend the poem in all its multiple symbolic nuances are now rules of pictorial composition. Space is still divided into planes and zones, but the delicate juxtaposition of proportions, enlarging and dwarfing, lose some of their subtlety and charm. The sense of balance and harmony in nature and the vibrant response of birds, animals and the natural flora and fauna to human emotion becomes a decorative design. And yet the links with 200 years of painting preceding these are clear and unequivocal. Occasionally there is a slight introduction of the linear perspective of a clear foreground and background but by and large the principles of pictorial composition are the same as in the 17th and early 18th centuries.

The arched bowers are enlarged to constitute rich lush woods and forests, the foliage becomes a tapestry of geometrical design and the figures of Radha and Krishna are often full-faced. The Kama figure disappears in the Darbhanga *Gita Govinda* altogether and is seen only twice in the two Jaipur sets. The sakhis sing and dance, but now not with cymbals (*manjira*) and the tambourine (*jhanja*); instead the sarangi and a pair of tablas accompany the rasa. Monkeys, symbols of Eros, continue to appear, but they are not half as impish as those in the Mewari *Gita Govinda* set in the Udaipur State Museum.

The deification of Krishna and Radha is clear from the halos and the adornment. The impact of the Chaitanya and the Vallabha sampradaya is also clear from the saint figures, particularly in the set located in the City Palace Museum, Jaipur.

Despite these derivative features, there are some remarkable innovations within the conventional style. The arched bowers are sometimes small and diminutive, hidden in branches of trees without trunks. These invariably represent dream or fantasy states. The time past and recollection is frequently portrayed through this pictorial device. The sakhi as the bridge between the separation of the two is brought home aptly by placing her outside the consecrated space of the arched bower. The image of the wagtails and does is slurred over, but peacocks are used as symbols of internal emotive states. All three sets use the pair of peacocks effectively to support and underline the nature of the dialogue of the human characters. There is very little evidence of the word-to-word or line-to-line relationships, between the verbal imagery and the paintings. The artist seeks to portray a whole prabandha or a sarga and not a particular phrase.

The colours undergo a great change. Although the colour symbolism of the dark Krishna (*shyama*) and the fair Radha, the blue sky and the *pitambara* continues, the tonalities are different. Lighter and brighter shades of blue and green are used. The Indian red of the early Mewari paintings becomes scarlet and crimson, and the orange gives place to yellow. Although white is used for the platform, there is a difference: now designs and floral decorations adorn the platform on which Radha, the sakhi and Krishna meet. This detracts from the symbolic purity of the white of the platform used in the Mewari paintings of the second and third phases. The red background of the bower also changes colour. Also the text is not written as superscription. The paintings accompany a text page as in the Saraswati Bhandar *Gita Govinda*.

And, finally, the comprehension of the text and its creative pictorial transfiguration are at the level of ritual rather than sensuous perception and spiritual experience. This is perhaps the most important distinction between these paintings and those of the second and third phases.

INTEGRATING THE NATURAL, THE DIVINE AND THE EROTIC IN *THE GITA GOVINDA* AND *SHIR HA-SHIRIM*

YUDIT K. GREENBERG

EROTIC LOVE IS the leitmotif that characterizes two of the best works of poetry ever produced, the *Gita Govinda*[1] and *Shir Ha-Shirim* (Song of Songs).[2] These lyrical poems are teeming with cultural tropes, and contribute to the richness of the cross-cultural study of religious love and desire. The *Gita Govinda*, the 12th-century Sanskrit poem composed by Jayadeva, depicting the passionate love between Krishna and Radha, is one of the most popular works in Vaishnava Hinduism. There are more than forty commentaries on the *Gita Govinda*, and its lyrics have been set to devotional music, dance and paintings throughout India. It is, therefore, not surprising that the *Gita Govinda* has been claimed as the Indian 'Song of Songs'. *Shir Ha-Shirim*—Song of Songs, comprising one of the Hebrew Bible's twenty-four books portraying the sensuous love between a shepherdess and a shepherd in the land of Israel—has been the most quoted biblical book, inspiring a plethora of literature, theology, liturgy, art and music.

While there are several compelling resemblances between the two poems that are worthy of examination, my objective is to initiate their comparative study with a focus on female desire and the role that imagery from the natural world plays in depicting the physical beauty of the lovers and their sexual desire.[3]

Eros has been understood by early philosophers such as Plato, Aristotle and the Neo-Platonists as passionate desire for union with the beloved.[4] Such love stems, to a large extent, from the physical separation of the lovers from each other.[5] While this dynamic dominates both the *Gita Govinda* and *Shir Ha-Shirim*, the nuanced features of erotic love represent unmistakable geographic locations and historical/mythological narratives of which these texts speak.

The *Gita Govinda*, consisting of twelve chapters and further divided into twenty-four songs, is a poem, not embedded in scriptures, yet deriving its inspiration from the sacred texts of the *Bhagavata*. While celebrating religious fervour intertwined with eroticism, the *Gita Govinda* explicitly introduces Vaishnava theology and references to deities, primarily to Lord Krishna.

The *Gita Govinda* has been expressed through dance for at least 500 years, in the Odissi dance style that originated in the Jagannath Temple in Puri. Not only in Bengal and Odisha but also in Nepal, the *Gita Govinda* is sung during the spring celebration in honour of the goddess Sarasvati in which worship is offered to the god of love, Kamadeva and his consort. In the Jagannath Temple as well as in other temples, the song is sung daily.

Shir Ha-Shirim comprises a series of dialogues spoken chiefly between the male lover and his female beloved and is an inimitable voice in the Hebrew Bible. Since the 16th century, *Shir Ha-Shirim* has played a performative and liturgical role in the weekly recitation by Kabbalists and Sephardic Jews on the eve of the Sabbath. Other occasions of the song's recitation include the last day of the spring holiday of Passover and at weddings.

In both the *Gita Govinda* and *Shir Ha-Shirim*, the woman's voice is the dominant one. This feature has led some scholars to suggest that *Shir Ha-Shirim* was composed by a woman.[6] Furthermore, contemporary feminist interpretations suggest that Song of Songs redeems the problematic rhetoric of gender and sexuality in the Bible. Scholars such as Phyllis Trible have suggested that *Shir Ha-Shirim* has engendered notions of positive sexuality and an egalitarian relationship, focusing especially on the portrayal of the woman lover who asserts her emotions and desires.[7]

A profound parallel in the *Gita Govinda* and *Shir Ha-Shirim* is the ubiquity of imagery from nature during springtime. The natural world is integral and woven into the fabric of the verses and interlaced with the moods of the lovers. To begin with, the rendezvous take place during the spring, and they occur amid nature's fecundity, either in the forest in Vrindavana (*Gita Govinda*) or the garden, the hills and desert of Israel (*Shir Ha-Shirim*). Furthermore, revelling in beauty and sensuality, the lovers' bodies, in both poems, are often described in the likeness to trees, fruits, flowers, animals and geographic areas. In the narrative, parts of the human body are often compared to aspects of fruits, trees and even animals.

In the *Gita Govinda*, the Vrindavana forest is the location of the lovers' rendezvous. Krishna and Radha's encounters occur on the banks of the River Yamuna, at the Mansarovar Lake and in the forest as the following verses reveal: 'O my dear friend, the mango trees in the forest groves of Vrindavana are covered with freshly sprouted buds because they are thrilled by the embrace of the restless creepers [. . .] Shri Hari is affectionately playing with young women in the pure water of the Yamuna that flows alongside those forest groves' (*Gita Govinda*, 3:34).

References to a variety of native flowers and scents abound in the *Gita Govinda* (5:4–8; 7:11; 15:23; 19:14):

Varieties of flowers are opening and tearing open the hearts of lonely lovers [. . .] Once, in the splendid spring season, when Radhika was pining for Krishna, she began to search for him in one forest grove after another [. . .] The nectar of spring flowers and the aroma of jasmine blossoms are enthralling [. . .] His tender lips are an enchanting soft reddish colour like the bud of a scarlet mallow flower [. . .] The blueness of my throat is not the effect of poison, but a garland of blue lotus flowers [. . .] The bow of fresh petal-like eyebrows [. . .] Your lips, as soft and red as bimba fruit [. . .] O Shri Krishna, my

sakhi Radha is behaving exactly like a deer [. . .] My beloved
Candi, O hot-tempered woman, your enchanting red lips are
friends with the lustre of a bandhuka flower. Your cool cheeks
have assumed the splendour of a madhuka flower. Your nose
is like a sesame flower. Your teeth are as radiant as jasmine
blossoms. O beloved, the flower archer Kamadeva worshipped
your face with his five flower arrows and then conquered the
entire universe.

In *Shir Ha-Shirim*, the lovers are assimilated into their environment
and are associated with specific locations in the land of Israel. 'I am
a flower of Sharon, a water lily growing in the valleys' (2.1–2). 'Your
hair is like a flock of goats moving down mount Gilead' (6:5).

The imagery of the land includes its native flowers and fruit trees
whose buds and scents joyfully announce spring. Of the fruits, the
pomegranate in particular, has a prominent place in the Song where
it appears six times. A native to the land, the *rimon* (pomegranate) is
used in metaphors for skin colour and wine drinking (*Shir Ha-Shirim*
4.3, 13; 6.7, 11; 7.13; 8.2). The multiplicity of its seeds is a known
symbol of fertility and its blossoms are a sign of the timelessness of
love in ancient Near East literature.

Therefore, the profusion of the natural landscape merges with
the personality and mood of the protagonists. The lovers are not
only an integral part of nature, they domesticate it as its stewards.
In the *Gita Govinda*, both Krishna and the *gopi*s herd cows, and
in *Shir Ha-Shirim* the lovers are referred to as a shepherd and a
shepherdess. The juxtaposition of exquisite human form and scenic
beauty in the *Gita Govinda* and *Shir Ha-Shirim* and the similes
of nature employed in both works of poetry reinforce and extend
the erotic beyond the sexual. At the same time, the *Gita Govinda*,
regardless of its abundant similes of nature, is imbued with direct
and transparent sexuality. Although Radha and Krishna suffer
from periods of separation from each other, their bodies are often
portrayed as if in the midst of a sexual experience that takes place in
the present, rather than as imagined and distant objects. Her eyes are
not only analogized as lotus-shaped but are 'languid with passion's

drunkenness' (*Gita Govinda*, 19:15). Other examples from the *Gita Govinda* of erotic bodies and sexual experience include: '[H]er fortunate body bears drops of sweat . . .'; '[U]pon a delightful-woman's face, where love has arisen where a lower lip is turned for a kiss . . .'; '[T]he pitcher of your breast is more heavy and full of juice than coconuts'; and '[O]h, you who bear the burden of firm breasts and thighs . . .' (*Gita Govinda*, 23:14).

Frequent and explicit sexual encounters in the *Gita Govinda* also include references to physical movement and experience during lovemaking, such as sweat, scratches, trembling and sexual exertion. For example: 'Punish me, lovely fool! Bite me with your cruel teeth! Chain me with your creeper arms!' (*Gita Govinda*, 19:11).

In *Shir Ha-Shirim*, there are clear references to kisses and touch, but these are often spoken in the future tense and couched as longing for such encounters. Take, for example, the opening line of the song: 'May he kiss me with the kisses of his mouth,' and 'He shall lie all night between my breasts.' Also, images of breasts as two fawns, hair like a flock of goats streaming down from mount Gilead, etc., embody the integration of the lovers' bodies with the sensuality of nature in the land of Israel.

The love language of *Shir Ha-Shirim* is a bit more suggestive of a sexual encounter, and is often expressed in botanical metaphors, rather than in direct and overt language, as indicated in the following: 'A garden is my sister, my bride; a spring shut up, a fountain sealed . . . Let my beloved come into his garden, to eat his pleasant fruits' (*Shir Ha-Shirim*, 4:12).

To reiterate, in both songs we find the preponderance of similes of the landscape of India and Israel. Furthermore, we note that the holiness of Jerusalem, Vrindavana and the Yamuna River serve as the backdrop for the lovers' erotic desire for each other. In the Hindu tradition, one of the holiest rivers is Yamuna, and Jayadeva makes abundant references to it in the *Gita Govinda*. Also, the forest of Vrindavana is a pilgrimage site in Vaishnavism for its association with the life of Krishna.

Weaving such sacred places into the poetry of the *Gita Govinda* and *Shir Ha-Shirim*, where the lovers meet, contributes to the allegorical and spiritual meanings of the text. While the entire land is holy for Jews, the holiest site in the land of Israel is Jerusalem. Thus, we read recurrent references to Jerusalem in *Shir Ha-Shirim*. The woman often speaks to the 'Daughters of Jerusalem', who appear seven times in the song. The wilderness of the forest, the open spaces of the hills and the desert, the dynamism of the fauna, and the lushness of the garden in the *Gita Govinda* and *Shir Ha-Shirim* underpin the unstable nature of erotic love. Radha and the Shulamite, the female protagonists, are often portrayed as lovelorn due to the pain of separation from their lovers. In the *Gita Govinda*, Krishna's rendezvous in the forest include numerous gopis who are enamoured of him. These trysts with women are portrayed quite explicitly: 'He hugs one, he kisses another, and he kisses another dark beauty . . . while Hari roamed in the forest making love to all the women, Radha's hold on him loosened . . .' Ultimately, in his deep love for Radha, Krishna repents, changing his demeanour and promising Radha absolute devotion.

In comparing the relationships of lover and beloved in both songs, we note the intensity of 'love in separation' (*viraha*) as a dominant motif.[8] While the cause of the lover's absence in *Shir Ha-Shirim* is often a mystery, in Krishna's case, his absence is due to his sexual encounters with multiple gopis until he is finally ready to commit to Radha. In contrast, even in the midst of acknowledging numerous 'wives and concubines', the male lover in *Shir Ha-Shirim* is never portrayed as desiring or being with them. In fact, he differentiates between his beloved and his other relationships: '[B]ut unique is my dove, my perfect one' (*Shir Ha-Shirim*, 6:9).

The *Gita Govinda* is, in its literal meaning, simultaneously about earthly, sensuous human love and also divine love—that is, between Krishna, a humanly incarnated god, and Radha, a humanly incarnated goddess. In the literal reading of *Shir Ha-Shirim*, in contrast, the shepherd and shepherdess are irrefutably human. Only in later rabbinic commentaries and interpretations of the Song is she allegorized as the nation of Israel, and he, as representing God. Interestingly, in a reversal of the common tendency to depict God as male, in some of the allegorical interpretations of the *Gita Govinda*,

Krishna represents the human soul that is subject to uncontrollable desires, whereas Radha is seen as the symbol of 'love from heaven,' as *prema*—divine, unconditional love.

With the focus on erotic love in the *Gita Govinda* and *Shir Ha-Shirim*, we uncovered similarities in the dominance of the female voice, and in the intensification of Eros provided by the imagery of nature. In its depiction of overt female sexual desire, *Shir Ha-Shirim* represents a welcome alternative to the representation of Eve, the female protagonist in the 'Garden of Eden' biblical narrative, who is the subject of temptation, sin and punishment. Still, the joy of sexual union eludes the lovers in *Shir Ha-Shirim*, despite the woman's deep yearning for her paramour. She remains in a state of desire and longs for the joyful fulfilment of her love. While both female protagonists suffer the pain of separation from their beloved, Radha and Krishna do attain ecstasy at the end of the poem when Radha finally conquers Krishna's heart, body and being. The very fact that Krishna and Radha are able to consummate their love offers the bhakti devotee an embodied and temporal image of ananda—the bliss achieved in the union of lovers, and in the union of the human soul with the divine.

BECOMING RADHA

ALKA PANDE

RADHE RADHE! I turned my head at the sound of the most attractive bass baritone greeting in the small village of Barsana. I see this small man raising his hand in salute, greeting his friend who responded with an equally musical Radhe Radhe. I was in Radha's birthplace, the village where the nayika of all nayikas was born and grew up. As I travelled through the place, I was intent on visiting the Radharani Temple—the only one in the country dedicated to Krishna's muse and Shakti—his beloved Radharani. The town where people greet each other by calling out Radhe Radhe. Even Krishna is not affixed or suffixed to the greeting. The next greeting is 'Radha Krishna' in one breath.

Goddess Radha was born to Vrishabhanu and Kirti. According to one legend Radha was the daughter of a king. While cleaning the floor for a yajna puja he found the infant Radha. Another tale goes on to say how Radha appeared in this world when Lord Vishnu was set to take birth on earth as Lord Krishna and he requested his family to accompany him, and so, as a lover and companion to Lord Krishna she emerged. She is always believed to be older than Krishna. But until Lord Krishna appeared in front of her, Radha as a baby did not open her eyes.

Om ajnana-timirandhasya jnananjana-salakaya
caksur unmilitam yena tasmai sri-gurave namah

I was born in the darkest ignorance,
And my spiritual master opened my eyes with the torchlight of
knowledge.
I offer my respectful obeisance unto him.

Radha is the essence of Krishna, she is his Shakti, the very core
of his being. Radha is a metaphor for many things: power, love,
bhakti and oneness. The oneness of Radha–Krishna is also similar to
the concept of the Shiva–Parvati manifestation of Ardhanarishvara.
In Vaishnavism it is seen as Ardhanarikrishna, as in Shaivism it
is Ardhanarishiva, in Shaktism it is Ardhanarishakti, and in the
acculturation of Shiva and Vishnu in the manifestation of the
Harihara image.

Legend has it that Lord Krishna used to visit his beloved Radha
and tease her and her *sakhis* (friends) on the day of Holi, which is
celebrated all over the country. Over the years, the Holi celebrations
of Barsana acquired a unique flavour and came to be known as
'Lathmar Holi'. On the first day of Holi, *gopas* (shepherds) from
Nandgoan (Krishna's village) come to Barsana to play Holi with the
gopis (shepherdesses) of the village. The gopas from Nandgoan are
greeted with sticks and most of them run away. The ones who are
caught by the women are then made to wear women's clothing and
dance in public.

Apart from Holi, Radha Ashtami is also an important festival
to celebrate the birth of Radha. Braj, Vrindavana and Rawal are also
some of the prominent places where Radha Ashtami is celebrated on a
grand scale after fifteen days of Krishna Janmashtami. It is celebrated
in the Bhadrapada month on the Ashtami of Shukla Paksha. As part
of the festivities, women keep a fast to seek the blessings of Radharani.
To please Radha, the temples are beautifully decorated and the idol
of Radha is dressed in new attire with jewellery.

This essay focuses on a set of theories pertaining to Advaita
(oneness), bhakti (devotion) and *samprada* (sect), where the merging

of Radha into Krishna and Krishna into Radha is validated. In the Indic tradition '*itihas* Puranas' follow a trajectory parallel with historical narratives and literary traditions. Whilst Bhakti literature is flooded with myriad examples of the 'becoming', the most lyrical observation on cross-dressing emerges from bhakti poetry, which often forms the sahitya (literature) of Indian classical dance and music. Numerous questions confront us about Radha: Was Radha a reality? Did the divine lovers Radha and Krishna actually cross-dress? Was it only a figment of the imagination of artists and poets alike? With this set of questions, this piece is an attempt to find their answers.

LEELA HAVA

Leela Hava emerges from the Indic philosophical concept of Advaita (oneness). Radha is the highest exemplary figure of true devotion and immortal love. She spends her entire life in the memory of Lord Krishna. Her fervent devotion of the Lord remains unmatched in the legends. An unknown poet in this verse says:

> *She wears his peacock feather;*
> *She sports his yellow garment,*
> *He wraps himself in her beautiful sari*
> *How charming the very sight of it . . .*
> *The daughter of Vrishabhanu [Radha] turns [into] Nanda's son*
> *[Krishna], and Nanda's son, Vrishabhanu's girl.*

The bodies of Radha and Krishna veiled under lotuses, except the faces, reinforces the Leela Hava, which is the archetypical artistic representation of Lord Krishna in a sportive mode. It highlights the state of mind rather than a physical act of the divine lover. To borrow from Dr Daljeet and P.C. Jain: 'The Lord of Creation, in Krishna's case hava is the ultimate for in his case hava does not precede leela— an act, hava itself is leela and itself the expression of joy of which Creation is the manifest form. Thus, Krishna, the Creator, does not create by act—leela but the Creation evolves out of his joy, and his joy seeks its expression in his leela hava.' Popularly, Krishna is depicted with the lotus flower. The lotus stands for the three cosmic spaces: earth (roots under the earth), water (body spread across the water) and sky (flower headed to the sky). Thus Krishna embraced with a lotus flower signifies that the entire Creation is part of Leela Hava. Radha as a manifestation of a dutiful devotee partakes in the pleasure of Leela Hava with Krishna. With the same dimensions as Krishna, Radha is an equal participant in this cosmic play.

Following the same concept is Leela Hava as espoused by Bhaktivedanta Prabhupada. Of the many sampradas, such as the Swaminarayan Samprada, the Nimbarka Samprada and the Vallabharcharya Samprada, within bhakti is the Chaitanya Samprada which has 'sakhi bhava' as part of its core philosophy, where even the male bhakta is a woman, i.e. Radha. Vidya Dehejia opines that the erotic aspect of Krishna is evident when he cross-dresses as a woman on numerous occasions to meet his beloved Radha: disguising himself as a bangle seller to be near his beloved or participating in the all-women Holi celebrations.

Among the many legends that prove Radha's oneness with Krishna, this story once again illustrates the eternal love shared between the two. In order to put the love between them to the test, Krishna's wives gave boiling hot milk to Radha, saying it had been sent by Krishna; Radha, without any sign of reluctance, drank it. But the prank took an ugly turn when Krishna started suffering from ulcers in his throat. This episode once again ascertains the fact that Radha and Krishna were the same. Radha was ready to do anything for Krishna and the latter was willing to undergo any kind of pain for Radha.

Swami Prabhupada in his philosophical interpretation of Radharani in the 20th century expresses the Leela Hava. The Hare Krishna movement follows the sampradaya system of passing Vedic knowledge from guru to *shishya*. Srila Prabhupada, as the founder of the movement, represents the Brahma–Madhva–Gaudiya sampradaya, which begins with Lord Krishna. In one of the lectures by Srila Prabhupada on 30 August 1968, he said: 'Srimati Radharani is as fully spiritual as Krishna. No one should consider Her to be material. She is definitely not like the conditioned souls, who have mental bodies, gross and subtle, covered by material senses. She is all-spiritual, and both Her body and mind are of the same spiritual embodiment. Because Her body is spiritual, Her senses are also spiritual. Thus Her body, mind and senses fully shine in love of Krishna.'

Moreover, according to Vedic scholar Nagaraj Paturi, in the Brahma–Madhva–Gaudiya sampradaya, there is a huge *aradhana* of Radha and Krishna where Krishna is not the avatar of Vishnu but Bhagwan (God) himself. According to Paturi, 'The relishing of Krishna comes from Radha herself. Radha is the relishability of Krishna. Krishna without Radha is unrelishable.'

Stri-Vesha

In Indian literature this exchange of clothes between Krishna and Radha is vividly expressed and narrated. As an identity marker of the couple, the exchange is not limited to the surface but stands as a personification of the deep Vaishnava philosophy of Advaita. Moreover, in Hinduism this sublime Oneness further subscribes to the concept of God as the *simghata* or *sammisrana*, the coalescence of male and female principles. It visualized God as being *ardhanara* (half man) and *ardhanari* (half woman), and this imaging was given the name Ardhanarishvara. The duality of the male and female principles has been recognized and paid due cognizance in literature, myths and in the mythological representation of the ancient and known world. In India itself there has been a variation in the themes that have influenced religious and philosophical projections in history and mythology. A perfect example is that of the *akshara*, or a letter of the Devanagari script. The akshara is understood to be mostly representative of the combined form of Shiva and Parvati, the letter representing the presence of Shiva, and the horizontal support indicating the presence of Parvati.

Indologist Devdutt Pattanaik states, '[I]n temples across India, amongst the many attires of Krishna is one called *stri-vesha*, where he dresses as a woman. Krishna is shown wearing a saree and women's jewellery. Some identify this as a form of Mohini, the divine enchantress, an avatar of Vishnu and Krishna. Some say this is Krishna dressing up like his mother, Yashoda, to amuse her. Some say this is Krishna being "punished" by the *gopikas*.' According to legend, the women of Gokul could not bear the mischievousness of Krishna and decided to take revenge by dressing him as a woman. The popular lyrics of the thumri 'Nar Ko Nari Banao' (Make the Lad a Lass) illustrate this. To dress him up as a woman, they make Krishna wear a ghaghra and choli. His hands are made red with *alta*, but instead of getting miffed with the gopis, Krishna goes with the flow and partakes in the pleasure. He eagerly demands jewellery and asks for *shringara*. In Indian literature the sixteen traditional adornments of a woman do not merely enhance her beauty—they are also an *arpana* (offering) for her beloved. This is an important aspect of shringara rasa. The retribution turns into a play, or *leela*, between the gopis and Krishna. In order to commemorate Krishna's love for Radha, he dons the stri-vesha. To give one more instance of cross-dressing, during 'Gore Gvala Ki Leela' (The Game of the Fair Cowherd), since Radha insists on feeling like Krishna, both of them exchange each other's clothes. Krishna is clad as Radha and Radha as Krishna. However, Radha declares, 'Oh, Krishna you can look like me but you will never know the pain in my heart when we separate.'

It cannot be denied that Radha and Krishna are one and not two different individuals. As Radha and Krishna are discussed in the light of the legendary donning of each other's garments, they become a symbol for the united self, and not two figures. Make-up becomes an important part of cross-dressing. It also comes in handy for the visual and literary depiction of the erotic shenanigans of Krishna and Radha since their entanglements inevitably involve Krishna dressing up as a woman—complete with make-up and flowers in the hair—in order to meet Radha. Pahari art form is passionately pursued by the Basohli artists of the 17th century and later in the 18th century by the artists in Kangra. The use of human forms adorned with lotus flowers largely prompts the artists to take Krishna and Radha as their immediate medium of expression. Closely, the rendition of Krishna and Radha is a point of emphasis of the same. It cannot be denied

that there are several variations on this theme within the gamut of
Kangra paintings (Menon 2002).

CROSS-DRESSING

Cross-dressing is given a legitimacy in the bawdy exchange through
song and colour. The power play between the two genders is yet
another assertion of authority. It is imperative to discuss the act of
cross-dressing as prevalent across the Western world and Indian
tradition to have a better understanding of it. Cross-dressing may
seem like a mainstream idea in the current times. But it is important
to note that the idea that seems so normal today had undergone strict
scrutiny in both India and the Western world. The Western notion
of cross-dressing is more about gender power-play, while on the other
hand the Indian cultural thought about cross-dressing is embedded
with the philosophical notion of oneness that comes from the fusion
of the two gender identities: male and female. Interestingly, when
Judith Butler, as the forebear of the critique on cross-dressing, states
that heterosexuality is 'both a compulsory system and an intrinsic
comedy, a constant parody of itself', she deploys the term 'comedy'
to reinforce how the society, like theatre, through repetitive attempts,
gauges gender norms. For occidental thought, the audience reaction
or spectacle plays a significant role in setting the definition of cross-
dressing. If Indian culture still shies away from cross-dressing,
Western culture is replete with artists who have cross-dressed to make
a statement of gender fluidity. For instance, Prince, Harris Glenn
Milstead, Nan Goldin, David Bowie, David Armstrong, to name a
few, have blurred and redefined gender notions. Artists have, time
and again, proved that gender identity does not remain confined by
the apparent form but is fluid.

Looking at traditional cultural practice, Koothandavar, in
Tamil Nadu, is famous for its annual festival of transgender and
transvestite individuals, which takes fifteen days in the Tamil month
of Chitrai (April/May). Here, the story of Aravan, a warrior who
had to be sacrificed during the battle at Kurukshetra, is pertinent to
understanding the different forms that Krishna may take. However,

Aravan did not wish to die without a wife who would mourn him. No woman wanted to marry a eunuch, so Krishna took on the female form named Mohini and became his beloved wife, who later wept copiously on becoming his widow. In the temple of Koothandavar, the sacrifice of Aravan and Krishna, in his role as Mohini, is enacted every year with full fervour near Pondicherry. The fluidity of gender is something that is still not accepted under the societal structures in much of India but Krishna easily broke this structure to reinforce the importance of the man–woman bond. Another old custom is known in Maharashtra, where Krishna is popular as Vitha-ai, Mother Vithal, thanks to the poet-saint Tukaram.

The act of cross-dressing, to a large extent, has been used as a representation of the unity of atman and *paramatma*, of oneness, particularly in the path of devotion or bhakti (Wulff 1982). So deep is the love of Radha and Krishna that it transcends gender identity. It is while role playing that Radha dresses Krishna as a woman, and Radha becomes Krishna, complete in their understanding of a shared unity. These two images from miniature handheld paintings, which suit the intimacy of bhakti, have been selected to illustrate the complete surrender to paramatma through the shringara bhakti of Krishna, when he becomes Radha, beyond gender. He is no longer the male god Krishna but one who has morphed into his Shakti Radha, who is within him.

The Emergence of Radha

16,000 gopis are mentioned in the *Skanda Purana*, with 108 gopis as the noticeable ones. However, from this lot of 108, eight gopis were further considered as the chief gopis, with Radha being the numero uno. The names of the eight gopis were Lalita, Vishakha, Champakalata, Chitra, Tungavidya, Indulekha, Rangadevi and Sudevi. It is believed that goddess Radha's love for Krishna is at the scale of spiritualism which is nothing short of divinity. Radha embodies true love. She is the individual soul and Krishna is the universal soul. And their union is the ultimate union of the atman and the paramatma. It is believed that like Brahma created the world through maya (illusion), maya

Radha and Krishna Dressed in Each Other's Clothes, circa 1800–25, opaque watercolour and gold on paper, 8 x 5 1/2 in., displayed at the Los Angeles County Museum of Art. (Kangra, Himachal Pradesh)

Leela Hava: Krishna and Radha Exchange Clothes, 1825, opaque watercolour, silver and gold on paper, 21.2 x 16.9 cm, displayed at the Museum of Fine Arts, Boston. (Attributed to the family of Nainsukh; Kangra or Garhwal style, Punjab Hills, northern India)

also becomes the Shakti energy of Brahma. Similarly, Radha is the energy of Krishna. However, Radha is also the epitome of true love.

This brings me to the question of whether there was a real gopi named Radha, or whether Radha is a metaphor for Krishna's shakti (power). While Krishna is a major figure in the Indian epic Mahabharata, Radha appears as an individual figure much after Krishna. It is only as late as the Puranic period—in the *Brahma Vaivarta Purana*—that Radha is mentioned as a relative of Krishna's father. But it was the 12th-century poet Jayadeva who actually visualized Radha as a beloved, as a nayika with his verses in *Gita Govinda*. Following Jayadeva was the trajectory of Bhaktivedanta, where, in the Sanskrit commentary *Chaitanya Charitamrita*, Radha is shown as the most devoted of the devoted devotees. And ever since Radha lives on as the muse of the innumerable artists—for instance, Suhas Roy from Kolkata, who has painstakingly painted innumerable Radhas. Radha epitomizes bhakti and love in every aspect from spiritual to physical. So intense is Radha's identification with Krishna that often the two are inseparable and devotees use a greeting in which the names are fused—*Jai Radhey Krishna*—with Radha being the prefix rather than the suffix.

The Bhakti movement started in south India with the Nayanars (worshippers of Shiva) from the 5th to 10th century AD and with the Alvars (worshippers of Vishnu) from the 6th to 9th century AD. By the 12th to 18th century AD the movement had spread across the nation. The Bhakti movement, as a spiritual movement in Hinduism, opened up ways to everyone to worship a particular deity, irrespective of caste and gender. The legacy of Bhakti literature reinforces the diversity: Meera Bai, Tulsidas, Kabir, Surdas, Lal Ded, Akka Mahadevi, to name a few. What makes this religious movement stand apart from the rest is the importance given to the presence of female devotees.

The Ashta-Nayika ('eight nayika'), or classification nayika-bheda, was first documented by Bharata in the *Natyashastra*, a key Sanskrit treatise on Indian performing arts, in the 2nd century BC. The subject of nayika is discussed in literary works such as *Kuttanimata* by Damodaragupta (8th century), *Dasarupaka* by Dhananjaya (10th century), *Gita Govinda* by Jayadeva (12th century), *Sahityadarpana* by Viswanatha Kaviraja (14th century) and *Rasikapriya* by Keshav Das (16th century). Even if Radha takes on the multiple role of nayikas, her nayaka remains Lord Krishna. Apart from canonical texts talking about Ashta-Nayika, the Indian arts, comprising painting, sculptures and dance, widely illustrate the Ashta-Nayika, which are:

1. Vasakasajja Nayika ('one dressed up for union')
2. Virahotkanthita Nayika ('one distraught by separation')
3. Svadhinabhartruka Nayika ('one having her husband in subjugation')
4. Kalahantarita Nayika ('one separated by disagreement')
5. Khandita Nayika ('one infuriated with her lover')
6. Vipralabdha Nayika ('one deceived by her lover')
7. Proshitabhartruka Nayika ('one with a sojourning husband')
8. Abhisarika Nayika ('one who goes to rendezvous with her lover')

Ritikavya is the genre of romantic poetry in Indian literature which, as opposed to the bhakti *kavya*, added a worldly and sensuous dimension to the earlier devotional Radha–Krishna poetry. Radha in the hands of the Riti Kal poets became the principle of shringara. In the Indian tradition, Radha is not an individual, rather she is a universal figure who has become depersonalized and symbolizes every woman who is in love. Riti poetry reached great heights with the works of the 16th-century poet Keshav Das. His *Rasikapriya* is a celebrated treatise on erotic love. The expression of shringara comes to the fore in the poet's description of the nayika:

> O sakhi, the nayika resembling the flame of the lamp ran to hide herself in the grove of sandal trees entwined by lovely clove creepers of undimmed leaves where she conceals the lustre of her limbs in her blue garment. Waiting for Krishna in the bower she looks like a caged bird.

In the 16th century, the Bhakti movement gave the shringara rasa further impetus in music. The *Bhagavata Purana* had already established Krishna as the prototypical romantic figure, but with Surdas's *Sursagar*, bhakti took a new direction, giving equal importance to the romantic, human and divine aspects of Krishna, investing the concept of devotion with a greater intimacy. Here Krishna stands as a divine form of love, with Radha's devotion as an earthly form of love. Their relationship is seen as the unity between the god and lover, the ultimate supreme divinity. This verse from Surdas says it all:

You become Radha, and I Madhava
Truly Madhava, this is the reversal which I shall produce
I will braid your hair and will put your crown upon my head.

Jayadeva's *Gita Govinda* is sung in temples dedicated to Lord Krishna and is quite passionately erotic:

O Shri Krishna, in a secluded place, Radha is painting a picture of Your captivating form in musk, considering You to be Kamadeva himself. After depicting You with mango-bud arrows in Your hand and riding upon a makara, She bows down to offer respectful obeisance to Your portrait.

Legend and oral history have a cultural significance. While most scholars believe that Radha was given a formal identity by the 12th-century bhakti poet Jayadeva in his *Gita Govinda*, there is always more to add over time. The noted Kathak exponent and researcher Uma Sharma imaginatively ended her film *Sri Radha*, with the words: *'Radha toh krishna ki kalpana hai. Mahabharat mein jab Krishna akele hotey hain woh Radha ko yaad karte hain, Radha unko miltey hi unmey gupt ho jaati hai'* (Alone, after the battle of Kurukshetra, Krishna remembers Radha, and Radha appears, only to be morphed into Krishna).

This becomes the ultimate metaphor for the oneness of Radha and Krishna, an integral part of not only Bhakti but also of Advaita philosophy.

7

RADHA: BELOVED OF THE BLUE GOD

BULBUL SHARMA

KRISHNA IS THE beloved of 16,108 women. Innocent village milkmaids and princesses of royal blood—they are all besotted with him and love him unconditionally. Still, from time immemorial, Krishna's name has always been linked with Radha's. They merge together like the petals of an unopened bud, and Radha–Krishna is always chanted together in one breath, as if it is one name—one single, lyrical word.

Radha–Krishna. Together they form a magical circle of dancing light which bestows eternal love and joy to the world. Though her name is forever linked with Krishna's—she is not his wife and there is no mention of her in the most important Purana dedicated to Krishna, the *Bhagavata Purana*. There are just a few mysterious lines about a *gopi* who was chosen amongst all the other maidens to go with Krishna to the forest. This made the chosen gopi very proud and, her heart swollen with vanity because now she considered herself the best of womankind, the gopi asked Sri Krishna to carry her. He agreed and asked her to climb on to his shoulders, but as soon as she touched him he vanished into the air, leaving her humiliated and repentant. That is all we learn about her, and years later this proud, fairest-of-them-all gopi is identified as Radha.

Radha's relationship with Krishna always seems to have fiery elements of pride, passion and longing. When we meet her as a fully developed personality many centuries later as the heroine of a poem by Jayadeva—the *Gita Govinda*, Radha is still feeling the pangs of passionate love, longing and hurt pride. The poet paints her as the lovelorn heroine always pining for her absent lover. Her restless eyes seek him everywhere and her soul is never at peace.

The dominant emotion of Jayadeva's *Gita Govinda*—a great poetic work created in Odisha during the 12th century—one that was going to influence poets and painters for many centuries to come, is the '*viraha* rasa', or love in separation. There is jealousy, anger and hurt pride too in the poem, and we experience them all in a short span of time. We see through Jayadeva's lyrical verses, how Radha loves Krishna with all her being, defying society, against her own will and knowing the fact that he is not always faithful to her.

'My mind counts the multitude of his virtues, it does not think of his roaming even by mistake, and it possesses delight, it pardons him his transgressions from afar; even when fickle Krishna delights among the girls without me, yet again my perverse mind loves him! What am I to do?' writes the poet Jayadeva, who sees this powerful love relationship of Radha and Krishna as a metaphor for the divine–human relationship. According to legend, Krishna himself came down from heaven and swiftly composed this poem when Jayadeva had gone to the river to bathe. The poet, a great devotee of Krishna, sees Radha as the worshipper who willingly gives up her entire being, her heart and soul, to become one with her beloved God.

It is after *Gita Govinda* is written, that Radha comes into her own but we still see her surrounded by a veil of mystery. Unlike Sita, she is not a consort, a crowned queen seated on a throne by her husband. In many mythological stories she is said to be older than Krishna, and a married woman. Her relationship with Krishna is fraught with danger and intrigue. Not for them a palace with a glittering court paying their respects to the couple. Radha always meets Krishna in the forest or in some secret grove hidden from the prying eyes of her family and the people of the village.

In one popular tale still narrated by Bengali folk singers, we see Radha stealing out in the darkness of night to meet her beloved. 'Abandon the noisy, capricious anklet, go to the dense dark grove; wear a dark blue cloak,' Jayadeva had written earlier, describing her tryst in the forest with Krishna.

Radha walks quietly through the dark, lonely forest but she is not afraid since she knows Krishna is waiting for her in the grove of trees. Soon they will be together in ecstasy. The heady scent of night blossoms makes her dizzy but she forces herself to walk faster and then suddenly she hears footsteps. She turns around and sees a group of women from the village following her. Her mother in-law, Jatila, is there too, glaring at her with angry eyes. 'Where are you going, Radha, at this late hour? Who are you going to meet in the forest?' the women ask suspiciously. Radha turns to them and says, 'I am going to pray to Goddess Katyayani at midnight. She stands in the middle of the forest in a bower. I pray to her every night. Let me go or the auspicious hour will pass.' Radha then quickly runs into the darkness. Krishna is waiting for her in the bower, his blue skin glowing in the dark. Radha falls into Krishna's arms, trembling with fear. 'I have lied to the women of my family. I told them I was going to pray to Goddess Katyayani in the forest. They will follow me here and soon find out that I lied,' she sobs. Krishna smiles and caresses her hair. He soothes her with gentle words. 'You told no lie, my beloved. You will pray to the Goddess,' he says, laughing, and takes her in his arms. Then suddenly the forest is set ablaze with a flash of blinding, golden light and there before Radha stands a beautiful image of Goddess Katyayani. When the village women reach the bower they see Radha bowing to the shimmering image of the goddess, offering her fruits and flowers. The women of the village go away sheepishly, feeling ashamed that they had doubted Radha. She is left alone in the forest to be with her beloved for the rest of the night.

Though the love of Radha and Krishna defied all social norms, in Bengal, Assam and Odisha she is worshipped in her own right by Vaishnava Hindus. Radha and Krishna idols form the inner core of many temples in the Chaitanya Mahaprabhu, Vallabhacharya and

Chandidas sub-traditions of Vaishnavism in Bengal. Here we often see Radha seated next to Krishna, bedecked in jewels like a bride.

Most mythological sources say Radha was never married to Krishna and is thus called a *parakiya*, or another man's woman. Yet, an episode from the *Brahma Vaivarta Purana* tells us a different story.

In this legend Radha's marriage to Ayan is shown as a trick of illusion, and it was really Radha's shadow that was wedded to Ayan. She was always Krishna's wedded wife.

This is how they first met.

Radha was born in Barsana, and a few years later, Krishna, as ordained, was born of Devaki, in captivity, and carried to the house of Nanda to be safe from Kansa. There he grew up amongst the cowherds, a beautiful, lotus-eyed baby. One day Nanda, Krishna's foster father, had taken his baby son along with him when he went out to graze the cows. He placed the baby on the grass and, as soon as he did that, the skies became overcast with dark clouds and a strange sapphire light filled the forest. Thunder and lightning began crashing all around them and Nanda ran around in fear. Just then, in a flash of light, he saw Radha standing under a tree. 'Do not fear. I will take care of your baby son,' she said, and reached out to take the baby. She carried him to the safety of a bower and as she held the baby in her arms, her face began to glow with joy. She shut her eyes and remembered her past life when she was Krishna's beloved in a celestial city high above Vaikunth.

As the storm, created by Krishna, roared around them and pillars of dust surrounded them like a wall, Radha recalled her glorious days of rapture with Krishna. She recalled the bed made of fragrant flowers in a palace of gold and she began to cry with happiness.

Suddenly she heard Krishna's voice and when she opened her eyes, he stood before her—a young boy of immense beauty. His skin was dark blue and his lotus eyes sparkled with love for her. As she gazed at him with wonder, he said, 'My beloved, remember the days we were together. You are dearer to me than my life. You are the container of the world and I am the cause. Therefore, O chaste one, come and occupy my heart. As an ornament bedecks the body, come and adorn me.' As his honeyed voice filled Radha with ecstasy, Lord

Brahma, the priest of the Gods, suddenly appeared. Trumpets and drums began to play and a shower of flowers fell from the skies as Radha and Krishna were married. 'Let us dance the eternal dance of love once more,' said Krishna and embraced her. The storm continued to rage around them but Radha lost her reason as thrills of rapture flooded her. She did not know if it was night or day any longer. Then the forest fell silent, the sky cleared and she opened her eyes. She could not find her beloved lord, her Krishna, anywhere. He had vanished in an instant.

The baby now lay in her arms, crying with hunger. With tears flowing down her face, Radha ran swiftly, carrying the baby back to his home. She handed him gently to Yashoda and turned away. Her heart was filled with a secret happiness because now she knew she was the true beloved of Krishna. She would always remain his true beloved. Had he not promised her that? 'In the sphere of the rasa, you will sport with me. As I am, so you are. I constitute your life and you constitute my life.'

In lyrical verses Jayadeva tells us about the turbulent love life of Radha and Krishna. Radha is in a jealous rage because she has heard from the gopis that Krishna has gone away with Chandravali.

Radha runs home in tears but takes care to hide her grief from the people who greet her. She stays awake all night, crying softly as she imagines Krishna with Chandravali. 'O cruel love, do you remember me at all as you make love to her? Or has she erased all memory of our love from your heart?' Radha watches the moon through tearful eyes and finally when dawn breaks over the groves of Vrindavana, she goes out. There, standing in front of her, is Krishna, his chest marked with vermilion streaks, his lips red and swollen. 'How he humiliated me by standing there, so openly showing the marks of his lovemaking on his body.' Seething with rage Radha walks away though Krishna tries to placate her with loving words.

The following day a sadhu comes to their house, begging. Radha's mother-in-law and some young girls go out to give him some alms but he refuses. 'I will only take food from a woman whose husband is living or else I will go away.' The women, afraid of the sadhu's wrath, cajole Radha to come out and give him some food.

The sadhu looks at her and says, 'No, you must give me what I want.' Radha suddenly sees Krishna standing before her, dressed in saffron robes. Only she can recognize him.

'Radha, Radha, give the holy man what he asks for,' say all the women, agitated.

Radha, bewildered, looks up at Krishna, 'What is it that you want from me?' she asks softly.

'I want your pride,' says Krishna.

Radha, overwhelmed with love, bows her head. She can no longer be angry with her beloved. Krishna takes the offering of fruit from her hands and goes away, promising to meet her at midnight in the bower. Their secret is safe and Radha's eternal dance of joy with Krishna, her divine love, continues in an endless cycle of Raas Leela.

ENJOYING GOD: THE DIVINE PARAMOUR

MAKARAND R. PARANJAPE

मेरी भव बाधा हरी राधा नागरि सोइ।
जा तन की झाँई परैं स्याम हरित दुति होइ।।

*Meri bhavabaadhaa harau radha naagari soi
Jaa tan ki jhaaim paraim syaama harit duti hoi.*

INTRODUCTION: THE RISE AND FALL OF RADHA

SRI RADHA, KRISHNA'S soulmate and paramour, is a unique phenomenon in the religious and spiritual history not just of India but of the world.[1] In no other tradition is there a female character quite like her, a humble milkmaid elevated to the supreme status of the erotic and holy beloved of the Supreme Godhead. What makes her story unique is that she is not mentioned in the classical sources or scriptures. Even later, during the medieval period, while the name of Radha occurs in various places, her rise to prominence as an important goddess alongside Krishna is actually a comparatively recent phenomenon. According to Charlotte Vaudeville (7), 'Her emergence in the cultic and devotional sphere of Vaishnavism as Krishna Gopala's beloved and shakti is known to have taken place rather late, certainly not much earlier than the 16th century.'

In the *Bhagavata Purana*, the source of much of the later Krishna cult, there is no reference to Radha.[2] The only clue to her identity is the single, unnamed girl with whom Krishna disappears in the Tenth Canto, which celebrates Krishna's amours in the forest on the night of the full moon. While all the *gopis* cavort with Krishna in that scene, there is one he takes aside, much to the consternation, even dismay, of the others. Perhaps, that exceptional partner gave our medieval myth-makers the germ of the story of Radha which Jayadeva narrates in the *Gita Govinda*. As Guy L. Beck (72) notes:

Within the entire Sanskrit canon that is accepted by normative Vaishnava traditions, Radha is actually never mentioned by name. In the earlier canonical texts there is only the suggestion of Radha's character, not her actual name, as one of Krishna's favorites among a number of 'unmarried' (*Harivamsa*) or 'already married' (*Bhagavata Purana*) cowherd girls (gopis) who nonetheless seek his attentions during his childhood life in Braj.

Thus it is to Jayadeva and his remarkable *Gita Govinda* that the real credit for creating Radha goes. As Valerie Ritter (180) says:

The *Gita Govinda*, a highly popular and influential Sanskrit poem by Jayadeva, thought to have been composed in the twelfth to thirteenth centuries CE, was the first to focus extensively on Radha, in a manner evocative of the courtly *nayaka* and *nayika* (hero and heroine) of Sanskrit poetry.

But when Jayadeva makes her a full-fledged nayika, or heroine, of his most influential poem, *Gita Govinda*, it seems as if we have always 'known' or at least craved Radha's presence, nay, predominance in the love story of Krishna.[3]

Once created by Jayadeva, Radha steadily rose in importance as Krishna's chosen paramour, partner, spouse (as she was later in

the Radhavallabha sect), and thus the supreme Vaishnava goddess.
Chaitanya Mahaprabhu (1486–1534), who gave the Krishna cult its
decisive form, at least in much of northern India, contributed a great
deal to the character and theology of Radha (Beck 180):

> Radha's presence in poetry and her theological importance
> increased with the growth of the Caitanyite sect of Vaishnavism in
> Bengal, which saw the integration of poetic theory of the *sringara
> rasa* (the erotic sentiment) and its taxonomies of the *nayaka-
> nayika* with theology concerning the love of Radha and Krishna.

But we cannot forget Jayadeva's fundamental contribution to this
apotheosis. According to Barbara Stoler Miller (quoted in Beck 73):

> The compounding of Krishna with Radha into a dual divinity
> is central to Jayadeva's conception of Krishna, not as an
> incarnation (avatar) of Vishnu, but as the source (*avatarin,
> dasavidharupa, dasakrtikrt*) of all the incarnate forms he himself
> assumes in order to save the world.

While the *Gita Govinda* institutionalized and legitimated Radha's
centrality in Vaishnavite Bhakti literature, her character, persona and
role was further embellished and moulded by eastern Indian poets
like Chandidas and Vidyapati, who created the platform for the great
devotional and political upsurge marked by the advent of Chaitanya.
But others, notably, Nimbarka, closer to Jayadeva, and Vallabha,
around the same time as Chaitanya, also played a crucial role.[4] Later,
most of the great Krishna-worshipping poets such as Surdas also
exalted Radha till she became almost secularized and universalized in
the Ritikal with poets like Bihari (1595–1664).

With the beginnings of modernity, Radha the goddess, underwent
another drastic modification, now coming more often than not to
represent illegitimate sexual desire. In the new puritanism fostered
during the so-called Indian renaissance, Radha and her dalliance with
Krishna proved an embarrassment to the agenda of social reform that
the proponents of Hindu modernity espoused. Yet, Radha persisted

in folk songs and, later, in many popular art and craft traditions. The final twist in the Radha tale was added by 20th-century feminists, who began to see in her a victim of the patriarchy or, even, the special symbol and voice of a male poet, as in Ramakanta Rath's celebrated *Sri Radha*.[5] Sometimes, Radha became a symbol of the degraded and exploited woman, or she was even depicted as a fallen or abandoned woman, her tale a cautionary reminder of what happens to such women in our society.

All told, the story of Radha is extraordinary, not only in itself, but in the larger context of the history of Indian art, culture, religion and spirituality. The reasons for the rise of Radha are not merely historical, but theological, metaphysical and spiritual too. If such a methodology has explanatory power, then it may also account for the decline of Radha, to which I shall come later.

RADHA'S PRIME

It might be appropriate to glance, briefly, at Radha in all her glory in the middle of the 16th century. Jayadeva's *Gita Govinda* has already been in circulation for nearly 400 years. Nimbarka and Vallabha have already accepted, even celebrated her, in their own compositions and in the theology of the church. But it is Chaitanya who really established the centrality of Radha in the worship of Krishna. As Graham M. Schweig observes (458):

> The divine couple, Radha and Krishna, comprise the essence of the Godhead. Radha is therefore acknowledged by Chaitanyaite Vaishnavas to be part of the very center of their theological doctrine, as reflected in their liturgical practices. Sacred images of the forms of Radha and Krishna, standing together side by side, are elaborately worshiped in Indian temples.

Chaitanya accomplished this by personally experiencing and exalting 'Radha bhava', the state of being Radha-like, which gave the cult of Radha its biggest boost. Now Radha becomes not just one of the gopis or even Krishna's chosen partner but, indeed, the preferred way of reaching or obtaining Krishna. Wherever Radha is, Krishna must be; therefore, every devotee must not only pay obeisance to her but, in being like her, attract the attention of Krishna, indeed, enjoy Krishna as Radha herself did. Since Krishna is the Supreme Godhead, the most desirable entity in the universe, that which enables us to catch Krishna must also be most valuable, most sought after. So important did Radha become that Krishna was sometimes given second place, assumed to be implicit to the devotees' adoration of Radha; a practice that still persists today.

So high was the general adoration for Radha during this period that even an otherwise 'secular' and largely erotic cycle of poems such as Bihari's *Satsai* of 700 (couplets) reflects this, as demonstrated by the opening *doha* (distich).[6] The *Satsai* of Bihari is arguably the most celebrated Hindi poem of what is called the Ritikal, or the age of courtly poetry. One index of its importance is that it has more than seventeen commentaries and was translated into Sanskrit twice. It was also illustrated extensively, especially by the Kangra painters, and its verses set to music. It thus came to occupy a central position in the literary and cultural life of northern India of the 17th century. That the opening doha is also used as a *mangalacharan*, or an auspicious invocatory verse, is quite significant. The placement of Radha in the invocatory opening verse of the most important poem of the period signifies that her apotheosis was by then complete. Radha in the early 17th century is thus a full-fledged goddess, the principal and chosen deity of the leading courtly poet of the time, and thus a central figure in the widely prevalent Vaishnavism of the times.

The meaning of the couplet is by no means simple. It is, on the contrary, complex, allusive and multilayered, thus making it difficult to render into English. The flattened and simplistic translations prevalent scarcely do it justice. For instance, consider Krishna P. Bahadur's translation for the Penguin (UNESCO) edition of 1990 (289):

> Gifted Radha, even a glimpse of you delights Krishna,
>   dispel my worldly sorrows I pray you.

Bahadur's rendering fails to do justice to the complexity of the composition arising out of its triple *shlesha alankara*, or equivocal figures of speech, somewhat like double entendres. Several key words in the couplet can be translated in at least three different ways according to their various meanings: for example, *shyam* (black, Krishna, or blackness = sin) or *harit duti* (green lustre, removed brightness, or removed effect, respectively).[7]

What follows is not a very much better translation but at least attempts to explain the meaning better:

> May that skilled Radha take away the suffering of my existence,
> by the shadow of whose body Shyam turns lustrous green.

Or:

> She who removes my existential distress is artful Radha
> By the glimpse of whose body Shyama's darkness becomes
> lustrous green . . .

So the second line of the couplet could also mean that the very shadow of Radha's body: 1) turns Krishna from black into luminous green; 2) steals Krishna's lustre; 3) removes the darkness or stain (of sin). Meaning 2) is somewhat hard to comprehend; why should Radha's very shadow steal Krishna's lustre? What is suggested is that Krishna is so overpowered by his attraction to Radha that even the shadow of her body can make him lose his self-possession or shine. In any case, the doha asserts the power, even supremacy, of Radha, not only in her ability to overcome Krishna, changing his colour or taking away his brightness, or removing the stain of sinfulness, but also in saving the poet himself by removing the latter's bhava *baadhaa*, or existential distress. If it is admitted that all of us suffer from some version or the other of the latter, then Radha as saviour or redeemer is indeed a very attractive and opportune figure.

The colour symbolism in the couplet has been captured in a modern-day painting in imitation of the precolonial style of Indian Rajput miniatures. Commissioned by Professor Harsha V. Dehejia in

2005, this painting is by Kanhaiyalal Verma of Jaipur. What caught the painter's imagination when he heard the verse is the fact that when yellow and blue colours are mixed the outcome is green. Krishna is *shyama*, or blue-black, while Radha is golden yellow in hue; their mixture leads, literally, to the greening of Krishna, portrayed in the painting most obviously in Krishna's face. But what of the theological implications of this colour chemistry? Clearly, colouring and dyeing are prevalent metaphors for spiritual transformation throughout medieval poetry. Falling in love and being united with one's beloved is often spoken of as being dyed in the latter's colours. When the devotee surrenders totally to the deity, she becomes imbued with the latter's hue. But in this case, it is Radha who gives her colour to Krishna, again emphasizing her importance in his lifework. Krishna's greening or blossoming is effected by Radha's love for him. It is she who steals his native lustre only to replenish it with her own effulgence. Radha it is who is responsible for the flowering of Krishna; she fertilizes him, amplifying his power and glory as none other could.

I have translated *naagari*, Bihari's unusual epithet for Radha, as skilled or artful in preference to Bahadur's previously mentioned 'Gifted Radha'. As we shall see, Bihari, the courtly poet, constructs Radha as Krishna's sophisticated, skilful, urban lover rather than an artless, guileless, naive milkmaid of Vrindavana, the epitome of pastoral innocence and unfallen beauty. Radha, by the time she becomes the fully developed protagonist of Krishna *leela*, or the play of the dark God, acquires a somewhat dual significance as being both artless and sophisticated all at once. As Valerie Ritter observes, 'In Braj-dialect Hindi literature (as well as other languages), Radha continued her double life as both a simple *gopi* and a sophisticated lover (*nagari*) of Krishna, in poetry comprising both popular devotional lyrics and courtly poetry' (180). No wonder Bihari, more courtly than devotional, crafts his Radha as adroit, not only in the arts of dalliance and love, but in saving souls such as his from the distress of worldly existence (*bhava baadhaa*). Anyone practised in saving us from worldly suffering is surely worthy of worship.

Radha's high status is also amply illustrated in other texts of the period, especially Surdas's famous *Sursagar*. Thus, instead of

Put a pattern on my breasts, make a design on my cheeks, fasten
a girdle on my hips, fix the mass of my braids with artless
garlands, put rows of bracelets on my arms and jewelled anklets
on my feet—thus directed the yellow-robed-one was pleased
and he did so.

By the end of the poem, Radha's triumph is thus complete.

This elevated status of Radha is prevalent to this day in the area
around Vrindavana, the legendary site of young Krishna's amorous
dalliance with the gopis, or cow-girls. These artless women become
the embodiments of the highest spiritual attainment and symbols
of supreme devotion to the Godhead. This is India's own pastoral
paradise, an Edenic, unfallen world in which Eros is not tainted
by lust, and God himself frolics with his devotees in never-ending
moonlit nights of ecstasy in the charmed forest clearing. Here, Radha,
as Krishna's love interest indeed rules. Even the normal greeting of
common people is 'Radhe Radhe'.

The rise of Radha was facilitated by the widely prevalent
Shakta cults in medieval India. Radha, 'aligned and identified'
(Siegel 121) with Bhagavati, or the Supreme Goddess, attained
a status higher even than Krishna. For example, in the *Devi
Bhagavata Purana*, Narayana is shown to worship Radha (cited in
Siegel 121):

Salutations to the supreme goddess, who resides at *Rasamandala*,
who lords over the Rasa and is dearer to Krishna than his own
life. Salutation to the mother of all the three worlds, whose
lotus-like feet are worshipped by gods headed by Brahma and
Visnu. Be propitiated, O Ocean of mercy.

Mother of three worlds, worshipped by all the male gods—these
are the typical descriptions of the Mother Goddess, applied clearly
to Radha, identified as the mistress of the *Rasamandala*. Radha as
Bhagavati is a Shakta appropriation, just as Radha as Lakshmi (Sri,
Kamala, Padma, and so on) was the more conventional Vaishnava
appropriation.

To return to the opening verses from *Satsai*, one of medieval north India's most important poems, it is easy to see how they mark the transformation of Radha from gopi to goddess, consequent upon the consolidation of the cult of Radha. Radha thus becomes Krishna's fittest spouse in the new Krishnology. But how and why did such a radical apotheosis take place? And what might its metaphysical and spiritual significance be? Radha, it would seem, is largely a medieval phenomenon. She doesn't exist in the classical world and doesn't quite survive as a goddess in the harsh dawn of modernity in India. The modern Radha is anything but a love goddess—she's the fallen woman, the exploited or abandoned woman, the seductress, or an erotic playmate, but no longer the supreme pastoral goddess and consort of Krishna.

WHY RADHA?

From the late classical to the medieval period, we notice a fundamental shift from the Advaitic orthodoxy of Shankara to the qualified non-dualism, theism and Vaishnavism of other acharyas, or founders of lineages, such as Ramanuja, Madhva, Nimbarka and Vishnuswami. Some of these schools built up a considerable devotional literature around Krishna in both Sanskrit and the vernaculars, with Krishna as the favoured avatar of Vishnu, thus worthy of worship equivalent to Vishnu. Tracing back their lineages to the Vedic period they created a new orthodoxy between 900–1300 AD, known as the Chatuh-Vaishnava sampradaya, or the four authorized Vaishnava schools. But the rise of Radha was propelled by newer and smaller groups who went even further, considering Krishna not just as the favourite avatar of Vishnu, but as the supreme Godhead, the only being worthy of worship, one who embodied all the divine perfection and grace in himself.

Between 1500 and 1600 AD, a number of newer but smaller Vaishnava sampradayas were founded or modified from previous sampradayas in the late medieval or Mughal period in which the status of Krishna was elevated further. These new movements generally favoured Krishna as the Supreme Being, over and above

Vishnu, and drew even more exclusively on vernacular poetry from within their respective traditions that exalted Krishna's childhood pastimes (Beck 71).

These groups established themselves around Braj, between Delhi and Agra, believing, after Chaitanya, that this was indeed the lost or forgotten site of the frolics of Krishna's boyhood. They thus imagined into being a new pastoral geography for the conquered Hindus in the very heart of the Mughal power, a feat that must have involved considerable political skill and ingenuity in addition to unprecedented devotional fervour. The legend of Vrindavana was thus born for which, I would argue, the figure of Radha was the key ingredient. The heterodoxy of these groups had a definite erotic component to it to which Radha was essential. Those who contributed to the rise of Radha were thus the champions of a new Krishnology and included 'the Vallabha sampradaya founded by Sri Vallabhacarya, the Radhavallabha sampradaya founded by Sri Hita Harivamsa, a revived Nimbarka sampradaya, the Haridasi sampradaya founded by Swami Haridas, and the Gaudiya sampradaya of Bengal inaugurated by Sri Chaitanya Mahaprabhu' (Beck 71). What distinguishes these sects is that they 'extol Krishna as the supreme Absolute Truth from whom all other deities, including Vishnu, evolve, and the *Bhagavata Purana* is presented as the epistemological authority in this regard' (Bryant 112).[8]

As the cult of Radha grew, these new Vaishnavite traditions converted Radha's illicit or adulterous relationship with Krishna to a much higher theological principle of the indivisibility of God's masculine and feminine aspects or of the soul's inseparability from God. Whatever the ruse, it was Radha who was worshipped alongside Krishna in innumerable temples, not one of his legally wedded wives. The exception to this is Rukmini, who is given the pride of place in the Vitthal cult in Maharashtra, where it is Vitthal–Rakumai, not Radha–Krishna, that forms the divine pair. But even in the Vitthal sampradaya, the Devi's temple is usually separate from the Lord's; they are rarely conjoint as in the Radha–Krishna coupling. Thus, over time, the more disturbing or heterodox aspects of the Radha–Krishna story were smoothened out. Yet, the slightly uneasy and a sex-positive mystical cult in which sexual fulfilment was very much a part of self-realization. After colonial intervention, Indian spiritual traditions took a decisive turn towards celibacy, from which we have not yet recovered fully, despite the silent but rather obvious sexual revolution that has overpowered India in recent times. Nearly every notable spiritual guru or leader including Sri Swaminarayan, Sri Ramakrishna, Swami Vivekananda, Mahatma Gandhi, Sri Aurobindo, Ramana Maharshi, J. Krishnamurti, Swami Sivananda, Satya Sai Baba, and so on, has been an open advocate or largely in favour of abstinence for serious spiritual practitioners. Some have been silent or hypocritical, saying one thing but found out practising another. Only Osho Rajneesh was openly contemptuous of the celibacy fetish; there is an impression that he was encouraging of sex as a way to superconsciousness, though that is not what he said. His followers, even those who took *sanyas*, or vowed renunciation, were not called upon to give up sex.

Thus, Radha not only defies the whore vs virgin-mother dichotomy that has plagued most cultures of the world in their fear and exaltation of female sexuality but she has also managed to embody an unfallen Eros, so rare in romantic traditions of the world. Unlike the other love stories of the world, the Radha–Krishna myth is not about the impossibility of perfect love on earth but rather its fullest expression and celebration. It is, however, another matter that Krishna must leave the gopis. In the story as canonized in the *Bhagavata Purana*, the gopis of Vrindavana have higher wisdom and status than *jnanis*, or knowers of Advaita (non-dualism), because, despite physical separation, they experience Krishna in their hearts and are, therefore, ever united with him. But unlike Catholic nuns, who are also supposed to be brides of Christ, the gopis have experienced physical union with Krishna, dancing in ecstasy with him in the heart of the forest on that special full-moon night that lasted a thousand years when Krishna united with each one of them physically. It is only the thus ravished gopis who have forever learned the lesson of undying union with the Lord, a wisdom higher than all other paths to know God.

The story of Radha and Krishna, at least in the *Gita Govinda*, is one of found–lost–found love, not of found and lost, or even, lost and found, love (Siegel 160):

[U]nion-separation-reunion is the conventional pattern in Indian erotic literature. But it is also the archetypal structure in Indian ontology . . . For the individual liberation is reunion, a return to the primordial Unity, a recovery of the unborn Self . . .

The poem ends with the supreme joy of oneness and physical rapture, not with tearful separation or sorrow, but with the promise of eternal union in the hereafter as either in Romeo–Juliet or Saleem–Anarkali, to name two different but equally powerful takes on romantic love on earth. Even in representations of Islamic or Sufi romantic love the last stage is *fana*, or death, often interpreted as the death of the separate self but usually depicted in physical fatality at the end of the story, whether in the legend of Laila–Majnu, Shirin–Farhad or Heer–Ranjha. It is only in the Persian story of Yusuf–Zulekha that the lovers enjoy earthly fulfilment after all their trials, but that too because the transfiguration of Zulekha, who represents the earthbound soul, happens on earth itself, when her good looks and youth are restored by God because of Yusuf's good offices. The story stresses her exceptional good fortune because ordinarily such a transformation or translation could only be possible in heaven, after her death. The traditional pattern in Christian love stories is also 'the separation of lovers, both temporarily and through various obstructions and permanently through death' (Siegel 137). The Radha–Krishna story, unlike all these, takes place on earth, in the enchanted space of Vrindavana, in a peculiarly bold and unprecedented kind of pastoral, available perhaps only in India, a world that is not prelapsarian, but radically unfallen, even infallible, because of the power and glory of the supreme Godhead sporting with his creation in a perfected human form. What has been effected is a reversal of the Platonic schema, with the idea instantiated here and now, right in our midst, though in sacred and mythical time, while even the heavens, ordinarily endowed with unearthly perfection and immortality, end up looking pale and second-best in comparison. The pastoral God-child, Krishna, defies Indra, the King of Heaven, several times, thus upturning the Vedic cosmology and hierophany. Earth is now superior to heaven; Krishna, or Vishnu in his perfect human embodiment, is superior to the gods in their heaven; the provisional delusion of separation which allows us to enjoy God is superior to non-dualistic monism, which is not only monochrome but without rasa, or relish.

Radha–Krishna shows us God as an object of sensual enjoyment in a way that such an experience at once turns suprasensual, defying the normal structure of human sensual experiences. What we see is neither an assertion of the supremacy of sense experience as the logical positivists might uphold, nor God as the transcendental signified, above and beyond all sense data. It is intense, pure-hearted and transformative love, such as the gopis felt for Krishna, that came to be concentrated in the single unique person of Radha, God's paramour, and that was endowed with the strange alchemy that could turn the suprasensual into the sensual and back again into the suprasensual, thus erasing the boundaries between them.

Unlike the shame of Adam and Eve on eating the fruit of the tree of knowledge, discovering their nakedness and covering themselves when they appeared before God, the gopis, bathing in the lake, though full of shame, consciously, deliberately and lovingly emerge from the lake to be utterly nude before God, thus not only losing their shame but gaining dignity and self-realization through such exposure to the divine gaze. Their love makes them pure and innocent, quite unlike the fallen Adam and Eve. It is not a case of innocence lost but rather of innocence regained. Loving surrender to God gives us back our pristine purity instead of making us fallen in our own eyes.

The male gaze, in this case, Krishna's, is not prurient, objectifying or oppressive, but elevating, innocence-bestowing, turning the merely carnal into the spiritual, destroying, in effect, the difference between them. It is this erasure or dissolution of the difference that truly ends duality, turning us ordinary mortals into gods and goddesses. Such is the potential and the power of human, sensual, even physical, love as demonstrated by Radha and Krishna. Such love purifies the passions and emotions, taking us beyond possessive, selfish and destructive desires to the highest levels of self-realization. The ill effects of the extreme jealousy, possessiveness and fidelity of the gopis are thus not just negated but reversed when the object of their attentions is God himself. The desideratum is simple: love with all your heart and it would be like loving God himself, even if the ostensible object of your devotion were a mere man or woman. To put it differently, love God as man and man as God. That is the secret of love as revealed in the story of Radha and Krishna.

The Radha–Krishna story is of loving attachment, rather than detached loving. The latter has been the preferred choice for the spiritually inclined in most cultures, but here we see the rare reversal in which attachment itself leads to God-realization. As Siegel points out (41–42):

> The religious system aims at release; but human love is bondage and aims at bondage, attachment. In Krishna the paradox of love is realized: bondage is release; the profane dimensions of love are wholly sacred.

This reversal is effected by means of a ruse: we must be attached to God with all our hearts, leaving no room for anything else. It is a special kind of monomania, which, in the end, is not so different from the way of renunciation. Yet, for the attachment-inclined, here is the way. The trick, of course, is that being attached to God or Krishna is not quite the same as being attached to an ordinary man or woman. This is made amply clear in the Krishnology that exalts Radha to such a high status. It is only because Radha is attached to Krishna that she is saved and transformed. To desire an ordinary mortal in a similar way might not result in similar gains. Yet, the temptation, if not the possibility, is always there to emulate the Radha–Krishna love in our daily lives, to exalt love, in other words, to such a level that it becomes a transforming experience. Radha–Krishna, like Lakshmi–Narayan, thus becomes the prototype of the ideal couple, which even flawed humans may aspire to copy if not replicate.

Similarly, the Radha–Krishna love gives pride of place to a distinctive world of emotional variety, richness and depth. Even though most of the situations that the lovers go through are severely conventionalized, they still distil the essence of passion—its tremulous longings, its multitudinous fears, its endless hopes and heart-wrenching sorrows and mind-blowing ecstasies. The whole package so resembles the gamut of our own human emotions that even though it is idealized, the family resemblance between the human and the divine is unmistakable. Hence, just as sensual and sexual pleasure are an aid to self-realization, so is the whole range of human emotions, which need not be shunned but directed by love to the highest object, that of obtaining a lasting and transforming union with the beloved. Indeed, some might argue that this variety of Krishnology degenerated into excessive, even maudlin, emotionalism and sentiment, in cloying and stereotypical gestures and modes of expression, which the social and religious reformers in the 19th century regarded as effeminate and emasculating. Whether in the songs of travelling Vaishnava bards, a staple feature in the new literature, but representing a now marginalized and residual tradition, or even in the Odissi style of dancing, what we see is a stylized enactment of standardized emotions of submission. Such cloying sentimentality found disfavour in the ethos of renascent India, especially in Bengal, where a new cult of masculinity began to be fostered as a precondition to nationalism. An ideology which regarded God as the sole male and every other creature as female, soul-wise, could easily be dubbed as conducive to subordination and slavery in a feudal age, as Ranajit Guha tacitly argues (50):

> Bhakti . . . is an ideology of subordination par excellence. All the inferior terms in any relationship of power, structured as Dominance or Subordination within the Indian tradition, can be derived from it.

Perhaps, this is why the Mughals found this variety of Hinduism non-threatening enough to permit its practitioners to set up a whole temple-city in the middle of their power base. Unarmed but effective in their politics of embrace, the followers of the Radha–Krishna cult managed to give beleaguered and conquered Hinduism a new locus standi in north India.

While it is standard practice to regard Radha as allegorizing the human soul and Krishna as God, what makes Radha so special is that she is not an ordinary soul, but a Krishna-catching device par excellence. There is no one superior to her in this respect. That is why, from the generalized attraction of the gopis for Krishna, and Krishna's own dalliance with numerous cow-girls, Radha emerges as supreme in her capacity to claim Krishna for herself as hers exclusively. When she wins him over all her other competitors, though, there is no jealousy or loss of status for the latter, they concede, even celebrate, Radha's triumph. That is because Radha is everything that the gopis are, taken to its logical conclusion; her victory over Krishna, therefore, gives hope to all other souls thirsting for God. Radha as Krishna's chosen paramour is exemplary, even as she is unique and exalted over all the others. What is so special about her that it is she who 'gets' the Lord? In a word, it is the quality and intensity of her self-offering. Krishna as the supreme Godhead belongs to everyone; all have claims over him. But it is Radha alone who can become his bride and then subdue him so that he serves her. Thus, the Lord bends low to worship and honours his own creation, this world of light and colour and ecstasy that is the reflection of his own glory. This world that is transient and relative is thus no 'less' or no different from the sheer majesty of the absolute, alone, self-shining and independent of all else though 'He' may be. Radha is Krishna; the world is God. There is no duality.

What, after all, is Krishna without Radha? Though, as the Purushottama, or the Supreme Being, he is already perfect, needing no other support or embellishment, Radha augments his power and divinity just as the halo of the sun makes visible and radiant the otherwise intolerable heat of the core of the sun.[9] Radha, thus, makes Krishna accessible to the rest of us. She shows us how to obtain our heart's desire, how to unite with the Lord, how to make him our very own. The Lord is perfect but he needs Radha to make that perfection visible and manifest. Radha delights Krishna as the world; when the world functions according to his wishes, she delights the

Lord. Radha, in completely surrendering to Krishna, also becomes indistinguishable from him. Where she ends and Krishna begins no one knows.

I have sometimes wondered what Radha would tell Gandhi if she were suddenly to encounter him, as he tries to purify himself and rid himself of all carnal desires. Perhaps, she would say:

> Bapu, to love Krishna the way I do, to long for the notes of his flute, to wait for days just to catch a glimpse of him, to desire above all to touch him, feel him, dance with him, dissolving in his embrace, to feel him inside one's body, quickening the very rhythm of one's heart, to be one with him, to experience the joy of union with him, to transcend one's sense of separation from him, to think, touch, taste and hear of him, to speak only of him, to praise him, worship him, and to be teased, touched, abandoned and reunited with him, to be his and to make him one's own, to conquer him, win his favour, subdue his fiercely independent nature—all this is also *brahmacharya*— the way of the vast. To love is also to grow vast, to love not only in the celibate, impersonal way, but to love in a deeply sensual, sexual and whole-being way, to love personally, even 'romantically,' is also to lose one's moorings and grow infinite, the circumference of one's being expanding till it embraces the whole cosmos. This, Bapu, is also a way of loving, a way of being, a way to reach God, not only through self-denial, chastity and renunciation, but through the fullest participation in the ananda-yajna that is life.

This way of loving does not bind one in the chains of causality or trap one in the endless eddies of *samsara*. Instead it is a special kind of maya, which in traditional Krishnology goes by the name of Yogamaya. As Edwin F. Bryant explains in 'Krishna in the Tenth Book of the *Bhagavata Purana*' (Bryant 131):

> Yogamaya covers the pure liberated souls in the *leela* with her power of illusion, such that they are unaware of Krishna's real

nature and thus relate to him not as God but rather as their friend, lover, or child, and so on. Were Yogamaya not to extend her influence in this way, the souls would realize Krishna's true nature and be incapable of interacting with him in *leela* in these intimate ways (10.7.32; 10.11.2 and following; 10.16.14; 10.19.14; 10.20.1; 10.42.22; 10.61.2). To put it differently, how could God truly play spontaneously and unceremoniously with anyone in the role of a son or friend, if everyone knew he was really God? Unlike that of her samsaric counterpart, Yogamaya's power of illusion, then, is a highly desirable and positive one obtained only by the highest yogis.

That is why of all modes of bhakti, or devotion, *madhurya*—the way of regarding the Lord as lover, partner, spouse and husband—is the best.

CONCLUSION

The rise of Radha coincides with the period when Vaishnavism, especially the post-Chaitanya ecstatic mode of Krishna bhakti, enjoyed the widest popularity in northern India. Its after-effects, albeit in a diluted and distorted form, are still evident in popular culture and imagination. Vaishnavism, before Radha, suffered from a particular goddess-deficit. The first three avatars—Matsya, Kurma, Varaha—are subhuman; Vaman is single and celibate; Narasimha, half man, half lion, though later paired with Lakshmi, had no relationship with her. With Rama we see the beginning of a real love story. The romance of Sita–Rama is, indeed, charming, especially their first meeting, the *svayamvara*, when Sita chooses Rama after he breaks Shiva's bow, then, despite Rama's banishment, it is Sita's accompanying him that changes the first years of that terrible forest exile from something akin to a death sentence to a real honeymoon. The image of Rama and Sita in Chitrakoota is etched in the cultural memory of India as an idyll of conjugal bliss. But then Sita is abducted and the focus shifts to the great battle between Rama and Ravana. Though the latter is vanquished and beheaded, Sita's subsequent humiliations, her trial by fire and, finally, her banishment when pregnant with Luv and Kush, turns the love story into a tragedy. It takes the peculiar double 'DNA test' of his sons first reciting incognito his own story to him, then vanquishing Rama to prove that they are indeed his sons. But the love story by this time is dead, as is Sita. Vaishnavism needed the special kind of love-goddess, whom Radha would make the most attractive and irresistible of the avatars. Krishna is God because he can satisfy all his devotees, not only his fabled 16,000 plus wives who come to him later, but right in his adolescence, Radha, the most demanding and devoted of all lovers. We all wish to enjoy and own God; only Radha knows and teaches us how to. It is only with Radha that Vaishnavism's goddess-deficit is met. There are other female worshippers of Krishna both before and after, Andal and Meera, for example, to name two historico-mythic heroines. But Radha supersedes the former and anticipates all those that follow her, showing how loved and adored she is. That is why Radha bhava is so significant, whether in Chaitanya or Ramakrishna—we have to become Radha really to know and enjoy God.

Related to the goddess deficit is the problem of the male-dominated theology of the Vaishnavas. Vishnu, the Supreme Person, is conceived of and depicted as a male. In Vaishnava iconography, there is the famous depiction of the Lord reclining on the sea of milk, shaded by the hooded snake, *sesha*, with Lakshmi, his consort, at his feet. Such a portrayal invites, indeed, a feminist critique.[10] Here, the goddess serves her Lord, pressing his feet, offering service, while he rests. It would appear that men have it easy in such a scheme, while women must serve them. But on closer scrutiny we see that a lotus emerges from the navel of the Lord, which contains the three-headed creator, Brahma. The implication is that the Lord is tired because he has just completed one cycle of creation, but even as he rests before his next act of bringing into being another universe, the process of creation has already been initiated. The goddess, his own power, pleased with his ability to generate another world into motion, ensures that he enjoys a moment of rest between his labour. Such iconography acknowledges the exertions of the male in the act of reproduction; he must exert himself to satisfy his female partner before conception can take place. After losing his seed, the male rests to recover his strength, while his spouse looks on, pleased, helping to put him to sleep. Despite such a favourable interpretation, Vaishnavism remains mostly male-dominant. But it is possible that the rise of Radha occurred because of the intersection of Shaktism with Vaishnavism. The Supreme Goddess, the divine Mother, thus infiltrates and re-engineers the male-dominant creed of the Vaishnavas as Radha. But she flowers not as Mother but paramour, lover, spouse. In that sense, Radha adds to the repertoire not only of Vaishnavism but of tantricism as well. But one might argue, to the contrary, that the gopis are only the older yoginis of tantricism, pastoralized and tamed. Instead of flying, powerful beings, they are now docile cow-girls pining for Krishna. The fierce, matriarchal harridans and witchlike spirits have now been domesticated in the new agriculturalist patriarchy in which women's generative and sexual powers are no longer feared or worshipped. The wild orgy in the forest and the ritual of the chakra puja becomes the more sedate and serene rasa mandala, with one Supreme male cavorting with all his adoring nymphs.

One of the unique qualities of Hinduism, as we have already seen, is its almost infinite capacity to create gods and goddesses. There is a standard ritual process for doing so, quite akin to *nyasa* of *pranapratistha*, the breathing of life into an image of stone, metal or wood.[11] What makes Radha so exceptional is that she is god(ess) not as father, mother, child, sibling or spouse, but as paramour, lover, beloved. The distinction between licit and illicit love is erased in madhurya; only love reigns supreme. Radha 'the lover of Krishna' is an empowered being who is able—in love, and as lover— to transcend all barriers and obstacles to reach Krishna. She is the classic *abhisarika*, the woman who ventures out in storm and rain, overcoming both shame and fear, to meet her lover. But here she is exalted to the status of a goddess for doing so, not stoned, lynched, pronounced whore, or forced to commit suicide. Radha's devotional and sexual prowess is celebrated. In her wake there are texts—such as *Radhika Santwanam* of Muddupalani, famously quoted by Susie Tharu and K. Lalita in their introduction to *Women Writing in*

India (Tharu and Lalita, 1)—where Krishna is taught how to satisfy Radha, which is one of his duties as her lover. Radha, then, does give us one more example of women on top, though by and large subdued and vanquished by the patriarchy. Radha's story suggests that the eternal feminine can never be fully suppressed, but rises in one guise or another to claim her rightful equality with the male principle as enshrined in Sankhya, one of India's oldest philosophical traditions.

Radha also represents Advaita, or non-dualism simplified. Doctrinally, Advaita, as propounded by Shankara and others, is quite deep and subtle philosophically, which is one reason that it was traditionally thought that women and Sudras should not be privy to it. But the Radha–Krishna relationship, modelled as it is on romantic human love, is easy for all of us to comprehend, even instinctively relate to. It is simply the story of a glorious and joyous union between two lovers as each one of us dreams of and craves on earth, born separate and lonely as we are. We each of us hope to find that perfect partner who can help us bear the sorrows of life and lift us out of our primal loneliness. Radha–Krishna is the celebration of two becoming one; wherever that happens is sacred, at least we believe so in India, where every confluence of two or more rivers is considered holy.

Radha–Krishna, then, stands for just such a holy confluence, the very contemplation of which puts us into the frame of mind to appreciate the perfectibility and perfection of not just all nature but of the human condition itself, so characterized ordinarily, as the great Buddha reminded us, by *dukkha*, suffering, duality, separation from self. We, the ordinary, suffering mortals, beholding the perfect bliss of Radha–Krishna in Vrindavana, may also retrace the fundamental sense of *purnatva*, or completion, whose memory still inspires us and which we know, at least unconsciously, is our true nature and original state. Radha–Krishna in Vrindavana is thus the iconic depiction of the initial wholeness which the Upanishads declare as the nature of the ultimate reality: '*Purnamada, purnamidam, purnat purnamudachyte . . .*'

I would like to end by re-invoking Sri Radharani, the queen of Braj, who also rules the hearts of all devotees of Krishna, this time in the words of Bilvamangal:

A building can collapse because of a single flaw—
who knows in what ways I, who desire to be
a palace for his pleasure, may be faulty?
And few are those who can restore what once is broken . . .
Distracted, I wander from place to place,
everywhere finding only anxiety.
Oh, to see his smile!
My love, whoever brings down the house of our love
will have murdered a woman!

Whether such things happen in real life or not, in the poem, Chandidas, the poet himself enters the world of Radha's fear and grief to offer the following reassurance in the concluding couplet, or the *bhanita*:

Chandidasa says, O Radha, you reflect too much;
without your love he could not live a moment.[14]

With Chandidas, we too need to believe that the very Lord will have to come down to earth when faced with love as intense and irresistible as Radha's. Even Krishna, normally so wayward or impersonal, must yield to such a great love as Radha's. He too cannot live even for a moment without her. So must it be in all stories of true love. Wherever love exists in its pure, concentrated and overpowering form it manifests as the Radha *tattva*, the essence that is Radha, which has the power to capture even the Lord of the worlds, Krishna himself, the supreme Godhead, the stealer of our hearts and the object of all our desires.

RADHA: THE PLAY AND PERFECTION OF RASA

SHRIVATSA GOSWAMI

Essence of beauty and rasa,
Quintessence of bliss and compassion,
Embodiment of sweetness and brilliance,
Epitome of artfulness, graceful in love:
May my mind take refuge in Radha,
Quintessence of all essences.[1]

AS 'QUINTESSENCE OF all essences' Shri Radha is the ultimate answer to the human quest—philosophical, theological, existential. The following interpretation of her significance reflects the views of the religious community of which I am a part, the Chaitanya sampradaya, those who look to Sri Chaitanya, the Bengali ascetic of the late 15th and early 16th century, as the complete avatar of both Radha and Krishna.

The final adequacy of the Krishna avatar has sometimes been likened to the sixteen degrees through which the moon waxes from nothingness to fullness in the course of a fortnight. These are called *kala*s, and it is asserted that Krishna contains them all, whereas other incarnations lack at least one. The kala they lack is kala in another of its meanings: fine art. They lack the fine art of love. Such avatars may have been motivated by love, but they were never the enactment of love itself, its full play.

When one claims such a fullness of love for the Krishna avatar, of course, it is not only Krishna about whom one is speaking. Without the highest *shakti*, Radha, it would all be impossible, for she is love's potency. Without the round dance that magnetizes the two of them—the rasa in which they equally participate—there would be no experience of rasa. There the divine grandeur plays a limited role at best: all melts away in the intensity of love. If it were not so, the human seeker would remain far from the divine presence: there would be no common meeting ground . . .

Love is a form of relation grounded in the innate attraction of the human senses for their objects. This attraction builds upon a fundamental identity between subject and object; love is thus 'a natural, intense desire of a subject for contact with its object'.[2] Beings whose essences are mutually exclusive, by contrast, cannot be attracted to one another. Hence all love, following from a community of essence, is ultimately self-love. Yet, in the process of love the distinction between subject and object does not collapse into total non-differentiation. On the contrary, love is by nature a relation that presupposes a state of identity indifference.

Human love may take any number of forms, but it finds its highest expression in the love of a man and a woman. Such love, in which two hearts melt into one, involves the highest degree of intensity, and provides a more complete union than is found in other modes of relation, such as those of servant with master, parent with child, or friend with friend. Amorous love (*kanta-bhava*) joins two lovers on the same level in mutual satisfaction. This equality coupled with intensity makes possible a level of rasa unknown elsewhere.

Because of its finite basis, however, this worldly love ultimately gives rise to feelings of disgust and aversion. It cannot lead to infinite and eternal bliss, and it is to this that the human quest tends. The limited phenomenal rasa must finally be transmuted into the transcendent, absolute rasa.[3] To attain such a rasa the devotee chooses a personally suitable mode of relation with Krishna from those exemplified by the people of Vraja. The deep, loving relationship is crystallized in certain conceits that a devotee may adopt. One may regard Krishna as one's master, charge, friend or beloved. Such conceits, remembered from dramatic situations in Vraja and gradually appropriated, give rise to permanent relationships. One comes to consider Krishna as a master (*dāsya*), a son (*vātsalya*), a friend (*sakhya*) or a beloved (*mādhurya*). When catalysed by ancillary factors, these modes of intense attraction and attachment (*rati*), the substantive causes (*sthāyi-bhava*) of love, culminate in the ultimate aesthetic experience of Krishna rasa. Such realization is the highest form of love.[4]

What is the form of Radha adored by those who aspire to such higher reaches of bhakti? On the one hand, Rupa Goswami tells us she is 'the supernal *hlādinī shakti*, established in the scriptures and especially in the tantras as the greatest of all shaktis. Yet, on the other hand, that very shakti is Radha, daughter of Vrishabhanu. As such, her form is exceedingly beautiful. She has sixteen ways of dressing and making herself up, and she bedecks herself with twelve different sets of jewels and ornaments.'[5]

Raghunatha Dasa Goswami draws out the inner meaning of the various aspects of Radha's splendid appearance.

Her body is the glowing touchstone of *mahabhava* [the highest state of love], which further shines with the unguents of her friends' love for her. Having bathed in the ocean of the nectar of beauty that flows with the current of youth and ripples with compassion, Radha makes even Lakshmi despair of her charms. Radha's inner silken garment is her modesty. Her body is delicately painted with the saffron of beauty and the musk of glowing *srngara-rasa* [amorous mood]. Her ornaments are fashioned of the nine most precious jewels: they are her trembling, tears, thrilling, stupor, sweat, stammering, blushing, madness and swoon. Her garland is prepared from the flowers of a select assortment of aesthetic qualities, and her garment is freshened with the pure, subtle perfume distilled from her exquisite virtues.

Her hairdo is devious like her hidden pique, and she wears a bright mark of good fortune on her forehead. Her ears are adorned with the glorious sounds of Krishna's name. She reddens her lips with the betel leaf of intense attachment, and the guile of love is her mascara. She is fragrant with the camphor exuded by her sweet smile and tinkling voice. Wearing on her heart the necklace of love's separation, weighted with a swinging pendant fashioned of the paradoxical feeling of separation-in-union, she reclines on a couch of conceit in the chamber of charm. Her breasts are covered with the blouse of anger and affection. The melody from the vina of her glory drowns out the noise [of envy] from the hearts and speech of her co-wives. Her lovely hands rest playfully on the shoulder of her companion. Adorned in this way Radha offers the honey of amorousness, which maddens even the Love-god.[6]

Even when bhakti blossoms into the highest state of love (*prema*), there is a further internal intensification of feeling. This ripening process begins with the stage of being confident of one's love, flourishes in a complex of moods that express her stubborn annoyance at her lover's inconstancy, congeals into a state in which the heart melts with excessive longing for the beloved and, in a love that is ever fresh, culminates in a supreme ecstasy (mahabhava).[7] This process resembles the various stages required to refine the juice of the sugar cane until it becomes a transparent crystal, the quintessential concentration of sweetness. External agents may encourage this refining process, but their presence does not affect the essential flavour. The love of the *gopis of* Vraja, and of Radha, first and foremost, is of this highest type.

Love by its very nature is manifest, realizing itself in infinite ways and moods, and Krishna experiences it in its total variety through his relations, with the panoply of gopis that inhabit Vraja. Yet, in a way that seems paradoxical, he is satisfied only in the company of Radha, love's ideal. The paradox is resolved when one realizes that the many gopis are but manifestations of the body of Radha *(kāya-vyūha)*. She complicates herself thus in order to satisfy her beloved in all possible ways: her friends are but instruments of rasa. All that expresses the fact that the love of Krishna for his lovers remains the same, while yet it varies in accordance with the receptivity and preparedness of his devotees. The love of the gopis, which symbolizes this devoted love at a higher level, is itself great. Yet, in the last analysis there is a further height, a level at which all feelings are fully explicit. This manifests itself as an excess of unmotivated jealousy and a deep contemplative consciousness even in the actual eternal union with Krishna. It occurs only in Radha: it is possible for no one else, since she alone is the essence of hlādinī shakti.[8]

Love is, by nature, a mutual satisfaction that is possible only when one negates oneself totally for the sake of the other. This self-negation involves the negation of sensuality and constitutes the height of spirituality. Its other-directed delight both includes and transcends personal and subjective pleasure. Krishna seeks pleasure in heightening the bhava of Radha and she is delighted in his delight.[9]

Thus, Radha and Krishna, the subject and object of love, provide absolute bliss to each other through their lovely dalliance (rasa). This supreme aesthetic experience is the ultimate stage of love, the goal of a devotee, where the two highest principles are coupled in one self-subsistent reality. Often this highest experience is described with the imagery of rain. Either Krishna is painted as the dark cloud pregnant with torrents of love's nectar (rasa, i.e. Radha), or Radha is envisioned as the receptacle and Krishna as the liquid content. Their mystical union is the ultimate rasa.[10] In it separation gives rise to the pleasure of union, and conversely union contains a loving feeling of separation. In such an intermingling the separate identities of lover and beloved dissolve into a single whole; two characters flow into each other; two separate entities become interchangeable . . .

From age to age one essence, two names:
    the joy of bliss is Śyāmā,
    the bliss of joy is Śyāmā.
From all eternity manifest
    as two in a single form
Two as one they come to Vrindavana,
    Rādhā–Krishna, Krishna–Rādhā,
    ever and unchanging,
Devastatingly beautiful.[11]

—Harivyāsa Deva

10

UNDERSTANDING
RADHA'S SYMBOLIC LOVE

SHUBHA VILAS

THIS ESSAY AIMS to explore the role of Radha, the feminine aspect of God, through the teachings of the bhakti saints in the Gaudiya Vaishnava tradition. Gaudiya Vaishnavas are those who worship Radha and Krishna in accordance with the teachings of Chaitanya Mahaprabhu, whom they worship as a divine avatar.

For the Gaudiya Vaishnavas, Krishna is the most comprehensive appearance of God. The *Chaitanya Charitamrita* (*Adi-Raas* 4.10–12) substantiates this.

> *pūrṇa bhagavān avatare yei kāle*
> *āra saba avatāra tāṅte āsi' mile*
>
> *nārāyaṇa, catur-vyūha, matsyādy-avatāra*
> *yuga-manvantarāvatāra, yata āche āra*
> *sabe āsi' kṛṣṇa-aṅge haya avatīrṇa*
> *aiche avatare kṛṣṇa bhagavān pūrṇa*

'When the complete Supreme Personality of Godhead descends, all other incarnations of the Lord meet together within Him. Of the multifarious energies, or *shakti*s, that Krishna has, two are prominent. They are the *bahiranga* shakti, or external energy, and the *antaranga* shakti, or internal energy.'

> *kṛṣṇera ananta-śakti, tāte tina – pradhāna*
> *cic-chakti', 'māyā-śakti', 'jīva-śakti'-nāma*
> *antaraṅgā', 'bahiraṅgā', 'taṭasthā' kahi yāre*
> *antaraṅgā 'svarūpa-śakti' – sabāra upare*

'Krishna has unlimited potencies, which can be divided into three main parts. These are the spiritual, material and marginal potency, [together] known as the living entity. In other words, these are all potencies of God—internal, external and marginal. But the internal potency is the Lord's personal energy and stands over the other two.'

Krishna never becomes influenced or affected in any way by his external potency more popularly known as Durga Devi. On the other hand, he is so intimately connected with his internal energy that he allows himself to be affected by it intensely. This energy is also called *swarupa* shakti or atman shakti. This is the energy that allows Krishna to be what he is. This internal energy manifests itself in three divisions—known as *sat* (eternality), *cit* (knowledge) and ananda (bliss). The sat feature, which is also called *sandhini* shakti, causes all expansions of Krishna into being. The cit feature, which is also called *samvit* shakti, is used by Krishna to cause everyone to know. The ananda feature, which is called *hlādinī shakti*, causes Krishna to feel bliss. Radha is the very embodiment of the bliss-producing feature of Krishna's internal—or antaranga swarupa—shakti. The culmination of hlādinī shakti is *prema* (pure love), the culmination of prema is bhava (ecstatic emotions), the culmination of bhava is *mahabhava* (highest emotions of love of God) and the personification of mahabhava is Radha.

Just like Krishna expands into a multitude of Vishnu and Narayana forms, Radha expands into complimentary forms of Lakshmi. In addition, the 16,108 queens of Krishna in Dwarka and the host of *gopis* of Vrindavana are also expansions of Radha. The *Chaitanya Charitamrita* (*Adi-lila* 4.74–77) substantiates this.

Kṛṣṇa-kāntā-gaṇa dekhi tri-vidha prakāra
eka lakṣmī-gaṇa, pure mahiṣī-gaṇa āra
vrajāṅganā-rūpa, āra kāntā-gaṇa-sāra
śrī-rādhikā haite kāntā-gaṇera vistāra

avatārī kṛṣṇa yaiche kare avatāra

aṁśinī rādhā haite tina gaṇera vistāra
vaibhava-gaṇa yena tāṅra aṅga-vibhūti
bimba-pratibimba-rūpa mahiṣīra tati

'The beloved consorts of Lord Krishna are of three kinds: the goddesses of fortune, the queens and, foremost of all, the milkmaids of Vraja. These consorts all proceed from Radhika. Just as the fountainhead, Lord Krishna, is the cause of all incarnations, Shri Radha is the cause of all these consorts. The goddesses of fortune are partial manifestations of Shrimati Radhika, and the queens are reflections of her image.'

Krishnadas Kaviraja Goswami, the author of the *Chaitanya Charitamrita*, uses a remarkable metaphor to illustrate the relationship between Radha and the gopis of Vrindavana (*Madhya-lila* 8.209).

Rādhāra svarūpa – kṛṣṇa-prema-kalpalatā
sakhī-gaṇa haya tāra pallava-puṣpa-pātā

'By nature, Shrimati Radharani is just like a creeper of love of Krishna, and the gopis are the twigs, flowers and leaves of that creeper.'

Rādhā kṛṣṇa-praṇaya-vikṛtir hlādinī śaktir asmād
ekātmānāv api bhuvi purā deha-bhedaṁ gatau tau

'Radha is a transformation of Krishna's love and his internal pleasure-giving potency.'

Radha is considered the highest devotee of Krishna and derives the greatest pleasure in serving Him. In fact, her name itself means 'one who is the greatest worshipper'. She is the origin of all the gopis and all the Goddesses of Fortune who are engaged in the service of the Lord. She is the mainstay, the ideal inspiration of all devotees embarking on the path of devotional service to Krishna. Her mood is that of sacrifice. She puts herself last and puts everyone else who can serve Krishna better than her ahead. She puts the needs of Krishna ahead of her own needs. Radha is an embodiment of love that sustains, surrounds and embellishes Krishna in every way.

Radha has many names according to her qualities and characteristics. Each name reaffirms another way she connects with Krishna. One name is Govinda-anandini, which means 'one who gives pleasure to Govinda'. Govinda-mohini means 'one who mystifies Govinda'. Krishnamayi means 'one who sees Krishna both within and without'. Of all the various names of Radha, one name that stands out is Veda-gopya, which means 'one who is hidden even in the Vedas'. This is because the subject matter of Radha is very confidential—so confidential that even the Vedas don't dare to talk about her openly. Radha *tattva* cannot—and should not—be discussed superficially and frivolously. A subject that even the Vedas hesitate to talk about openly should be considered with great care and precaution. Just as Radha is the confidential associate of the Lord, her glories remain confidential in the pages of the Vedas.

It is generally understood that God is male. In fact, one need only browse the various revealed scriptures of the world to note that God is always addressed as being male. Gaudiya Vaishnava literature, however, makes it clear that in the ultimate sense God is both male and female. It is Krishna who represents the male aspect of Godhood and Radha the female aspect. However, the two are not in the strictest sense, considered to be separate. Rather, Radha and Krishna are one, but have separated to enjoy each other's company.

Radha and Krishna are not two different personalities but one, having taken different forms to reveal to the world the eternal principles of divine love. Krishna represents the masculine aspect of divinity and Radha the feminine. Without understanding the feminine aspect one cannot claim to know God in his entirety.

Krishna is the energetic and Radha is the energy. Without the energy the energetic would have no meaning and completion.

Without Radha there is no meaning to Krishna and without Krishna there is no meaning to Radha.

In traditional Vaishnava literature, Krishna is compared to the sun and Radha to sunshine. Both exist simultaneously and yet one is emanating from the other. Still, it is a misconception to say that the sun came prior to the sunshine. As soon as there exists a sun, there has to be sunshine too. More importantly, the sun itself has no significance without the sunshine, heat and light. And conversely, heat and light do not exist without the sun. Thus, the sun and the sunshine coexist, each equally important for the existence of the other. It may thus be concluded that they are simultaneously one and different. Krishna, therefore, is described as the *shaktiman*—the energetic source, whereas Radha is the shakti, or the energy. The shaktiman is never addressed separately but rather along with shakti. For instance, Krishna is always addressed as Radha–Krishna. The calling of the shakti first is significant; it signifies that to approach the Lord in any of his forms, we must first go through their energies or, more appropriately, their consorts.

Radha exhibits such a vast variety of emotions that sometimes Krishna is mystified. He is at times lost in finding the appropriate way to reciprocate aptly with her. He then takes the help of Lalita, another principal gopi who is again an expansion of Radha, to find out the best way to reciprocate the current mood Radha is exhibiting.

Krishna is a balance of law and love. But Radha is filled to the brim with only love. Therefore, in the bhakti tradition it is recommended we approach Krishna through the agency of Radha. Connecting to Krishna directly could be risky, as he may choose to look at you through the eye of law and your flaws may be focused on. But Radha is a divine mother who never focuses on the flaws but on the desire to serve and connect with Krishna. Thus, she aptly assists in kindling that connection with Krishna.

The Vedic culture extends respect and reverence to women for the simple reason that they represent the feminine energy of God. There is a Vedic saying, 'Where women are worshipped, there the gods dwell.'

One of Radha's many names is Janagati, which qualifies her as the goddess of all goddesses. She portrays the divine feminine love and beauty. Thus, in the material world, we can see her divine reflection mirrored in all that is feminine, elegant and pure. Just by being aware of her qualities, we can experience the spiritual dimension flowing in the material world.

Radha embodies the quintessence of all the feminine qualities in completeness, each of which has a story. Rhythm, flow, creativity, inspiration, intuition, sensuality, beauty, receptivity, mystery, magic and wonder, bewilderment, attractiveness, magnetizing, flexibility, compassion, understanding, expansive, complex, multitasking (multidimensional), detail-oriented, caring, attentive to everyone's needs, visionary, nurturing, nourishing, creative, innovative, connected to a purpose, healing, sweet, charming, comforting, exciting, passionate, soft, warm, stress-relieving, tranquilizing, delightful, humorous, organized, creating a beautiful environment, communicative, sensitive, unconditionally loving, having parenting instincts, responsibility for parents, the ability to bear stress, humility, emotional intelligence, nursing, non-violent, expressive, honest, kind, forgiving, elegant and confident. This is just a fragment of the plethora of feminine qualities Radha epitomizes.

This is also why spiritual advancement is known to balance the female and male energies within oneself. When there's harmony within, peace and joy prevail.

There is a story which goes thus—once Radha confided in her *sakhi*s about Krishna's love for her. When they asked her how she knew this, she explained, 'Whatever I want him to do, he does. Whenever I want him to do it, he does. From this I guess he loves me a lot.' The gopis asked for an example, at which Radha remained quiet. The gopis were surprised and requested one example, at least. Radharani said, 'That's a big dilemma actually. The problem is whatever he does is to my liking. I'm not sure if he does what I like, or I like what he does! My mind thinks what he has done is what I want.' Radha's heart poignantly reveals the non-difference between her and Krishna.

THE HEART-THROB OF CHAITANYA

HARSHA V. DEHEJIA

IN A PERSONAL letter to me, Edward Dimock on 15 April 1998 wrote:

> The proposal of a relationship between religious and aesthetic experience, the use of aesthetic theory to gain understanding of the nature of God and worship, is an extraordinary contribution by the Vaishnavas to religious thought. It seems to me a unique contribution . . . that the poet must be in an exalted state before the creation of poetry is possible, and that when poetry is created in that exalted state, it is by definition true. Rupa Goswami and others of the Vaishnava tradition who gave shape to this understanding have been, I think, too little appreciated for the creative nature of what they did.

I have pondered about this cryptic, personal but pregnant statement of Dimock for many years. He was referring to Gaudiya—or Bengal—Vaishnavism, which, while following much of the basic tenets of orthodox Vaishnavism, departs from it in two fundamental areas. One is the insistence that Krishna and not Vishnu is the ultimate Godhead and, second, that Krishna is an androgyne and Radha is an essential part of Him. We will be mostly concerned with the second assertion in this essay and explore the presence of Radha in Gaudiya Vaishnavism.

While taking his stand on aesthetic experience Dimock was pointing to another experience which he called true. He firmly believed that to the Vaishnavas of Bengal *shringara* rasa, or celebrating Krishna as the paragon of love, is dual: it is pure aesthetic experience and enjoyment on the one hand as well as pure devotion at the same time—one leads to the other. It is in his evocation of shringara rasa that the Bengali poet becomes the spokesman of truth. It becomes clear that Rupa Goswami, the foremost of the Gaudiya philosophers, takes rasa out of the literary context and gives it a religious texture. Rupa takes the rasa doctrine a significant step further than Abhinavagupta. Until now rasa was the cornerstone of aesthetic experience, arising from the arts, and even though transient, it was capable of leading the *rasika* to *rasananda*, the bliss of rasa, a state that was described as the twin brother of *brahmananda*. In a little more than 500 years, the Vaishnavas of Bengal had brought Krishna at the centre of rasa. He was *Raseshwar*, the *ashraya* and repository of rasa, nay, He was rasa itself. Rupa Goswami asserts: *'Devadi vishayaa ratihi bhaktihi'*—that when it came to Krishna, shringara rasa became shringara bhakti. This was a major contribution of the Gaudiyas but we will not visit this issue in this essay.

The contribution of Jayadeva in the creation of Radha cannot be overemphasized as it was foundational. However, there were important political factors in medieval India that must also be considered in the transformation of Radha from a *gopi* to a consort, especially in Gaudiya Vaishnavism. The concept of kingship asserts that the king is the earthly representation of divinity and this automatically brings in the idea of the king's consort, or queen. The *Vishnu Purana*, dated the 4th century AD, regards Lakshmi as the consort of Vishnu. Regal Vaishnava dynasties of ancient India regarded the king as the terrestrial reflection of Vishnu and, by the same token, his queen as the earthly representation of Lakshmi. When in and after the *Bhagavata Purana* Krishna replaces Vishnu as the central Godhead of Vaishnavism it was but natural that once Radha came into being in the post-Bhagavata period and was romantically connected with Krishna that she came to be accepted as Krishna's consort. The concept of Radha as a consort thus was to a certain extent the direct result of the Vaishnava royal dynasties.

Wherever she came from, Radha is crucial to the development of the Vaishnavism of Bengal. To poets, she is a warm, touchingly sincere woman in love. To all Vaishnavas, she is the symbol of true love, or *prema*. To the Sahajiya Vaishnavas in particular, her presence on earth and in all human beings gives mankind a way to experience the divine.

However, the greatest contribution in the making of Radha not only as a consort but even more as a goddess is the Shakta tradition of Bengal and Odisha. It was around the 8th century that the conception of Shakti comes into prominence in the Vaishnava tradition, and it moves significantly away from Shankara's concept of maya. The Shaktas believe that the universe comes into being because of the association of the male and the female principles and that at the end of the cosmic cycle the created universe returns to its source when Shakti comes to repose in the male. The *Lakshmi Tantra*, which is a Pancharatra text compiled between the 9th and the 12th centuries, asserts the primacy of Lakshmi in the veneration of Vishnu; it is she who possesses *kriyashakti*. At about the same time dualistic Vedanta philosophers like Nimbarka were moving the tradition away from Shankara's Advaita, and because of Dvaitic formulations the concept of Shakti was gaining ground. The stage was now set for Chaitanya to take his stand on the *Gita Govinda*, accept Radha as a consort and formulate Gaudiya Vaishnavism and exalt Radha from a gopi to a consort.

It is significant that after the initial formulation of shringara bhakti *within* the framework of Advaita in the Bhagavata, the only Vaishnava tradition to uphold the Advaitic standpoint was Vallabha and the Pushtimarg sampradaya, where initially there is no Radha and even when she enters the tradition it is because of the influence of the Gaudiyas. All other traditions that followed the *Gita Govinda*, whether it was the Gaudiya Vaishnavism of Bengal, the Ritikavya tradition of courtly poetry of Keshav Das and the Ritikal poets or the Warkari tradition at Pandharpur, all of these uphold only the Dvaitic tradition, where Radha or Rukmini become consorts and cease to remain gopis. The shringara in the Dvaitic traditions has a different tone and texture. This is entirely due to the presence and persona of Radha and her love for Krishna.

Chaitanya was born in Nabadwip, a centre of learning, on the *amavasya* of Phalgun in 1486. Chaitanya's childhood name was Vishvambhara, which he later changed to Krishna Chaitanya, to which his followers added the honorific Chaitanya Mahaprabhu. His family were pious Vaishnavas, and Vishvambhara was educated in the traditional Brahmin fashion. He passed away in 1533.

Chaitanya was an enigmatic person and the details of his life are sketchy. He was neither a theologian nor an organizer, he was a god-intoxicated person and wanted to experience Krishna here and now. The immediacy of realizing Krishna was his mantra. What is more important is that he did not leave anything behind in writing and, therefore, what we know of him is from anecdotal evidence and the writings of his disciples, especially the *Chaitanya Charitamrita*. What is even more significant is that Chaitanya remained a controversial figure even in his lifetime, and his brand of Vaishnavism was considered socially deviant by the orthodoxy. It is said that one day a kirtan was taking place in the house of Srivasa, a neighbour of Chaitanya's, and people in the neighbourhood gathered and were burning with rage as they did not like the whole ethos of the kirtans. Chaitanya did not accept caste hierarchy, and the orthodox Brahmins of the day felt that he was changing the social control of society and this was another factor that invited displeasure. There are many anecdotal accounts of Chaitanya's life but these are not as important as his own persona. Chaitanya was considered not just an avatar of Krishna but Krishna himself, not the Krishna of the *Bhagavata* or the *Gita Govinda*, but he was the coming together of Radha and Krishna, Radha externally and Krishna internally. 'In the body of Chaitanya the two are one, undivided' (*Chaitanya Charitamrita* 7.111).

As Dimock puts it:

> He was Krishna internally, Radha externally, his golden colour was
> that of Radha; his deep love and longing for Krishna were those of
> Radha; yet within he had the full divinity of Krishna. When Radha
> and Krishna were two, neither could experience love to the full . . .
> When they became one in Chaitanya their joy was doubled.[1]

Chaitanya very often dressed as Radha, he would sing and dance, go
into a trance and ecstasy. For Chaitanya, bhakti to Krishna was the
defining feature of his brand of Vaishnavism and not social norms
and practices, or rites and rituals. He said, 'Things are pure because
they are sacred to Krishna, not because they are thought to be pure
by men' (*Chaitanya Charitamrita* 7.74). Sin, according to Chaitanya,
is the denial of Krishna as the highest god (*Chaitanya Charitamrita*
6.72). Chaitanya's Vaishnavism was, therefore, quite distinct even
from the orthodox Vaishnavism of Bengal and Assam, which was
based on the Bhagavata and Sahajiya Vaishnavism, which took its
stand on the tantric tradition. This does not rule out that there was
intersection and cross-fertilization of the three types, but despite this
Chaitanya's Gaudiya Vaishnavism remains unique.

The story is told among the devotees of Chaitanya that once
the devas came to Krishna and complained that the Kali Yuga was
an age of wickedness and that mankind was in trouble. On hearing
this Krishna told Radha they must go down to earth together and
become avatars. Radha refused, for she said that all she required for
her happiness was the company of Krishna in the eternal Vrindavana,
as she could not bear another separation from him, reminding
Krishna that he had left her in Vrindavana. Krishna assured her that
there would be no *viraha* this time. In their previous incarnation
on the earthly Vrindavana, Krishna said we were one soul in two
bodies, but in the present avatar in Chaitanya's Vrindavana, we will
be in one body—Krishna internally and Radha externally. This is
the unique formulation of the Bengal Vaishnava androgyne nature
of the Godhead and differs significantly from the *ardhanarishvara*
concept of Kashmir Shaivism. Radha, in the Chaitanya system, is
the *hlādinī shakti* of Krishna and is engaged with him emotionally

and not intellectually; she loves Krishna and does not just venerate Krishna.

The keynote of Bengal Vaishnava theology is that the relation between *jiva* (mankind) and Bhagavat (God) is the same as the difference between Shakti (Radha) and Shaktiman (Krishna). Jiva Goswami calls it *achintya bhedabheda*, same yet different, one that cannot be comprehended by the human mind. This homologous relationship is carried one step further, for just as Radha is the perfect devotee of Krishna, we as humans can do no better than be perfect devotees of Radha–Krishna. Radha is the perfect devotee of Krishna, so devoted is she that even though she resides in the same body as Krishna she feels pangs of separation from him, so extreme is her viraha. The presence of Radha and Krishna in one body is a recurring refrain and is the credo of Bengal Vaishnavism.

While the main tenets of Bengal Vaishnavism are elaborately laid out in the writings of Jiva and Rupa Goswami, and these texts are indeed very erudite, it is in the padas that the persona of Radha comes through. The singing of mystical songs is an established tradition in Bengal. Wandering mystics, temple singers, groups of singers that go from home to home or from one festival to another are a feature of Bengal. These songs express profound truths in simple language and reach the common people. Not only do they perform a social purpose in getting people together but they keep the religious tradition alive at the ground level.

Chaitanya, it is said, was influenced by Jayadeva, Vidyapati and Chandidas. Apparently, there were many poets who were called Chandidas, but the one text that Chaitanya read was Chandidas's *Srikrishna Kirtana*.

> Come, let us go to see the fair one, in all his beauty;
> Come, let us go to Nabadwip, to see his wondrous form.
> His body glows like melted gold,
> and waves of tears swell in the ocean of his eyes.
> Let us look upon the golden columns of his arms
> reaching to his knees, and on the cloth
> coloured like the dawn, around his waist.

Let us look upon the jasmine garland
swinging to his feet.
Vasu says: Come! Let us worship the living God.

The following dialogue was recorded between Chaitanya and his
disciple Ramananda.

Chaitanya: What is the goal of life?

Ramananda: To follow the rules and injunctions followed in
the scriptures.

Chaitanya: This is only an external part of religion, only a
means, not a goal.

Ramananda: Surrendering the fruits of action to Krishna.

Chaitanya: This too is external.

Ramananda: Realizing that devotion arises from self-surrender.

Chaitanya: This too is external.

Ramananda: Realizing with knowledge.

Chaitanya: This too is external.

Ramananda: Acquiring the spirit of service to Krishna.

Chaitanya: That is good. Go further.

Ramananda: To love Krishna as a friend.

Chaitanya: That is very good. Go further.

Ramananda: To love Krishna as a child.

Chaitanya: That is also good. Go further.

Ramananda: To love Krishna as a beloved bridegroom.

Chaitanya: This is no doubt the goal. But tell me if there is any
attainment further than this.

Ramananda: My understanding does not go further than this.

At this point Chaitanya stopped Ramananda from speaking,
indicating thereby that the highest truth, the highest secret, must not
be divulged. According to Chaitanya *premvilas vivarta* is the truth of
mystic union, wherein there is no longer a distinction between the
lover and the beloved.

In Gaudiya literature, Krishna is compared to the sun and
Radha to the sunshine. Thus, both exist together, independent and

yet dependent, what is called achintya bhedabheda. They assume different forms to enjoy each other. Our role as rasikas and bhaktas is to identify with the sakhis. Gaudiya texts elaborate on the role of sakhis. The gopis are divided into five groups, the most important being the parama-preshtha-sakhis, or the eight primary gopis. These gopis are named: Lalita, Vishakha, Chitra, Indulekha, Champakalata, Tungavidya, Rangadevi and Sudevi. Gaudiya literature provides many details of their lives and service, including each one's parents' names, spouse's name, skin colour, age, birthday, mood, temperament, favourite melody, instrument, closest girlfriends, and so on. These elements form the substance of an inner meditation, or sadhana, which is designed to relieve the practitioner of the spiritual amnesia that afflicts all conditioned souls. It helps them to realize who they really are in terms of their eternal identity in the spiritual realm. Through this meditation one gradually develops prema, or love for Krishna. Among the gopis there is a class of gopis called manjari, also called prana-sakhis or nitya-sakhis, and their love for Radha is called bhavollasarati. A manjari is totally dedicated to Radha and even helps her in her amorous sports with Krishna. If Vrindavana, the spiritual realm, is compared to a lotus flower, and Radha and Krishna are acknowledged as the centre, then the gopis may be compared to the petals and the manjari to the stamens.

A common Gaudiya mantra is:

Atapa-rakita suraja nahi jani
Radha-virahita Krishna nahi mani

(Just as there is no such thing as sun without heat or light, I do not accept a Krishna who is without Sri Radha!)

12

RADHE RADHE

MADHUREETA ANAND

'RADHE RADHE', NOT Hare Krishna, not Jai Shri Ram, but 'Radhe Radhe' is the greeting of those who live in Vrindavana. Being a film-maker and keen traveller, it was strange that I hadn't been to Vrindavana before. Here I was for the first time—in a city famed for love. Not for lovers but for love. Love in the way it was when Radha and Krishna were said to dance their Raas Leela—spiritual, deep, never-ending and immortal.

And yet at first sight, all one sees are quiet streets so narrow that even time and its ravages couldn't make its way in, temples with distant clanging bells, mercenary monkeys that trade stolen glasses for boxes of juice, and widows. Thousands of ladies clad in white, their bodies stooped with age and furrowed by the forces of survival—they seem like the same person multiplied. They scurry through the lanes from one bhajan *sabha* to another, receiving the few rupees to help them survive.

What is apparent physically probably stems from their shared story—almost all of them are from Bengal, arriving here when their husbands died and they grew too old to work—their families decided there was no place for them any longer in the homes in which they lived their entire lives. Sons, grandsons, brothers-in-law all cut them off because they didn't have the right male relative by their side any more. Some of them were brought here and abandoned—because who can explain to a distraught woman that all relationships, money and social life were a mirage created by a living husband. And now that he's gone, so has all that.

And so then one has to wonder how it came to be that the greeting here is 'Radhe Radhe'—celebrating the woman who was the lover of Krishna but a wife to another? A woman who clearly had it all and celebrated it with no attachment and no apologies—where was she? Why use her name as a greeting when she was no longer here? If one scoured Vrindavana, one couldn't find any *gopi*s and certainly no Radha—those ladies clad in bright attire, singing and dancing in celebration of a beloved, living in the ecstasy of love.

And, yet, we find things in the most unexpected places.

I was making a film for the Paramhansa Yogananda Trust, which is doing some wonderful work to not only restore physical health to the widows but, most importantly, also giving them their dignity back by giving them their right to demand and control their lives. They have managed to create a sea of bossy, happy ladies, but the supply of the abandoned widows does not stop and so their work is continuous.

It was lunch break during our shoot when I stepped outside to ponder this deep contradiction: the heartbreak of remembering Radha, and now seeing women who stood as symbols of freedom lost in the sand of superstition and deep patriarchy.

It is then that I noticed her.

To my side stood a woman. About seventy years of age— swaddled in a white sari, stooped—and, like myself, also in deep thought. She looked distinctly worried and anxious. I watched her for a few moments not sure what to do. Not able to bear the deepening concern on her face I asked if everything was all right. There was no answer. I then asked her if she had eaten lunch—hoping that a neutral question would break the ice. What it did was break the dam. She turned and looked at me, exasperated—'How can I?' Why?—I asked, she replied, 'Because he hasn't eaten a thing all day.'

I smiled, guessing, approximately, who she was referring to but still asked her anyway—who are you talking about?

She looked at me like I must be the stupidest person on earth. 'Him . . . my thakur—you know his name? Don't you?' Yes, I said. His name is Krishna. She nodded. 'That's one of his names.' She shook her head and said, 'I made kheer, he didn't eat it, I made dal, he didn't eat it—you can't eat palak every day.' I nodded in understanding and said in sympathy that that was pretty stubborn of him.

She replied, 'Yes—he knows I love him so he likes to tease me sometimes,' and then she smiled . . . And there she was. Radha— the cosmic dancer with her lover—transmuted and transfigured but definitely her.

Perhaps, then, we have got so used to seeing joy and love in a certain way that we do not recognize its other forms. Like a monochrome shadow becoming more real than the body, we search for the image we know.

And it was this encounter that unfurled Radha in Vrindavana to me and suddenly she was evident everywhere.

In the widows, showing me their shrines. In the clothes they stitch for 'Him'. In their rendition of 'Hare Krishna', which is not just a song but a call. A call so deep that it must surely be heard and must vibrate in the heart of the one that they call to.

Driving back to the hotel—someone casually pointed to a square where they said Uddhav met with the gopis. Krishna's cousin Uddhav, a knowledge-driven seeker, needed a lesson in devotion and so Krishna sent him to Vrindavana on the pretext of teaching the gopis about God.

Uddhav's ego is stoked at the prospect of being a teacher and he explains to the gopis that their search for God is incomplete because they have not read the scriptures. That instead of saying Krishna's name all the time, they should spend time gaining some knowledge. The gopis listen carefully and then one of them speaks: 'My heart, my mind, my entire body is filled with Krishna—where would I put your knowledge?' Uddhav watches the love-absorbed gopis and is brought to tears. It is from them that Uddhav learns that transcending the ego is a crucial step towards God. That devotion and love is a direct path to enlightenment.

And so, perhaps, the greeting of 'Radhe Radhe' is not a greeting but, in fact, a call to invoke the Radha quality in those who inhabit and visit Vrindavana—because in each of us resides that quality of surrender that is the path to joy and love.

Later that day we were to film the widows playing Holi—the festival of colour that was famously played by Radha and Krishna. We were to recreate the festival in the month of April—four weeks after the actual festival.

Mounds of rose petals, marigold flowers, red *gulal*, pink and yellow colours of decorative powder lined the periphery of the central courtyard of the care home for widows. Ladies of advanced years sat in chairs in the corridor waiting for us to set up and start. Many of them racked by ailments were finding it hard to sit this long. And I was concerned that perhaps it was all too much for the ladies.

A warm shaft of light fell on the courtyard—dappled by the trees overhead. And the music was turned on—a simple lyrical Krishna bhajan—'Hare Krishna, Krishna Krishna, Hare Hare . . .' As if propelled by another force, the ladies rose and danced—a dance of ecstasy, of joy, of celebration. They coloured each other, sometimes Krishna, sometimes Radha they smeared each other in red, pink and yellow. They bathed each other in flower petals. The colour flew up and filled the air and mixed with the raining petals—the light held them in its thrall and under this umbrella the widows in white became the gopis in colour, dancing and swaying and whirling— showing their true form. It seemed like their physical bodies were attire they had worn to live in a material world and here they had discarded them. Naked and revealed they were Krishna's lovers. Here, now and forever.

And then one of the ladies objected to the filming crew being left out of the revelry. And in a moment I stood coloured and engulfed. Becoming one of them. Becoming one.

13

THE BLUE-NECKED GOD

INDIRA GOSWAMI

TRANSLATED FROM THE ASSAMESE
BY GAYATRI BHATTACHARYYA

SAUDAMINI TRIED TO get familiar with this new life and adjust to it. She was inquisitive by nature so she was curious about everything around her: the life of the *radheshyamis*, the new temples and the ancient ones, the ruins of Bilwamangal Kunj, the Sringar Bot Temple, Sakshi Gopal, and she lost no time acquainting herself with it all. She even visited those ruined heaps that had once been impressive ancient monuments. Those ruins that were now entwined by jungles of thorny shrubs. For days, Saudamini wandered in those places, quite bewitched by their history and mythology. Indeed, she felt, these ancient ruins and temples of Braj had a peculiar charm that could touch the core of one's heart. Like those old stone statues of the Raj Bhawan in Jaipur that were now covered with moss, one could still hear their heart-rending voices if one had the desire.

Aurangzeb had long ago ordered the swanlike necks of the priceless statues of Krishna's companions, the *gopis* carved on the ancient Govind Temple, to be broken to pieces. But even now, if one sits in meditation inside the broken old temple built of red stone, and listens intensely, one can hear the plaintive tunes of sorrow and torture.

In the meantime, Dr Roychoudhury had started working in the dispensary. So he was mostly away from home. Saudamini started to pass her time, particularly the afternoons, roaming around the *akhaara* (ashram) and its neighbouring areas. There was a strange locality on the right-hand side of the akhaara, in the small lane facing Harabari, and near this was the temple of Beharimohan Kunj.

One day, she crossed the roof of this temple, intending to go to this mysterious place. But as she was about to go down the steps, the sadhus who stayed in the temple said to her, 'Since you are new here, it will be better if you do not go there.' These words from the sadhus who slept on string cots on the roof and who passed their spare time playing the *pahkwaz*, only increased Saudamini's curiosity.

Bowing respectfully in front of the priests, she replied, 'Every inch of Brajdham's land is of interest to me.'

She climbed down the broken and faded old steps. She saw an old unused well, the top of which was covered with a few moss-covered wooden planks. Nearby were some small and dark dilapidated rooms that looked more like pigeon holes than human habitations. A large group of widowed radheshyamis dwelt here. They were grossly undernourished, and wore dirty and faded old dhotis. But their foreheads shone with *bibhuti* (sacred ash) and lines drawn with holy sandalwood. Seeing Saudamini, the old women came out of their pigeon holes and surrounded her inquisitively.

'Ladies, how do you make your living here?' Saudamini asked.

The 'ladies' looked at each other. Then one of them, sunken eyes shining with the brightness of the sun, replied, 'When necessary, we sit at the gates of the Tortoise Temple and at Rangaji and beg. When there is no other way, we spend the whole night in front of the temple, waiting and hoping for the *malcha* offerings.'

'But if you had become radheshyamis singing bhajans in the temple, you would have been assured of at least two square meals a day,' said Saudamini.

All the women cackled with laughter on hearing this, and one of them started singing mockingly, 'Sethbari's bhajan ashram, Gopinath's bhajan ashram, Borbag's bhajan ashram, the stable's bhajan ashram!'

'Listen,' she said, 'the accountant got so fat on the radheshyamis' money that he cannot get up now. You must be new here not to know this. This fat man sat and watched all the radheshyamis, their thin hands and feet and starving bodies. He came to know which of them would kick the bucket, and when! He also came to know which dying radheshyami had how much money, and where. He found out everything. Everything!'

Again the old women cackled with laughter.

'One day, this wicked man was observing our legs. As soon as we knew this, we fled and saved ourselves. Otherwise he would have kicked us out. See, look at our legs.' And they pulled their tattered clothes up to their knees and exposed their legs.

Saudamini hurriedly stepped back a few steps in fright and shock. All these women were sick! They had leprosy.

'My dear girl, we like begging at the Banke-Behari lane, at the doorway of Shahji Temple, on the steps of Daman Mohan . . . People like you go there.' And saying this, one of the women started stroking Saudamini's hand with her own hands. Saudamini went stiff with fright! But the ghostly woman seemed to get a peculiar satisfaction. Encouraged by the act of the first woman, another one started touching the gold bangles on Saudamini's wrist, while another came near her and said, 'Give us some donation to keep us alive. You people live to eat, but we need to eat something in order to live. Give us something to keep us alive.'

In the meantime, another group of old women came out of the small rooms and surrounded Saudamini. They started feeling and touching her soft young body, and then started scratching her all over in a strange and feverish excitement. Saudamini's hair came loose and cascaded down her back, her blouse was almost ripped off and, if some sadhus had not arrived at that moment, the women would have probably taken on the nature of wild wolves.

One of the sadhus shouted at the women, 'Get out! Get out, you demons! Do you think there is no one to help her?'

Immediately all the old hags disappeared inside the pigeon holes.

The sadhu rebuked Saudamini, 'Did I not tell you that you should not venture alone to these places? These old women can devour people. Come, I will see you on your way. And let me tell you another thing. These women are very unfortunate. I am told that you have come with the intention of making Braj your permanent home. Give some thought to the welfare of these women whenever you have the opportunity.'

Saudamini wiped the perspiration off her neck and face as soon as she stepped on to the main road of Gopinath Bazaar. The bhajan ashram here had not yet closed its doors and an old widow was standing in the middle of a group singing bhajans to the accompaniment of small cymbals. A sentry sitting at the doorway, whose function it was to keep the accounts, was silently chanting the Lord's name with prayer beads. Ever so often he would open his eyes and observe the radheshyamis, to see whether they were all really singing. These women were compelled to sing even if they were starving. They had to sing the Lord's praises as loud as they could, even if they were on the verge of choking. Saudamini noticed that, although they sang without stopping, very often their eyes would turn to the line of vegetable vendors. She noticed that the only buyers of the rotting, dried-up vegetables that were heaped on one side were the poor radheshyamis.

Saudamini returned home and entered her dark room again. She was trying her best to forget her loneliness, but it was not easy. Sometimes she would scrutinize her own body. She had a lovely, soft, young body. Even the mental imbalance and torture of the past seven years had not been able to leave any permanent mark on this lovely body. Try as she might, she could not come to terms with the condition of her life or her situation. Was there anyone else, she wondered, who had suffered as she had, who had been compelled to face a situation like hers?

14

KRISHNA: THE PLAYFUL DIVINE

PAVAN K. VARMA

IN POPULAR PSYCHE, Krishna and Radha became the universal symbol for the lover and the beloved. Krishna was the ideal nayaka (hero) and Radha the ideal nayika (heroine). The use of the word ideal should not be interpreted to mean a monotone image. On the contrary, they were the ideal precisely because their *shringara*-leela could accommodate a thousand variations. All lovers could not but reflect in their own personality some part (*ansh*) of the divine love between the two; conversely, the two incorporated in themselves the personality of all lovers. The canvas of their love was seamless, a painting which amplified and mutated itself in a myriad of reflections. For this reason, but also as a facade for the expression of human prurience, an invocation for their name became a password to sanction the description of all contact between the sexes.

Keshav Das (1555–1617) in his celebrated work *Rasikapriya* does precisely this. He was the court poet of Raja Madhukar Shah of Orchha, in present-day Madhya Pradesh. Rai Parbin, the accomplished courtesan of Orchha, was his mistress. The *Rasikapriya*, written in Hindi, was a treatise on erotics. Using traditional tools—rhetoric and verse—Keshav Das systematically analysed the kinds of heroes and heroines, their moods and emotions, their meeting places and their personality dispositions. In basic content, his work was not entirely original. Bharata's *Natyashastra*, a seminal treatise on dramaturgy dating back to perhaps as early as 100 BC, had classified nayikas into eight categories and dealt with the essential bhavas (emotions) and specific emotions of women (*havas*). Bharata had also discussed the ten stages of a woman's love, the meeting places of lovers and the functions of female messengers. Keshav Das elaborated on this framework. But the real originality of his contribution lay in the fact that he made Krishna and Radha the all-purpose models to illustrate the content of his work. The structure of the *Rasikapriya* essays a nayika, or a situation, or an emotion through a *doha* (verse) remarkable for its lyrical brevity, and then follows this with an illustrative example. In these instances, almost without exception, it is Krishna and Radha who are the nayaka and nayika.

For Keshav Das it was not enough to treat shringara as a general category. He sought to desegregate its elements. In doing this he used the scientist's tool of clinical observation, and apparently seemed to rather enjoy the very process of classification and the giving of labels to each constituent so identified. Shringara, according to him, was of two types: *samyoga* (love-in-union) and *viyoga* (love-in-separation). Both samyoga and viyoga could be either secret (*prachchanna*) or manifested (*prakasa*). A nayaka was defined as a young and handsome man, proud but sensitive and refined, and accomplished in the art of lovemaking. He could be any of four types: *anukula* (sincere and devoted), *dakshina* (one who distributes his affection equally among his lady loves), *satha* (cruel and unreliable) and *dhrishta* (shameless). Women were of four basic types: *padmini* (lotus-like), *chitrini* (variegated), *sankhini* (conch-like) and *hastini* (elephant-like). The padmini woman exuded the fragrance of the lotus from her body, had a golden complexion and was slim and beautiful. She was intelligent but bashful, cheerful but not wanton. Needless to say, for Keshav Das, the best illustration for the padmini nayika was Radha. Nayikas were also classified according to age: up to sixteen (*bala*), from sixteen to thirty (*taruni*), from thirty to fifty-five (*praudha*) and over fifty-five (*vriddha*). Depending on their relation to the nayaka, nayikas could be *svakiya* (one's own), *parakiya* (another's) and

vigil for the night. There was such a crowd that not a corner of the house was left unoccupied. The women sang and danced and played on musical instruments . . . In this situation, Radha slept in the bed of Krishna: he came and laid himself there, as if it was the night of his honeymoon.

Meeting on an excuse of illness (Vyadhi Miss Milan)

Having diagnosed the cause of the disease, offerings of gifts were made to placate the evil stars. Medicines were given but the disease showed no signs of abatement. 'Hurry up, O Krishna! You have been called, the condition of Radha is precarious. The pain of which you cured her last time has recurred.'

Meeting on the pretext of an invitation (Nimantrana Miss Milan)

Yashoda invited Radha to supper at her house . . . After the meal, chewing a betel, Radha went upstairs to see the house and encountered Krishna. Seeing the handsome Krishna, she ran back, but he, taking courage, caught her by her snake-like tresses. Taking her into his lap, he caressed her and did what he liked. And then, having taken off her nose ring, he rubbed her face with saffron to conceal the marks of his passionate love and let her go.

Meeting at water sports (Jala Vihara Milan)

Every day in the summer month, cow-boys and cow-girls play in the water of the Yamuna. Cow-girls are on one side of the river, and Krishna with a crowd of cow-boys is on the other. The two groups of lovers dive into the water like fish, and having met each other underwater, they emerge on their own side of the river. In this manner they satisfy their longings with craft, apparently remaining away from each other.'

Radha and Krishna were also the actors in Keshav Das's explication of the 'external indications of emotion'—havas—that are manifested in love-in-union. He enumerated thirteen havas produced by the love of Radha and Krishna. When the over-burgeoning of love made Radha and Krishna oblivious to those around them, they displayed *heta*-hava; when they sported, mimicking each other's manners or exchanging their clothes, they were in the grip of Leela Hava; when they attracted each other through their speech of laughter or looks or gait, they evoked *lalita*-hava; when the love of one for the other produced arrogance in either, it was the prevalence of *mada*-hava; when in sheer delight of rushing to meet each other, they got muddled in their action, they manifested *vibhrama*-hava; when at the time of meeting, modesty overtook one or both, it was the play of *vikrita*-hava; sometimes one gesture or glance could indicate a silent invitation; this produced a flutter of delight—*vilasa*-hava; the arousal in love of several contrary emotions all at once—such as anger and joy, desire and pride—reproduced *kilakinchita*-hava; when indifference to each other was feigned, it was the influence of *bibboka*-hava; when they met in attire starkly simple, shorn of any ornamentation, they demonstrated *vichchitti*-hava; when erotic feelings enhanced by dalliance were suddenly required to be arrested or camouflaged, the outcome was *mottayita*-hava; resorting to simulated quarrels to enrich the texture of love-play created *kuttamita*-hava; finally, a secret love message from one to the other in the form of a symbol or a riddle, when understood, gave birth to *bodhaka*-hava.

Keshav Das's illustrations of each have shown a delightfully fertile imagination. For instance, the meaning of vibhrama-hava is brought out by the example of Radha wearing her necklace on her waist, her anklets on her wrist and collyrium on her cheeks when, on hearing of Krishna's sudden arrival, she rushes out to meet him. Bibboka-hava—the affectation of indifference—is illustrated thus:

Aware of Krishna's approach, Radha lay down, feigning sleep. Not wanting to rouse her, Krishna sat silently by her side. Taking courage, he touched her leg, which caused the hair of her body to stand up on end. When he proceeded to unlace the cord of her ghaghra, Radha got up, startled and—though recognizing him—upbraided him in annoyance like this: 'O

ill-bred cow-boy, you graze the cows the whole day, how dare
you approach another woman's bed at night?'[2]

Kuttamita-hava—the simulation of a quarrel—is brought out
through a description by Radha's *sakhi*:

> Simulating anger and with obstinacy she (Radha) walked away,
> having turned her back on him. He (Krishna) leapt and held
> her again, although she struggled hard to free herself from his
> hold. He now pricked her flesh with his nails and teeth, and
> fondled her bosom, treating her worse than an enemy and
> transgressing all limits.

> 'Now he sits by her side, giving her betel leaves to eat.
> Perverse are the ways of love, O sakhi.'[3]

It is obvious that the nayika rather than the nayaka was the real
focus of the *Rasikapriya*. For this very reason, it was Radha more
than Krishna who emerged as the central figure of the work. The
Rasikapriya's eightfold classification of nayikas (*ashtanayika*) on the
basis of their emotional state in love appears to be but an attempt to
sketch a multifaceted elaboration of Radha's personality as profiled
in the many moods of her love with Krishna. The eight nayikas
described are: *svadhinapatika* (one whose lover is devoted to her),
utkanthita (one who yearns for her lover), *vasaksajja* (one who waits in
readiness with the bed made for the return of her lover), *abhisandhita*
(one who allows a quarrel to stand between herself and her lover),
khandita (one wronged by an unfaithful lover), *proshitapatika* (one
whose lover is abroad and has not returned at the expected time),
vipralabdha (one who waits the whole night for a prefixed rendezvous
but whose lover does not turn up) and *abhisarika* (one who boldly
sets out, braving all odds, to meet her lover).

The defining characteristic of each of the above nayikas could be
found in Radha. She could be any one in exclusion, but she could also
be all. The motif here is of an eight-spoke wheel, revolving on a single
pivot: Krishna. It was in relation to Krishna and as a consequence of

her love for him that her personality underwent mutation: secure in his love she was the svadhinapatika-nayika; wronged by him she was the khandita-nayika; pining for his love she was the utkanthita-nayika; waiting for him she was the vasaksajja, or (depending on the circumstances) the vipralabdha or proshitapatika-nayika; angry with him, she was the abhisandhita woman; and, when, unable to bear the pangs of separation any more, she set out boldly to meet him, she was the abhisarika.

15

RADHA IN NAZRUL GEETI

REBA SOM

Shyam! If only you were Radha
Like me you would have chanted, day and night, the name of Shyam
The burning anguish left by Krishna's scandals
Would then appear as malati *garlands*
And yearning for Krishna's love would
Make you pray, life after life, for a return to Brajdham.
How devoid of compassion is the music of your flute
How cruel is your failure to understand the women of Braj!
Like the tears you have reduced me to
Could I but make you weep too!
Only then would you realize
The endless heartburn born of a guru's neglect[1]

THIS REMARKABLE SONG, replete with all the nuances of a lover's quarrel, was penned by Kazi Nazrul Islam. Born in 1899 in Churulia, a village in the Burdwan district of West Bengal, Nazrul was the son of an imam of a mosque. Raised in poverty he was named *'dukhumian'*, the sorrowful one. Early in life he joined *leto*, a folk musical group, with whom he travelled to neighbouring villages composing musical skits and becoming conversant with Hindu mythology and the folk culture of Bengal.

One of the most powerful cultural influences in Bengal was Shri Chaitanya (1485–1534) during the reign of the liberal Husain Shahi kings. The fair-complexioned Chaitanya, often called Gauranga, was also popularly called Nimai. Born in a Brahmin family that originally came from Odisha, Nimai's father migrated to Nabadwip, a renowned centre of Sanskrit learning and pilgrimage. Chaitanya's life and work signified a new direction in the history of Vaishnavism since Krishna, the Hindu divine god, came to be worshipped now as the embodiment of the universal creator, abandoning the plethora of rituals and caste rules which had been laid down by the religious orthodoxy. True to the bhakti tradition, Chaitanya's Vaishnavism drew within its fold men and women across caste divide, who sought to communicate with God through chants, devotional songs and frenzied dance without the intermediation of Brahmin priests. Many Muslims came under his influence, among them, his favourite disciple, Haridas.[2]

This revolutionary approach made its mark on Bengali language, literature and culture. Chaitanya's Radha–Krishna cult was influenced by the romantic and devotional poems of Jayadeva and Vidyapati in Sanskrit and Chandidas in Bengali. Chaitanya, from all accounts, was not a theologian but a god-intoxicated person who saw Krishna and not Vishnu as the ultimate Godhead. Moreover, this was not the Krishna of the Gita but an androgyne, signifying the coming together of Radha and Krishna in one body—Radha externally and Krishna internally.[3]

This unique formulation of the Bengal Vaishnava androgynous nature of Godhead entered the folklore tradition of Bengal so deeply that Kazi Nazrul Islam, writing five centuries later, could carry in his song 'Tumi Jodi Radha Hotey Shyam' a refrain of an age-old dearly held belief.

There was in Nazrul both a mystical and a revolutionary streak. During a chequered school career he was able to learn both Sanskrit and Persian, both of which gave him the ability to comprehend Hindu and Islamic texts.[4] Although he received some training in classical music in school, it was his inborn musical talent that made him a powerful singer and a prolific songwriter with over 3000 compositions. During the First World War the revolutionary streak in Nazrul made him sign up for a regiment of the British Indian Army. Though he never saw action in battle, his enforced stay in Nowshera and Karachi exposed him to Persian studies and ghazal music, which he introduced in Bengali for the first time using Arabic and Persian words liberally in his unique compositions.

Nazrul is perhaps best known for his stirring patriotic songs such as 'Kandari Hushiyar', which inspired generations from Subhas Chandra Bose and the Azad Hind Fauj to the freedom fighters in the struggle for Bangladesh. However, it is perhaps in his kirtan songs, where the Radha lore is prominent, that we see best his compassionate, sensitive and romantic aspect. Drawn to communism from his early years of working as a journalist, which saw him bringing out several stirring news publications, Nazrul's ideas revealed a refreshing acceptance of all religions. His Islamic songs were composed in tandem with his Kali sangeet. Though his marriage to a Hindu, Pramila Sengupta, was socially boycotted by many, his secular beliefs made him insist that his wife did not need to convert to Islam. Each of his sons was given a hyphenated Hindu–Muslim name.[5]

Nazrul's treatment of Radha in his songs reveals a sensitive understanding of a woman's inner cry. Many of the songs were unabashed expressions of earthly love, conveying love and longing, dejection and despair. At a time when Tagorean restraint as well as morality advocated by the Brahmo Samaj conditioned the literary style, Nazrul's poetry verses on free love such as 'Madhobi Pralap', 'Anamika' and 'Gopone Priya' brought on a literary storm. *Kallol* and *Kali Kalom*, the journals where these were published in 1926, stood behind Nazrul and other writers, who chose to write on sexually explicit themes in a wave of new literature. As a rejoinder, *Shonibarer Chithi*, edited by Tagore's protagonist, Sajanikanta Das, launched a counteroffensive; Tagore, as always, sought to mediate. Affectionate towards Nazrul, to whom he had dedicated his play *Boshonto*, Tagore in his essay 'Sahitye Nobyota'[6] advised that though he was not a moralist he feared that aesthetics would disappear in needlessly provocative writing.

In the following selection of five songs can be seen Nazrul's sensitive handling of woman's emotions through the idiom of the Radha–Krishna romance, lyrically composed in a woman's voice.

In the song 'Aami Jaar Nupurer Chhondo Benukaar Shur' there is a total blending of the two personas of Radha and Krishna conveyed in the voice of Radha with exquisite metaphor.[7]

Set in Taal Kaharba, this song has a fast, rhythmic beat that echoes the dancers' anklets. The musical accent is on the word *ke*, meaning 'who', sung in a quick succession of ascending notes. The juxtaposition of the man and the woman, Krishna and Radha, through delicate imagery marks this rare composition. Radha is so much a part of Krishna's divine dance that she becomes his rhythm, melody, poetic inspiration, and takes the form of a peacock to be his dancing companion in the rains. Krishna, on the other hand, binds her in the embrace of the jewellery adorning her body.

Who is he, that Beautiful One?
I find myself resounding in the rhythm of his anklet
In the melody of his flute
In the pain of parting on the Jamuna front
I find myself as blossoms in his songs
In the distant unseen
Who is he, that Beautiful One?
The secret inspiration behind my Poesy
Alas! Where is he?
I appear in the rains, as the blissful peacock to be his dancing
    companion
As he appears as the bracelets and ornaments on my body
Who is he, that Beautiful One?

The song 'Bodhu Ami Chhinu Bujhi Brindabaner Radhikar Aakhi Jauley', set in Taal Dadra, speaks of a woman's anguish in unfulfilled love. Radha's deep sense of hurt at Krishna's departure from Vrindavana and realization that they are not destined for union is captured in the lyrics of Nazrul, with matching pathos in the musical composition. Sung in the voice of a despondent woman who internalizes the dejection of Radha and sees herself in Radha's unshed tears, or in the scattering petals of jasmine flowers that could never be strung as a garland for the lover, Nazrul creates a powerful image of dejection in love.

Bodhu Ami Chhinu Bujhi Brindabaner Radhikar Aakhi Jauley[8]

Dearest, I lay perhaps amidst the teardrops of Radha in
    Brindaban
Or perhaps, as the jasmine blossom of a monsoon evening
I had descended on earth.
And so, when the desire of union rises
You hide like the moon behind the cloud of farewell
While I scatter in the eastern breeze as jasmine petals, just as
    they bloom
Dearest, alas, in this play of destiny, union is not for me
Only for a chance encounter can I crave
Destined for eternal separation, union is not for me
Never will I visit on a spring evening fragrant with *madhavi*
Only in the rains will I come, only to scatter
In a relentless shower drifting away in a current
Never to be strung in a garland around your neck.

The popular song 'More Ghumo Ghorey Eley Manohar',[9] set in Taal Dadra, is an unabashed confession of a woman in love, who dreams of her tryst with her lover. Nazrul invokes the imagery of Krishna, the divine lover, in this composition. Yearnings of the body are stated boldly in a manner hard to find in the love songs of Tagore, which were generally addressed to both God and the beloved. The voice in this song is that of a forsaken Radha dwelling on her dreams.

More Ghumo Ghorey Eley Manohar

In my deep slumber you appeared as a charmer

To you I offer my salutations
Against the monsoon clouds my Krishna dances,
Jhamjham, ramjham, jhamjham
You sat near my head and kissed my eyes
My body through vestments revealed itself
Like a *kadamb* in bloom, unparalleled, alluring
My garden was replete with so many flowers
I collected them in a basket of offerings for my god
Alas, you took them not, shame O shame
Instead you unravelled my tresses and took the floral string binding them
In my sleep I know not what I said that made you go away
Waking up I cry for my god, my dearest beloved.

The song 'Tumi Haath Khani Jaubey Rakho More Hather Paurey'[10] is a powerful expression of a woman's reflection on the ecstatic moments of nearness with her beloved, contrasting with her despair at his absence. She seems to epitomize the elation and dejection of Radha in Vrindavana. Set in Taal Kaharba, the song is set to a racy rhythm in a unique musical composition where pathos and ecstasy are equally captured.

Tumi Haath Khani Jaubey Rakho More Hather Paurey

When you place your hand on mine
Melody pours like the Ganges from my throat
In your kohl-lined eyes behind heavy lashes
Sways the shadow of farewell
The sky-blue of your apparel touches the blue of the skies
On days when I find you not,
Find not your nearness, find not your touch
It seems the whole wide world holds no one and nothing.

16

LOVELORN RADHA, FORLORN GOD: TAGORE'S *BHANUSINGHER PADAVALI*

LALIT KUMAR

Vasant Aaval Re (Spring Is Here) (Translation mine)

Spring is here!
Humming black bees
woods covered with
flower-laden mango trees.
Listen to me, friend,
my joyous heart goes restless . . .
Decked with the beauty of spring
mocks the universe
'O lovelorn Radha, where is your beloved, Madhav?'

Maran (Death) (Translation mine)

You are my sole companion, Death
What fear do I have now?
All my anxieties are put to rest.
Show me the way now.
'Fie, fie, you fickle-hearted Radha', says Bhanu,

121

'Madhav is your lord, not Death
Now see for yourself.'[1]

THE CURIOUS TALE OF BHANUSINGH

The story behind the publication of Rabindranath Tagore's
(1861–1941) *Bhanusingher Padavali* (Bhanusingh's Verses), a
collection of love songs, is as intriguing as the poems themselves. In
1877, a Calcutta-based periodical called *Bharati* began to publish
a series of poems (twenty-two in all) on Radha and Krishna by a
newly discovered Vaishnava poet Bhanusingh. The identity of the
mysterious poet continued to remain a secret for many years. The
truth was eventually revealed, and Bhanusingh turned out to be a
pseudonym for the precocious poet Rabindranath Tagore. The name
Bhanu, a synonym for the sun, was conferred on Tagore by his sister-
in-law Kadambari Devi, who remained Tagore's muse till her suicide
at the age of twenty-three.[2] The enigma behind the name Bhanusingh
therefore may have evoked the curiosity of readers and critics in the
public sphere, but it was an open secret within the Tagore family.

To reinforce the authenticity and historicity of the unidentified
poet, Tagore, in 1884, wrote a fictional biography of Bhanusingh
in the journal *Navajivana*.[3] The biographer commented on the
similarity in the poetic craft of Bhanusingh and the 14th-century
Maithili poet Vidyapati: 'Many have said that his poetry is written in
a fashion after Vidyapati, but that only elicits laughter. No one has
tried to discover if he does or does not have anything in common
with Vidyapati.'[4] Since the short biography is characterized by
playfulness and irony, Tagore, in all likelihood, intended his readers
to believe exactly the opposite of what he literally conveyed. It seems
that, on the one hand, he wanted to hint at the similarity between
Vidyapati's poetry and his own craft and, on the other, he desired the
question of authorship to be widely examined and speculated upon
by contemporary intellectuals.

However, years later, in a chapter titled 'Bhanusingh' in his
autobiography, *Jiban Smriti*, a fifty-one-year-old Tagore reminisces
about this episode. One day the young Tagore, inspired by the

British poet Chatterton,[5] approached a friend and pretended to have discovered a tattered manuscript by some ancient poet named Bhanusingh from the Brahmo Samaj Library. The friend praised the verses profusely and exclaimed that the poems were better than anything composed by even Vidyapati[6] or Chandidas. An exuberant Tagore could not conceal the truth any more and said that the poems were, in fact, his own creation. The friend immediately ceased to share Tagore's enthusiasm and said, 'Not bad at all.'[7] Before pulling this prank, Tagore had attempted to read a collection of old Vaishnava poems, titled *Prachin Kavya Sangraha*, compiled by Akshay Chandra Sarkar and Saradacharan Mitra. The difficulties he encountered in comprehending the language of these poems, a blend of Maithili and Bengali, drove him further to initiate his foray into writing poetry in a similar fashion.[8] As a result he composed on a cloudy afternoon 'Gahan Kusum Kunja Majhe' (In the Dense Flowering Woods). The composition made him immensely happy and became the foundation for the further poems of *Bhanusingher Padavali*, written in Brajabuli (different from Braj Bhasha). The employment of Brajabuli, 'a mixture of Maithili and Assamese/Bengali/Oriya by the Vaishnava poets of the eastern India to celebrate the *leela* (divine sport) of the lord Krishna,' writes Sisir Kumar Das, is extremely significant to understand the 'development of Indian Literature in a multilingual situation'.[9] Tagore's *Padavali* is a fine imitation of the medieval Bengali Vaishnava poets, in general, and of Vidyapati of Mithila, in particular.

WHY BRAJABULI AND NOT BENGALI? PSEUDO-VIDYAPATIS OF BENGAL AND A 'BASTARD LANGUAGE'

In 1881, George Abraham Grierson had produced the first grammar and chrestomathy of the Maithili language, in which he compiled nearly all the Maithili literature, including the songs of Vidyapati on Radha and Krishna. These songs through the Vaishnava poet Chaitanya and others, writes Grierson, became as popular in the Bengali households as the Bible is in England. But this popularity gave birth to a curious problem to which a curious solution was immediately found. For a common Bengali reader, Vidyapati was difficult to comprehend. So his hymns were twisted and distorted into a kind of 'bastard language', which was 'neither Bengali nor Maithili'.[10] Moreover, a host of imitators of Vidyapati sprung up, who composed songs in this newly invented language. Their compositions lacked the finesse and felicity of expression of the original poet. These songs, nevertheless, increasingly became indistinguishable from old Bengali, and naturally became more popular in Bengal than the original poems of Vidyapati. Consequently, the songs of the Maithili poet were gradually wiped out from the memory of Bengalis.

These spurious songs produced in the name of Vidyapati were widely compiled and circulated. One such compilation was *Prachin Kavya Sangraha*, which had inspired the young Tagore to compose *Bhanusingher Padavali*. Tagore confessed later in his autobiography that Bengali interspersed with Maithili in this collection of ancient poetry was beyond his comprehension.[11] One of the co-editors of this work Saradacharan Mitra produced *Vidyapatir Padavali* in the same year, which Grierson refuses to acknowledge as the work of the real Vidyapati. Whether or not Tagore was aware of the controversy surrounding the real Vidyapati versus impostors, or to what extent the songs of the former had inspired Tagore's Radha, could be questions of further debate and research. Grierson's analysis of a contentious subject nonetheless helps us understand the influence of Vidyapati on Bengal and its poets in the 19th century.

ORIGINS OF RADHA IN EARLY INDIAN LITERATURE

The *Bhagavata Purana* is one of the first, if not the first among the Indian texts, to celebrate Krishna as a humanized God, a child, a cowherd boy, an accomplished flute-player and, above all, a playful lover. The tenth book of this Purana is especially dedicated to Krishna's birth, his early heroic exploits and his Raas Leela, or the famous dance with the *gopi*s, the cowherd maidens of Vrindavana. Though the book became the foundational text of the Vaishnava movement in north India in its equal emphasis on the divine and the mundane, on the religious and the erotic, the name of Radha is not mentioned here, among the gopis of Vrindavana.[12] Tracing the emergence of Radha to *Gita Govinda*, Sisir Kumar Das writes that the greatest achievement of Jayadeva is 'his creation of Radha, who became the central figure in Indian love poetry, in fact, the symbol of eternal lover'.[13] In all possibility, the character of Radha, in its embryotic form, existed in the folk songs of the cowherds, but Jayadeva in his Sanskrit epic merged the Radha of religious literature and Radha of folk literature into one.[14] In Jayadeva, 'Radha is neither a wife nor a worshipping rustic playmate. She is an intense, solitary, proud female who complements and reflects the mood of Krishna's passion.'[15] The poem captures the lovers' longing for each other, their separation and union. The later Vaishnava poets, in particular, Vidyapati from Mithila, Chandidas from Bengal and Tagore's pseudonym Bhanusingh, have added new dimensions to the character of Radha and created the legend of a lovelorn woman for her.

COMMENTARY ON *BHANUSINGHER PADAVALI*: LOVE-IN-SEPARATION

Sambhoga or *samyoga* (love-in-union), *vipralamba* or *viyoga* (love-in-separation) and *pranidhana* (total surrender to God) are the themes of Bhanusingh's *Padavali*. *Viraha*, the pain of separation, is the dominant trope in Vaishnava poetry as well as in Tagore's. In these poems, a young Tagore inhabits the persona of Radha's experienced confidante, called Bhanu, who attempts to give solace to the inconsolable Radha. The poems have been composed in the form of dialogue between Radha and Bhanu, whereas Krishna mostly registers his presence through prolonged absence except in his brief tryst with Radha.

A LOVER'S COMPLAINT: 'I WILL POISON MYSELF'

The first poem of the *Padavali* is set in the spring against the backdrop of the humming of the *madhukar* (black bees) and blossoming of flowers. Radha's heart becomes restless in Krishna's absence; she is being mocked by the entire universe, 'O lovelorn Radha, where is your beloved, Madhav?' (Translation mine).

The poetic persona prophetically warns Radha of the pain of separation that awaits her; Bhanu expostulates, 'Go wait for him in the last shreds / of your innocence, crazy girl / until grief comes for you.' (Poem 1, p. 17, *The Lover of God*).[16] As the story of separation unfolds further, her agony escalates, 'I am budding and blooming at once / and dying, too.' The prolonged absence of her lover and endless pain make her express a death wish, 'He will leave me. If he leaves me, I will poison myself' (Poem 3, p. 23). The self-annihilating impulse gives way to anger and remonstration against the absent lover, who, being driven by political exigencies, has gone to Mathura. Anger leads to sexual jealousy (Poem 4, p. 27):

> You are cruel, Lord of the lonely dark,
> so far away in Mathura.
> In whose bed do you sleep?
> Who slakes your thirst upon waking?

REUNION: 'YOUR FACE UNDOES MY PAIN'

Separation and intense longing are eventually followed by reunion and Radha's lacerated heart is put to ease immediately at the sight of her lover, 'Your face undoes my pain' (Poem 6, p. 33). The pain of viraha is replaced by the erotic, and *shringara* rasa becomes the dominant motif in representing Radha's much-awaited reunion with Krishna, her lover and her God, combined into one. The poetic persona Bhanu seeks the permission of readers for suspending modesty so as to capture the consummation of their love (Poem 11, p. 47):

> May I dispense with modesty, friends?
> Look at their beautiful bodies . . .
> even though he's undoing
> the knot she protects with her hand.

If spring is a metaphor for separation in Tagore, the rainy season symbolizes reunion that happens on a cloudy night amidst incessant rain and thunder. Longing and amorous embraces are replaced by care and affection, and it is Radha who seems to be in total control while authoring the script of love (Poem 14, p. 57):

> Come, you are drenched, Madhava,
> drenched again . . .
> Take off your clothes. Let me dry you. I will untie my hair.
> Come lie with me among the stalks of lotus,
> skin cold and thrilled.

Celebrating the significance of the erotic, Rupa Goswami, a 16th-century Vaishnava poet and contemporary of Chaitanya, divides 'bhakti rasa' (sentiments of devotees) mainly into five kinds: *preyas* (friendship), *vatsalya* (parental love), *prita* (faithfulness), *santa* (serene) and *madhura* (erotic).[17] Although each of them provides a means to approach Krishna, the erotic stands at the top of the hierarchy of love and subsumes all others. It is driven by an unparalleled passion, and being complete in itself, is the most satisfying to Krishna.[18]

From Shringara Rasa to *Karuna Rasa*: 'When Pitiless Madhava Leaves for Mathura'

Reunion and separation seem to affect Radha's persona as well, for Tagore's Radha is characterized by an ambivalent feeling, a hallmark of lovers. She constantly oscillates between anger and affection, complaint and forgiveness, and petulance and passion. Her tone varies from being accusatory to supplicatory, and karuna rasa replaces shringara, when Madhava eventually decides to leave for Mathura.

A heartbroken Radha pleads piteously before her lord at his departure, 'Stay, Shyama, my love Shyama, stay / Stay with me. I have no friend but you / no love, Madhava. No one but you' (Poem 16, p. 61). Her earnest entreaties go in vain, and though her lover does not melt, the poetic persona Bhanu does and empathizes with Radha's dejected self, 'Weeping for Radha, I say that life is pain /

If there were no love, there would be no grief' (p. 63). She is also painfully aware of the fact that though Shyama is her lone object of desire, there are hundreds of Radhas who yearn for him.

Once Krishna leaves, cloud and darkness, which had witnessed the consummation of their love earlier, become a metaphor for death. An utterly devastated Radha contemplates death as an alternative to love. In the poem titled 'Maran' (Death), a forlorn Radha vents her grief, *'Maran re, tuhun mam Shyam saman'* (O Death, you resemble my Shyam; translation mine). The desire to achieve liberation through death is not a recurring trope in Vaishnava poetry. Yet this permeates not only *Bhanusingher Padavali* but also *Gitanjali* and some of Tagore's later poems.[19] In the English translation of *Gitanjali* (Song 91), Death has been personified as the lord and bridegroom. The poetic persona expresses the desire to meet her last hope, 'O thou the last fulfilment of life, Death, my death, come and whisper to me! . . . After the wedding the bride shall leave her home and meet her lord alone in the solitude of night' (*Gitanjali*, pp. 59–60).

Tagore's Radha, nonetheless, is a resilient devotee and lover, who ceases to pay attention to thoughts of suicide and her social disgrace. Radha puts everything at stake in love, including her family honour, friendship and, above all, her soul. She surrenders before God in all humility and expects infinite pleasure, 'Radha is the Dark God's mistress / May her pleasure be endless!' (Poem 22, p. 85). She laments, however, that she does not know the art of seduction. Radha also emphasizes the class–caste difference in a self-deprecatory tone and addresses herself as belonging to *'dukhani* Ahir jati', a distressed woman from the 'Ahir jati'.[20] Her ambivalent feeling towards Krishna continues as, on the one hand, she expects to remain happy even in separation, but, on the other, she reflects on her miserable existence.

A Lovelorn and Forlorn God: Radha in Tagore, Vidyapati, Jayadeva and Bharati

Unlike Tagore, Vidyapati foregrounds Krishna's vulnerability in love too. In the songs of the Maithili poet, a humanized God reciprocates Radha's passion fervidly and conveys his pain through

Radha's friend, *dooti* (the messenger), who says, 'Hey friend! The agony of Krishna's heart is immeasurable / Forgetting the world, all that he utters is Radha, Radha' (Vidyapati's *Padavali*, 'Krishna ki Dooti', p. 85; translation mine). In his *Padavali*, Vidyapati seems to be mediating between the lovers, and here his sympathies overtly lie with the forlorn Krishna, 'A half-dead Madhav cannot survive, says Vidyapati / Unless he drinks the nectar of your lips' (87; translation mine). In describing Krishna's longing for love through the trope of a messenger, Vidyapati seems to be inspired by Jayadeva.[21] In a poem titled 'Lotus-eyed Krishna Longing for Love' in *Gita Govinda*, Krishna utters his total helplessness before Radha's friend, 'I will stay here, you go to Radha / Appease her with my words and bring her to me!' And then, the news of her beloved's pain is conveyed to Radha:

> Your neglect affects his heart,
> Inflicting pain night after night.
> Wildflower-garlanded Krishna
> Suffers in your desertion, friend.[22]

But in Tagore, the dark lord does not seem to languish in love and neither does he express his intense longing, for Krishna mostly remains an absent presence in his songs. The endless agony of Radha is juxtaposed against the endless indifference of 'heartless Krishna' in the concluding section of Tagore's songs, and the question of love and separation remains an open-ended one. It is perhaps this lack of a neat closure in various mystical–erotic narratives on Radha that induces the poets to revisit and retell the story of unrequited love. The eternal nature of their legendary love has been beautifully captured by the acclaimed Hindi poet Dharamvir Bharati in his work *Kanupriya* (1959), where a self-assured Radha addresses her lord Kanu/Krishna in absentia (p. 37; translation mine):

> Since eternity, in endless directions
> I have been your companion; I shall be your companion.
> I cannot recall the birth of this journey, neither can you
> And there is no end to this odyssey, my consort.

132   PICTURING RADHA

17

RADHA: THE UNFADING
MYSTIC BLOSSOM IN OUR MIDST

RENUKA NARAYANAN

LIKE MANY OTHERS, I grew up knowing that Radha and Krishna were supposed to have conducted their love-play in the hospitable and sweet-scented shade of the *kadamba* tree. It was something our gods did—make passionate love—and it's interesting how we just accepted it all so matter-of-factly as children and teenagers.

As for Radha's kadamba, its truly immortal moment surely came that golden day on the banks of the Yamuna when the *gopi*s went to fill their clay water-pots at the river? Once they filled their water-pots, perhaps they looked meaningfully at each other and at the cool, laughing water. Perhaps there was time for a quick bath? Shedding their skirts and veils, the laughing band must have plunged into the Yamuna and enjoyed a pleasant frolic in her waters. When it was time to come out though, they found that a dark-skinned rogue in a yellow dhoti had hung their clothes out of reach on the kadamba tree that grew over the riverbank.

How Krishna insisted that they shed their shame and come out naked to receive their garments is endlessly portrayed in song, story, painting and artefact. My favourite visual depiction of this scene is the Pahari miniature from Kangra, possibly by the artist Nainsukh.

131

It is so vivid and charming that you feel you are in the scene yourself, perhaps as a curious songbird on a kadamba branch at Krishna's own blue elbow, having quite forgotten how to chirp amidst all these strange goings-on.

We were never taught to look at this scene pruriently or as a patriarchal fantasy of sexual harassment. Instead, we were told that we needed *sanskar*, or spiritual merit, to understand it as a dramatic metaphor or allegory for how the human soul must shed all baggage and approach God with total surrender and vulnerability. Is that the living magic of being Indian, do you think, that the old stories never go away but just pick up new tellings and we go with the flow?

No wonder the dour Scots missionaries who traipsed about India during the British Raj in the 19th century grumbled in their journals and diaries that they were making very poor headway in their attempts to convert 'the Hindoos' because 'we cannot match their myths with our own'.

In case the matter teases, the kadamba's botanical name is *Anthocephalus cadamba* and *Nauclea cadamba* of the Rubiaceae family. It's a leafy tree with wide, spreading branches and yellow puffball flowers that scent up the air. You can propagate it from its seeds. It figures in medicinal listings because its bark is used for tonics and against fevers.

Against these arguably prosaic material facts, you wonder why our ancients gave the kadamba so much spiritual significance as a divine favourite, for it is right up there in scripture, especially in the *Srimad Bhagavatam* or *Bhagavata Purana*, also familiarly called the *Bhagavatam*, Sri Krishna's life story. This scripture celebrates the kadamba and details the creation of the Maha Raas, or Krishna's mystic circular dance with the gopis or milkmaids of Vrindavana. It even takes the place of the idol in a number of temples in north-east India after the great reformer Sankara Dev of Assam popularized Krishna worship in the region.

The kadamba also comes up in verses that praise the Devi, or Mother Goddess, where she is described as 'Kadamba-*vana nilaye*' and 'Kadamba-*vana vasini*' (Dweller of the Kadamba Forest).

So both north India and south India venerate the kadamba with the interesting difference that the north associates it with Radha and Krishna, while in the south it is categorically known as the 'Parvati Tree', which is also its trade name in the timber business.

Regarding this, I once saw a three-foot statue of Ganesha carved to order from Jaipur for the modest price of several lakh rupees.

'It looks so like sandalwood,' I said, knowing that it couldn't be, since sandalwood is protected, but I was amazed at how sandalwood-like the polish made it seem.

'Oh no, it's kadamba—doubly lucky as the sacred tree of both Shaivas and Vaishnavas', said an expert.

In fact, this apparent difference expresses a deeper spiritual unity. Radha is said to be a manifestation of Lakshmi, the consort of Vishnu, whose eighth avatar was Krishna. Since Lakshmi and Parvati are both aspects of the Devi, or Parashakti, the supreme sacred force, the kadamba, by deduction, is essentially associated with the same persona.

'Radha', then, is the mystic blossom of Krishna lore. Her name means 'auspicious' and 'wish-fulfilling'. It is said that the eastern poet Jayadeva is the man who made Radha really famous in the 12th century with his Sanskrit poem *Gita Govinda*, which celebrates Radha and Krishna's love through intensely intimate verses set in the poetic form called *ashtapadi*. It 'spread like wildfire across India' and was translated into sixteen languages. Two poems from it are enshrined in the Guru Granth Sahib, the holy book of the Sikhs. The popularity of Jayadeva's ashtapadis in Odisha, Bengal and north India is well-documented, as is the fact that the *Gita Govinda* is the official liturgical text of the great Jagannath Temple at Puri.

The seventh ashtapadi, *Mamiyam chalita*, is possibly the first verse, or even the first instance, of a poem that has God pining for a human being's love (Radha's) and reproaching Himself for not understanding her anguish that He does not 'belong' exclusively to her. This is interpreted as the Para (Supersoul or God) longing as much for the love of devotees as devotees long for God's love. It resonates with Advaita, the ancient Indian philosophical notion that the individual soul, Jivatma, is part of the Supersoul, the Paramatma.

My mother, a classical dancer, never tired of pointing out the grandeur of spiritual humility in this fact, that an apparently simple, unlettered milkmaid like Radha was worshipped across India as the personification of divine mutual love. She explained Radha and Krishna's love as an example of God's *saulabhyam*, or accessibility, the gift of divine mercy, and taught me to sing and dance to Radha–Krishna songs in Tamil, Hindi and Sanskrit. Indeed, my earliest memory of being onstage is as Krishna at age five. There was always a cultural programme for Dussehra and Diwali in our neighbourhood, and I was installed as Krishna on a high stool, ankles crossed, with a peacock feather in my hair and a flute held to my lips while the big girls did a 'gopi dance' around me.

In my growing-up years, Jayadeva's ashtapadis were very much in the air in the Bhajana sampradaya, or devotional-song genre. Its beloved 20th-century exponent was the singing sanyasi Swami Haridhos Giri, born at the temple town of Tiruvannamalai in Tamil Nadu, which is famously associated with the sage Ramana Maharishi. Swami Haridhos Giri travelled widely across the Indian peninsula and to eastern countries like Malaysia, Singapore, and so on, drawing huge, ecstatic crowds with his emotionally charged renditions of ashtapadis and bhajans like 'Brindavan Mein Kunj Bhavan Mein Naachat Giridharlal'. He made 'Radharani' come alive in *madhurya* bhakti, or 'honeyed devotion' to millions in south India until the day in 1994, aged about sixty, he reportedly took *jalsamadhi*, or voluntary death by drowning, in the holy waters of the Alaknanda, at Koteshwar Mahadev, near Rudraprayag, in the Himalayas.

Nobody found it strange that a sanyasi sang of Radha's love in Jayadeva's sensuous ashtapadis, for he 'became' Radha in his fervour; and men and women of all ages were irresistibly drawn into his intense devotion and became Radha with him. It was a 20th-century mass Maha Raas. Other notable bhajan singers after him have kept the tradition literally rocking. Some, like Vittaldas Maharaj today, are capable of making a crowd of over ten thousand people at Tirupati get up and dance spontaneously to songs like 'Radhe Radhe, Radhe Radhe', 'Radhe Govinda' and 'Hari Re Rangam Majhi'. Moreover, 'Radha Kalyanam', or Radha's Wedding, is a regular cultural event across south India even today; blissful evenings of song and ceremony and showers of rose petals.

In my view, a foundational reason for south India's glad receptivity to Radha is the wistful figure of the girl saint Andal, who is believed to have lived in the Tamil region in the 8th or 9th century, well before Jayadeva in the 12th century and Meera Bai in the 16th century. Andal was found as a baby girl mysteriously left on the ground like Sita, by a priest who brought her up as his daughter. Andal saw Krishna as her husband and is believed to have 'merged' into the massive idol of Vishnu at Sri Rangam, the southern centre of Vaishnavism. Her songs remain hugely popular in 21st-century India. Andal, who sang of herself as a gopi, was a great influence on the luminous 10th-century founder of Srivaishnavism, Sri Ramanuja.

The legend goes that Andal had composed a prayer at Azhagar Kovil, the temple to Vishnu at Madurai, which went, 'O Lord Hari, if you accept me, I will offer you a hundred pots of sweet rice-pudding and a hundred pots of pure white butter.' Shortly after making her promise there, Andal had gone back to her village, Srivilliputhur. She had been found out soon after, by her saintly father, in an act of vanity. She had taken to wearing the garland of flowers she wove every day for Vishnu before giving it to her father to offer in worship. One day, her father had spotted a long black hair caught in the flowers and had made Andal own up. But her father had then had a strange dream in which Vishnu had appeared to him and said that it was perfectly all right. It was only Andal's pure and intense love that had made her wear 'His' garland.

Events had moved swiftly after that for the young devotee, and one day when she had gone to Sri Rangam temple, she touched the feet of Vishnu's idol there, swung herself up to sit on them . . . and disappeared. Everybody in the Bhakti community believed this then and believes it now. Andal's yearning and her unkept promise to Krishna was fulfilled 200 years later by Sri Ramanuja to honour the spiritual debt he owed her.

Here, it is fascinating to see how the cultural dotted lines run across India. Sri Ramanuja's legacy went north with Sant Ramananda, the guru of Kabir, who in turn was cherished by Guru

Nanak. Ramanuja's influence on the Bhakti movement is profound and other legatees of note include no less than Tulsidas, whose *Ramcharitmanas*, 'the people's Ramayana', changed the history of religion forever in north India.

And it was at Sri Rangam that Chaitanya Mahaprabhu, the founder of Srivaishnavism in Bengal 500 years ago, made his longest stay during the four months of monsoon called *chaturmaas*. This was during his travels to holy places for six years after taking *sanyas*. He went every day to the Sri Rangam temple after bathing in the Kaveri River, and it seems entirely likely that his host, Venkatesh Bhat, told him all about Andal.

Sri Chaitanya then set out to rediscover and map the long-lost physical locations of Vrindavana where Krishna was believed to have played and where the idylls and miracles of his childhood took place. This map is still followed by millions of pilgrims. Sri Chaitanya also conjured an inner landscape, of a life absorbed in the thoughts of Krishna, which he called the 'hidden treasure of the Vrindavana within'. He urged that the path to the treasure lay in the practice of *naam*, in repeating Krishna's names, particularly the refrain *'Hare Rama, Hare Krishna'* and in singing kirtans in Krishna's praise.

It was Chaitanya who had famously added new lustre to the *jatra*, the old travelling folk theatre of the land. Chaitanya had preached the equality and brotherhood of all men, whatever their caste, and thrown himself into religious ecstasy as he sang and danced to Krishna with his followers on the streets of his home town, Nabadwip. One day, he had told his disciple Chandrashekhar that he wished to perform the play *Rukmini Haran*. This famous love story described how Krishna stole away Princess Rukmini of Chedi after he received her desperate love-letter asking him to rescue her from being married to someone else. Chaitanya had wanted the costumes, make-up and jewellery to be perfect. He had played the role of Princess Rukmini, transforming himself so completely that nobody could make out that it was their guru. The performance had gone on through the night at Chandrashekhar's house and ended only in the morning. This pattern is similar to that of the other performing art forms like

Kutiyattam, Kathakali, Kuchipudi, Manipuri and Sattriya, which are 'musical dance-drama', or balletic-operatic, in nature.

So the depth and range of this great sweep of devotional, artistic, philosophical and lifestyle influence can actually be traced back to Andal-Radha. We could go so far as to say that it was the seed influence of Radha-Andal or Andal-Radha which kept religion alive in India through the tumult of history, putting out deep roots, wide-spreading branches and intoxicatingly perfumed flowers.

Going by the 'Radha logic' we have attempted to trace here, the choice of the kadamba does make sense. It blooms in profusion not only across the land but in many minds, in poignant acknowledgement of Radha's mystic idyll, and of how every pilgrim's heart becomes Radha, too, in quest of Krishna.

18

RAIKAMAL

TARASHANKAR BANDOPADHYAY

(TRANSLATED FROM THE BENGALI BY ARUNA CHAKRAVARTI)

A SMALL *AKHAARA* surrounded by a wattle fence. Through the gaps one can see a stretch of verdant green dotted with mango and guava trees, towering neems and bamboo clumps. In the centre of this charming garden is a little cottage with a couple of rooms and a yard swabbed smooth and clean with red earth. At one end of the yard a *madhabi* and a *malati* have formed a natural bower. Locked in an embrace they have flung leaves, stems and tendrils over a bamboo machan. And, taking turns, they cover it with flowers throughout the year. The akhaara is named Kamal Kunja.

Two women live here. Kamini, the Vaishnavi, follows her caste profession of gathering alms by clinking her cymbals outside the doors of the villagers and singing of the love of Radha and Krishna. And her daughter, Kamalini, whose face is like the lotus after which she is named, swabs the yard, waters the garden and takes singing lessons from the elderly Baul—Rasik Das. His akhaara, Rasa Kunja, is a short distance away but he spends most of his time here.

Rasik is the tallest man that ever lived. His neck is like a stork's, and his arms and legs so long and loose they jerk with every movement. His hair is tied in a knot on the top of his head and his beard carefully plaited into a braid. Kamalini can't resist giggling whenever she sees him. 'Stork Babaji! Stork Babaji!' she teases. Kamini is mortified at her daughter's lack of manners. *'Mar mukhpuri!'* she curses. 'Huge, hulking girl of fourteen! Do you have no sense?'

'Na go na.' Rasik smiles. 'Don't scold her. Her spirit is infused with the joy that was Radharani's. She is no ordinary Kamal. She's Raikamal.'

'Kamli!' Ranjan calls from beyond the fence. Kamal jumps up and runs out of the yard.

'The song . . . the song,' Rasik cries.

'Bother the song. I'm off to eat *kul* berries.'

'Na . . . na.' Kamini runs after her. 'Come back, you foolish girl. Don't you know what people are saying about you?' Then turning to the smiling Rasik, she asks angrily, 'Is this something to be merry about, Mahanto?' Rasik sways his stork neck from side to side and sings in a high, quavering voice.

Rai Kamalini unfurls her petals; black-bee Krishna hovers near.
People taunt and slander her. She does not care; she knows no fear.

Ranjan, the headman's son, was a couple of years older than Kamal. As children, playing house-house under the banyan tree, he would insist on being Kamal's husband. A scene from the past:

Half lying on the spreading roots Ranjan mops his forehead and
calls out in the voice of a seasoned householder, 'Bou! O Bou! Light
my hookah and fan me for a while. It's so hot . . .'

'Aa ha ha ha!' Kamal makes faces at him from behind
her veil. 'As if I have nothing better to do! Light your hookah
yourself . . .'

'Mind your language, woman!' Ranjan roars at her.
'Remember that a sun-scorched peasant and a burning coulter are
equally deadly. Another word from you and I'll break your bones.'

Kamal marches up to him and thrusts her bare back under his nose. 'Break my bones,' she dares him. 'Let's see what a big man you are!'

Ranjan takes up the challenge. Twisting her thick braid with one hand he deals half a dozen blows on her back with the other. Whereupon Kamal picks up a handful of dust and, flinging it in Ranjan's face, bursts into a fit of weeping. 'How dare you hit me?' she howls, her face red and streaked with tears.

Soft-hearted Bhola takes her side. 'It's only a game, Ranjan,' he says. 'You shouldn't have hit her.'

'Hmph! I'm her husband. What sort of man will stand by quietly when his wife humiliates him?'

'Husband!' Kamal lashes out at him between sobs. 'What sort of husband are you? Useless as a provider. Only fit to beat me and order me about. Ja! Ja! I won't be your wife any more. And I won't talk to you ever again.'

'Don't cry, Kamli,' Bhola takes her hand tenderly in his. 'I'll be your husband.'

'And I'll be your wife.' Pari, the grocer's daughter, looks up adoringly into Ranjan's face.

'No, Pari.' Ranjan shakes his head gravely. 'I'm not getting married again.'

Kamal looks up. She stops crying and, withdrawing her hand from Bhola's, moves slowly towards Ranjan. 'Take care,' Bhola calls out a warning. 'He'll beat you again.'

Kamal sighs then, assuming the weary voice and manner of the married women she saw around her, she says, 'Well, he may beat me or love me. It is his will. After all, I married him, and a woman, however ill-treated, cannot marry twice—can she?'

The game is resumed. Kamal beats her forehead with a tiny hand and sighs, 'There's no rice in the house. No salt. No oil. But does my husband care? Radhe! Radhe! What a worthless man I've married! Does he expect me to go out and earn money and buy the provisions myself?'

At this a faint smile appears on Ranjan's gloomy countenance. He moves to Kamal's side and whispers in her ear, 'I won't beat you again, Bou. Never again. I promise.'

Today Ranjan is a strapping youth. His eyes are tinged with the awakening of a dewy morn in spring. And Kamal is a lotus bud on the verge of bloom. It will take her a while longer to unfurl her thousand petals. But the promise is in the air. It is visible in the slight halting of her dancing footsteps and the shy mist creeping into her flashing, bird-wing eyes. She's still wild and restless as a forest doe. Yet, a veil of restraint, fine as gossamer, is perceived in her words and movements . . .

Reaching the kul tree Ranjan clambered up the trunk and proceeded to shake the branches. *Tup tup tup* the berries dropped like rain. Kamal ran this way and that collecting them. 'O Ma!' she exclaimed, biting into one. 'This must be the sweetest kul I've ever tasted.'

'Don't eat it all.' Ranjan jumped to the ground. 'Give me the rest.' Then, chewing on the half-eaten berry, he smiled at his companion. 'It's as sweet as sweet can be. That's because you bit into it first.'

'*Bol Haribol!* Is my mouth made of sugar?'

'Hunh? You're my Sugar.'

'And you're my Pepper.' Kamal giggled. Then, sobering down, she added, 'Do you realize what you've just done? You've lost your caste.'

'I don't care a crow's leg for my caste.' Ranjan took her hand in his. 'I'll happily become a Vaishnava if you marry me.'

'Arré! Arré!' Kamal snatched her hand away and ran home. But she kept looking back at him, her face glowing with joy.

Ranjan's mother loved Kamal for her pretty face and winsome ways and gave her a share of the sweets and toys she bought for Ranjan. But on that day her love changed into intense hate. '*Daini! Haramjadi!*' she screamed curses at the absent girl, 'Wait till I catch you. I'll give you such a lashing with my broom! And where's that good-for-nothing boy? O Ma! What'll I do now? My caste is lost and . . .'

'*Chup*, woman, chup!' her husband cautioned in an undertone. 'Stop screaming your head off. If the truth is revealed in the village we'll be thrown out of our clan. We'll be ruined.'

For the kul-eating incident hadn't gone unnoticed. There was an eyewitness. A person none other than the headman, Ranjan's father.

Ranjan walked in nonchalantly a few minutes later. 'O ré O mukhpora!' was his mother's loving greeting. 'Have you taken leave of your senses? What were you thinking of . . . you scum of my womb?'

'Serve my meal,' Ranjan growled. 'I've come home because I'm hungry. Not to listen to abuses.'

His mother's face twisted with disgust. 'Hasn't Kamli's half-eaten berry filled your stomach? Well, then, I'll fill it. I'll stuff your mouth with ashes hot from the hearth.'

The fire in Ranjan's eyes died out. Hanging his head he stared at the floor. 'You should have died the moment you were born,' his father's voice hissed in his ear. 'But I know how to deal with wayward sons. I'll cast you off without one paisa. I'll drive you out of the house . . .' He stormed away with a furious clacking of khadams.

'I've decided to get you married next month.' The mother tried to soften the blow. 'I'll find a girl so beautiful—Kamli will be nothing to her.'

'No.'

'No?'

'I'm not marrying anyone else. I've decided to become a Vaishnava.' The mother stared at him, speechless with shock. Then, flinging all caution to the winds, she screamed in panic. 'Come back! Come back! Hear what your son just said . . .'

'Mahanto!' Ranjan called from the bamboo gate of Rasa Kunja. This was a place where all manner of men, young and old, rich and poor, Vaishnavas and non-Vaishnavas, congregated. Rasik Das was a good host. The young ones could smoke as much tobacco as they wanted. The elders opted for ganja.

'Ah!' Rasik exclaimed. 'It's Raikamal's Ranjan at my door!' Then, peering sharply into the boy's face, he said, 'You look hungry.'

'I am. Can I eat with you?'

'You can. But you'll lose your caste.'

'I don't care. I'm becoming a Vaishnava.'

The old man nodded and smiled. Wagging his beard he began humming a song . . .

Faith, honour and line I held not dear. At thy feet I lie . . . a slave

'*Dhat!*' Ranjan cried, blushing furiously. 'What's wrong with you?'

'Rasik's heart is filled with joy. Joy that knows no bounds. It is spilling over in song.'

'Stop your nonsense and listen to me. I want to become a Vaishnava. Will you initiate me?'

'If Raikamal tells me to—I will.'

'Why? Is Kamli your lawyer?'

Rasik swayed his head, a mysterious smile on his lips. Ranjan waited for a few minutes. 'Very well. I'll go and ask her myself.' He stomped off in a huff.

Kamal was sitting under the flowering creepers of Kamal Kunja, sorting through a pile of berries, when Bhola tiptoed in and took her hand. 'Let go of me, you dolt!' Kamal giggled and tried to pull her fingers away. But Bhola wouldn't let her. 'Kamli,' he whispered, his voice charged with emotion. Kamal took a handful of berries with her other hand and squashed them against his face. 'Hee! Hee! Hee!' The sight of the boy, his cheeks, chin and nose spattered with kul pulp, sent her into gales of laughter.

'Sugar!' Ranjan's voice called softly from the wattle hedge.

'Oh! It's my Pepper!' Kamal exclaimed. But the sound of Ranjan's voice struck terror in Bhola's heart. He jumped up and ran out of the akhaara. 'Come back, Bhola!' Kamal ran after him. 'Why do you run away?' Ranjan took in the scene with lowering brows and, turning his face, strode rapidly in the other direction. Kamal was puzzled and cried out to him to return but he didn't look back, leave alone reply. This infuriated the girl. 'Go wherever you like,' she shouted after both of them. 'I don't care one bit. I'm no one's slave.'

That evening Ranjan's father burst into Kamal Kunja. 'We both have children,' he cried, clutching Kamini's hands in his. 'Give mine back to me.'

'What do you mean?'

'Ranjan says he will not marry anyone else. He will become a Vaishnava.'

Kamini's face paled. 'If indeed it has gone so far,' she murmured uneasily, 'can I break my daughter's heart?'

'I'll give you two bighas of land. And . . . and money—'

'*Chhi!* Is my Kamli's happiness on sale?'

Suddenly there was a loud thud, as of something heavy falling to the ground. Kamini ran to the door. Kamal stood outside, her sari soaking wet, the mud pot in which she had fetched water, lying in shards at her feet. Her face was white and she was shaking like a leaf. Kamini put her arms around the girl. 'Never mind the pot,' she said. 'Come inside and change your sari.' As mother and daughter entered the door a shadow slipped past them. It was the headman.

'Ma,' Kamal said after a while. 'Some people from our village are going to Nabadwip for the Raas festival. Why don't we go too?'

'Y . . . yes. We could go . . . I suppose.'

Kamal sprang up and ran out of the house. 'Where are you going?' Kamini called after her.

'To fetch Stork Babaji. He must come with us.'

Kamal was back within minutes, dragging Rasik by the hand. He looked puzzled but didn't ask any questions. 'An excellent idea,' he said, falling in with Kamini's plans at once. 'We'll leave tomorrow at dawn.'

Reaching Nabadwip, Kamini bought an akhaara and made it neat and comfortable. The garden she planted with flowering bushes and vines. And, every evening, she invited the local Vaishnavas to hold discourses and sing kirtans. Rasik was charmed by the young men and women who came to the akhaara. 'Aa ha ha ha!' he exclaimed. 'My eyes have never beheld such beauty before! This land is blessed. Haven't our Mahaprabhu's feet touched every inch of this ground? Isn't the air still redolent with his breath?'

'Aa ha ha ha!' Kamal mimicked, doubling over with laughter. 'My Stork Babaji is feeling the need of a Vaishnavi at last! Choose one from the beauties here and hang a garland around her neck as fast as you can.'

The days went by. The evening gatherings in the akhaara swelled with more and more young men hovering like bees around a newly blossoming lotus. But Kamal seemed unaware of them. She lived in her own world and thought her own thoughts. She wasn't pensive or withdrawn. She laughed and chatted with all but chose no one for special attention.

'Kamalini!' Subal, the fairest and most perfectly formed of all the Vaishnava youths, came upon her one morning. 'You seem lost in your thoughts. Won't you share them with me?'

Kamal looked up. 'It's mid-morning,' she said. 'I was wondering why my Subal Sakha hasn't come to me on his way to the pasture.'

Subal trembled at her words. Seizing her hands he murmured in a voice choked with emotion, '*Sakhi* . . . sakhi . . .' Kamal disengaged them gently and murmured, 'Is this conduct becoming of my beautiful Subal Sakha?' Hurt and embarrassed, Subal turned to leave but Kamal stopped him. 'Why do you go away? You are my friend, are you not?'

Weeks passed into months. The year was almost over. But Kamini refused to leave Nabadwip. 'Why go back?' she asked wearily whenever Rasik proposed returning to the village. 'Isn't it better that we spend our last days in this holy land and die breathing the air of the Ganga?'

The lotus bud, in the meanwhile, had burst into bloom; her thousand petals quivering with life. She no longer tossed and danced in the unruly wind. She floated serenely on the ripples, sending eddies of perfume into the air. Rasik gazed at her in wonder. Sometimes he sang snatches of an old Vaishnava love song . . .

Kamini was able to fulfil her last wish. She died in Nabadwip. She didn't suffer much. Just four days of fever. 'The thought of death doesn't sadden me, Mahanto,' she said. 'I'm filled with bliss at the thought of leaving my mortal remains in Ma Ganga's lap. At Gourango's feet. Only . . .'

'Why do you talk of death? What's wrong with you?'

'Nothing. Yet everything. I feel I'm going far . . . very far away. But one thought pulls me back. My daughter . . .'

'If it comes to that,' said Rasik, eyes glittering with tears, 'I'll take care of Kamal.'

Kamini sighed. 'I knew that, Mahanto. Still . . . I wanted an assurance.'

'Ma!' A sobbing Kamal flung herself on her mother's breast.

Kamini placed a trembling hand on the girl's head. 'Don't weep, child. Parents don't live forever. Promise me . . .'

'What is it, Ma?'

'The creeper that doesn't cling to a tree lies, weak and vulnerable, on the ground. It has no strength. Animals nibble at it . . .' Her voice choked on the words.

'I know. I give you my word . . . I will marry.'

'Don't take a son away from his parents.'

'I won't.'

'Jai Radhe! Radhe!' Rasik cried, making sure his voice reached Kamini's ears.

'Gobindo . . . Gobindo,' the dying lips murmured.

Time, like a mother, sings an unending lullaby that erases memory and soothes the suffering mortal into a state of blessed oblivion. The pain of loss eased with every passing day. Kamal laughed once more. And her laughter found an echo in the old man's breast.

'Raikamal,' he ventured one day. But he seemed unable to go on.

'What is it?' Kamal was surprised. 'Why don't you speak? Do you have a fishbone stuck in your throat?'

Rasik swallowed, then, making a great effort, blurted out, 'It has to do with your marriage.'

Kamal's face paled. 'I understand,' she answered softly. Then, looking up at the sky, she muttered, 'The day is almost done, Mahanto. Let's wait for the night.' Rising, she went into her room and locked the door. Weeping bitterly, she called out to the One she believed to be her true friend and guide. 'Gobindo! Gobindo! My heart and mind are another's. To whom shall I give this empty shell?' But all she received in reply was a chilling silence. Abandoned even by her God the bereft girl sought the answer herself. *She had to deceive someone. Who would it be?* Faces came and went before her eyes.

Rasik was sitting in the yard when Kamal came to him, the red-gold of the setting sun glowing in her cheeks. 'We'll need flowers for the garlands, Mahanto,' she said.

'I'll go at once.' Rasik rose to his feet.

He returned in a while, his *dhuti* dripping wet, holding a sheaf of lotus buds in his arms. 'Raikamal,' he called out to her happily, 'I've brought lotus as befits . . .' Kamal came and stood before him. The rest of the sentence died in his throat. She wore a tussore sari with a deep-red border. Her hair hung loose down her back like a rippling river, and the caste marks of her sect were etched in sandal paste on her delicate nose and brow. He had never seen her look so beautiful.

'Change your dhuti,' she said. 'Wear the one I've kept in your room.' Kamal took the flowers and began stringing them into a garland. 'You string one, too, Mahanto.'

'A good idea. I'll fetch Subal as soon as the garlands are done.'

Their task completed, the two rose to their feet. Kamal slipped her garland over Rasik's head and said, 'Won't you give me yours?' Taking up the bowl of sandalwood paste she adorned his wrinkled forehead.

'You throw away a silver rupee,' Rasik said sadly, 'and tie a copper pie in your *aanchal*. Is that wise, Raikamal?'

'Copper and gold are often mistaken for one another. I've found gold.'

Rasik smiled and placed his garland around Kamal's neck.

Rasik prepared the flower-bed that night, strewing the brightest, freshest blooms on one side and wilting, decaying ones on the other. 'You and me,' he said.

'Yes.' Kamal lowered herself on to the withered side. 'The fresh flowers are yours, Mahanto—the stale ones mine.' Her laughter rang out like a peal of bells. Rasik took up a lamp and held the light to Kamal's face. He gazed at her so intently—it seemed as though his eyes would never have their fill. 'The more I see you,' he murmured, 'the greater my awe and wonder! Radharani works in inscrutable ways but her bounty is immeasurable.'

Kamal lay on the wilted flowers, her eyes hard and dry. Rasik, on the other side, slept peacefully. Around midnight, she felt herself being drawn to the old man's breast. His shrivelled arms had the strength of a crazed elephant; his skeletal fingers the tensile grip of a hangman's rope. Kamal was frightened. 'Mahanto! Mahanto!' she shrieked fearfully . . .

The arrival of dawn saw Rasik sitting in the yard, motionless as a statue. His limbs were still, his eyes fixed. It seemed as though he had stopped breathing. Kamal's heart melted. She wanted to comfort him but couldn't find the words.

'Kamal.' It was Rasik who broke the silence. Kamal looked up in surprise. Why had he called her Kamal? A strange feeling came over her. She felt slighted, diminished. 'Kamal,' he said again, 'I'm made of flesh and blood.'

'We all are. But, today, you've turned yourself to stone.'

'Yes. Yes . . . like Ahalya.'

'Tear off this garland of embers, Mahanto,' Kamal said softly. 'Free yourself from this curse.'

'I tried to escape last night but couldn't. My feet were willing but my eyes wouldn't leave your face. This . . . this shame is my burden and I must carry it. But don't abandon me,' he gripped her hands and pleaded. 'Don't leave me . . . ever.'

'Then let's go somewhere else.' Kamal wiped her streaming face. 'Someplace far away.'

'Where?'

'Vrindavana.'

'No . . . no!' A shiver passed over the ancient frame. 'I cannot show this face, blackened with shame, to the moon of Brajdham.'

'Why, Mahanto? Is loving me such a great sin?'

There was no answer.

'Very well. We'll have no destination . . . no home. We'll wander aimlessly from village to village, seeking alms on our way. The open sky will be our roof and the shade of trees our resting place.'

The stone statue quivered into life. 'Let's go, then.' He rose to his feet.

Stepping out into the open Rasik heaved a sigh of relief. He could inhale the fragrance of the lotus beside him but its tender stem wasn't fastened around his neck like a noose.

Leaving Nabadwip behind, the two walked mile after mile till, hungry and footsore, they stopped by a pond at the edge of a village. 'I'll take a dip and cook a meal,' Kamal said like a seasoned housewife. 'But there's no salt in the bundle, Mahanto. Go into the village and buy some.'

Rasik returned an hour later to find Kamal sitting before a fire of twigs, stirring rice in a clay pot. Her long, wet hair was drawn to the top of her head in a knot. The ridge of her nose and gleaming forehead were etched in sandalwood paste. A group of people stood around her, staring and nudging one another.

'What a beauty! Who is she?'

'She doesn't seem to belong to these parts.'

'What is your name, Vaishnavi?' One of the men addressed her directly. 'Where do you live?'

Kamal didn't deign to reply. But Rasik stepped forward. 'Her name is Raikamal,' he announced, 'she lives in Rasa Kunja.'

'Where did this one spring up from? Who on earth are you?'

'I'm the husband, go! The Vaishnavi's Vaishnava. My name is Ayan Ghosh.' His lips twitched in a smile.

The crowd melted away. Rasik twanged his *ektara* softly and hummed a love song.

Days passed. The two walked, apparently without direction, but whether it was from the twists and turns of the road or the hidden promptings of the two hearts, they arrived one afternoon, at the gate of Rasa Kunja. Tears sprang to Rasik's eyes as he saw the ruin that had once been his beloved akhaara. Kamal Kunja hadn't fared any better. The walls had crumbled to the ground, the thatch blown away. But the bower stood intact, its canopy vibrant with blooms. 'I'm glad to be home, Mahanto.' Kamal lay down on the fallen flowers. 'I don't want to leave . . . ever.'

'Neither do I. The sky, air and earth of my native village are tying me with unseen bonds. Only . . .' Rasik said, hesitating a little, 'you must let me live in Rasa Kunja.'

'So you shall, Mahanto. So you shall. Rest assured, I won't disturb you with my presence.'

'But I shall come to you. We'll swing together under the clouds on Jhulan. I shall adorn you with flowers on Raas and sprinkle saffron and kumkum on your face on Dol.'

'You've thought of all the *leelas*. What about the difficult one? The bearing of Govardhan Mountain?

'That will be the first. From tomorrow morning I'll begin repairing the walls and thatching the roof of Kamal Kunja. But let's go to the village, now, and collect some alms.'

The two went from door to door, greeting old acquaintances and filling their satchels with rice. Reaching the headman's house Rasik's steps faltered. 'We have enough for today,' he muttered uneasily.

'But this is where my Pepper lives,' Kamal cried gaily. 'He'll be hurt if I don't stop at his house . . .' Rasik glanced at her face. It was as radiant as the moon. Rasik felt a stab of jealousy ripping his chest. His eyes burned with tears he dared not shed. Forcing a smile on his wan lips he twanged the string of his ektara, blending it with Kamal's high, sweet voice. 'Radhe Krishna! I've come for some alms, ma!'

A young woman opened the door. From the *ghumta* on her head and the sindoor on her brow and parting it was obvious that she was the daughter-in-law of the house. 'Sing a song, Vaishnavi,' she demanded. The proud tilt of her head and the sparkle in her eyes told Kamal that she was a happy, fulfilled woman. She hadn't been denied her husband's love . . .

Rasik's hard work turned Kamal Kunja into the serene, beautiful akhaara it had been during Kamini's time. Kirtan was sung every evening. Kamal's childhood friends, Bhola, Binod and Panchanan, came. Only Ranjan stayed away. 'I've requested him so many times,' Bhola grumbled, 'but he says . . .'

'What does he say?'

'Leave it. It isn't meant for your ears.'

Kamal saw the compassion in Bhola's eyes. 'Tell me,' she insisted. 'I want to hear.'

'He said . . . *to look on her face is a sin*.' Seeing the tears gather in the girl's eyes he added tenderly, 'Shall I speak to him again?'

'Chhi!'

A few days later Ranjan saw her at the bathing ghat. She had just stepped out of the water. Her wet sari clung to the curves of her exquisite form. Her face, framed by her long, wavy hair, was like a dew-washed lotus. Ranjan couldn't tear his eyes away.

'Sugar,' he called imperiously.

Kamal looked up. A powerful, well-built man stood before her. His arms were tense with muscles, his chest a stone wall. Kamal's eyes dimmed. Was this the tender youth she had known and loved? Her heart was torn with pity at his lost innocence. With the keen instinct of a woman in love she looked into his soul. She searched long and deep but found not a trace of light. It was a hollow shell: dark and empty.

Ranjan came and stood by her. So close she could feel his fevered breath licking her cool, wave-washed body. She remembered her bridal night. The terror of Rasik's arms coiling and writhing about her limbs like snakes; his bloodshot eyes gazing into hers . . . Picking up her water-pot Kamal walked away in the opposite direction. *I had so little left*, she thought sadly, *even that little has been taken from me. With what shall I sustain myself?*

'Mahanto!' Ranjan called loudly from the gate of Kamal Kunja that evening. Kamal started. Dropping her cymbals she ran into her room. Rasik's love song froze in his throat. *This is the beginning of the end*, he thought, glancing at the sinking sun. A few minutes later he stood outside the girl's door. 'Raikamal,' he called, 'Ranjan is here to see you.'

'I can't come out. I have a headache.'

'Chhi! What will he think? Is he not your best friend?'

'I beg you, Mahanto.' Kamal burst into tears. 'Don't torture me with your kindness. I'm a weak woman. I cannot bear the weight of your love.'

'Listen to me . . . Kamal.'

'Leave me alone for tonight. I'll hear all you have to say . . . tomorrow.'

'Tomorrow might be too late.'

'So be it. As of this moment let all words cease between us.'

'Shall I stroke your forehead and make the pain go away?'

'No! No! No!'

Rasik turned. Leaving the door open he walked out of Kamal Kunja. The sky above his head was dark and starless. The night was silent. Only a faint moaning of the trees echoed Kamal's pain. A sound unheard . . . only sensed.

Ranjan tiptoed in through the door Rasik had left open. *Sin is like a snake. It lives in a secret hole and creeps out in the darkness of night.* 'Sugar'. . . his whisper entered Kamal's ear like the deadly hiss of a forked tongue. She sprang up with a shudder and ran out of the akhaara not stopping till she reached Rasa Kunja. Her clothes and hair were dishevelled; her eyes wide with terror. 'Mahanto! Mahanto!' she called and banged on the door till it opened. Rasik stood within. 'Are you . . . happy, Raikamal?' he asked.

'Ranjan came . . .'

'You . . . sent him away?' A smile, like a shaft of moonlight, blew away the clouds from Rasik's face. But Kamal noticed that his hands were shaking and he was having trouble articulating his words.

'What have you done to yourself?' she cried out fearfully.

'Poison! Ranjan and you . . . I couldn't bear the thought . . . Death was preferable. But now . . . now that you are here . . . I want to live. Save me, Raikamal . . . save me!'

'Ma go!' Kamal shrieked. 'What will become of me? My sin . . .'

'The sin was mine. You are Raikamal . . . cast in Radharani's mould . . . Can sin touch you? Oof!' His face was contorted with agony. Foam gathered at his lips.

The night waned. The sky pearled with the first touch of dawn. Kamal sat outside the door of Rasa Kunja with Rasik's limp body in her lap . . .

Rasik's mortal remains find a resting place in the bower of Kamal Kunja. Kamal lights a lamp there, every evening, and sings the songs he loved. Her friends come to see her. Only Ranjan does not come.

'Shall I bring him?' Bhola asks.

'He'll come on his own . . . some day.'

An elderly Vaishnavi says to her, 'We are going to Vrindavana. Why don't you come with us?'

'No. I've had my fill of pilgrimages. I'm happy where I am.'

'Gobindo! Gobindo!' the woman touches her ears. 'What Vaishnavi will throw away the chance to go to Brajdham? The village women are right. You're a harlot.'

Kamal smiles and sings:

They call me a harlot; I'm in love with the name, dear friend.
Spurning it . . . shall I lose my beloved Shyam?
Radha comes before Shyam. They cry out . . . 'Radheshyam!'

Lighting a lamp at the mound covered with madhavi and malati flowers she touches her brow to the ground and murmurs, 'Guru . . . guru . . . guru.'

19

A FLUTE CALLED RADHA

DEBOTRI DHAR

RADHA DRAWS IN a deep breath and waits. Tonight the Yamuna will not speak to her. Tonight it flows silently, sulkily, without smell or touch or tears. The night has emptied out its stars and holds no forgiveness. Radha knows she must not move too much, lest the sky crumble. 'It crumbles so easily nowadays,' she mutters to herself in irritation. Like the other day, when some of the village boys raced through the ripening fields to shoot cardboard arrows at the sky and it split into so many shards of lightning. Later they lay noiselessly scattered everywhere, but when she bent to pick one up, it snapped forth and bit her, drawing blood. Radha looks down at her finger, bandaged with a grubby strip of cotton shot with dark splotches of red. Her hand itself is hard and veiny, nothing like the soft, white lilies he would often compare them to when he laid his head in her lap. And when she laughs, it is no longer the silver tinkle of anklets on moonlit marble. No, it is laughter from another time and place, a stranger's laughter that he cannot possibly love. But, then, he always had a way with words. Radha cocks her head from side to side, trying to remember. Some of the memories are smooth and easy, like his touch. If she closes her eyes tight enough, she can feel his fingers play expertly on her skin. She can feel the rush of blood to her forearm

154

where he rubs it deliciously. Her fingers are at war with themselves, kneading through his hair, pulling him close and pushing him away. When he kisses her, her lips swell like the bee-stung *champa* blossoms of Vrindavana. 'Radha, Radha,' he murmurs in agony, hounded by his own demons. I'm tired of being God, he wants to whisper. Radha knows. She folds him into the night, cradling him in her arms like she did when he was a child. The moment passes. He is once again Krishna, God, skilled lover, centre of the universe. He rubs the perfume of *raat-champa* into her smooth, flat belly. They love each other on the riverbank, to the slow music of the Yamuna, their bodies entwined, their souls flushed.

The stars look down and smile sadly, while Vrindavana sleeps.

'I am yours, my Krishna.'

'Radha, Radha,' he says in response.

Say, *And I am yours, my Radha,* she wills him with her stormy eyes.

But by the time he does, it is too late. Radha puts her hands over her ears, trying to shut out the sounds of drums and chariots and victory and loss. And Radha, old woman, madwoman, laughs and cries.

~

She arrived on the first day of *vasant*, bringing with her the bloom of roses and the lilt of the breeze. 'She is the most beautiful bride in all of Barsana and they say her skin glows like moonlight,' two women of Nanda whispered enviously among themselves. 'But what good did her beauty do? All that her destiny had to offer was the stammering cowherd Ayan with the thick belly and thicker mind,' laughed a third.

The gossip went on and on relentlessly through the day, but when it was evening they wore their most pious faces to the house where the young bride Radha had come to stay with her relatives for a while. The women sat in a circle and talked about this and that till Radha came out to light the evening lamps. Her hair shimmered all the way down her waist, her silver cummerbund was a lithe rope around the curve of her waist, and the mirrors on her choli glinted. *Is she lighting the lamps, or are the lamps lighting her,* the women wondered.

'Come and sit with us. Tell us about your wedding night,' one of them called out in good humour.

Everyone laughed. Radha smiled and shook her head, her doe eyes calm but cautious, and went indoors. And Yashoda's kind heart brimmed over. She got up, pulling the child Kanha by the hand, and followed Radha inside the house. Radha was folding bedclothes and looked up shyly at the plump, motherly woman and her young child.

'I am Yashoda, wife of Nanda and mother of this naughty son.' The older woman gave her a reassuring look.

'Welcome, didi,' Radha said, dazzling Yashoda with her smile.

'I hope your husband knows how lucky he is,' Yashoda murmured as she walked across to Radha to tilt her face upwards to the light of the lantern. Then, turning to Kanha, she winked at her child. 'So, would you want a bride as beautiful as her?' The child looked at Radha, mesmerized. 'There, now your beauty has achieved the impossible,' laughed Yashoda. 'Your face has even managed to silence the reigning terror of Nanda!'

Radha smiled and kneeled down to look deeply into the child Kanha's eyes. 'Do you think I am pretty?'

Eyes full of wonder, Kanha stretched out his hand and touched Radha's cheek. 'Yes. Will you be my bride?'

The two women laughed till tears started pouring out of Yashoda's eyes. Wiping them away with the corner of her *aanchal*, she put her arms around the younger woman's shoulders.

'Please don't be upset.'

'Oh, why, he's just a child,' exclaimed Radha, bewildered.

'No, I mean the women of the village.' Yashoda's tone was serious. 'We had all heard of your beauty and everyone was curious to see you. And you know how it is with us women. Sometimes we want to know all about . . . everything.'

'What do you want to know?' asked Radha quietly. 'That I was married off against my wishes to a man old enough to be my father? That he is good and kind, but I feel no love, no passion? That till the day I die, this is how God has willed my life to be? Is this what everyone wishes to know?'

'Be quiet,' Yashoda admonished, aghast. 'These are not the right thoughts for a new bride. Radha, as women, we must accept that which we cannot change. And we must learn to be happy with what we have, for on our happiness depends the happiness of our men and children. Our household is our universe, and you must always remember that.'

Radha looked at Yashoda and shook her head slowly, defiantly. 'No, didi. I will not learn to be happy with what I have. My household will not be my universe, for there is a much larger universe outside of my kitchen and my courtyard that I want to hold in my palms. I want to pluck stars from the skies, I want to dance with the sun!'

'Radha, my child,' Yashoda murmured soothingly, at once amused and worried. 'The sun and the stars, the universe and us— we all have our own paths. Don't fight the laws of nature, for the sun that snugly cocoons us from cold, faraway skies can just as easily turn into a cruel fire that burns to ashes those who dare to go too close.'

Radha smiled, her eyes shimmering with unshed tears. One errant drop broke free and rolled down her cheek. Kanha stretched out his palms and caught the tear as it fell.

'Look at him,' his mother said softly. 'I have never seen him so grave before. As if he understands all about women's woes!'

Radha stretched out her arms and pulled the boy close to her. Then she turned to Yashoda. 'Could I take him with me when I go to fill my pitchers tomorrow?'

'Yes, by all means. At home, all he does is get in my way,' laughed Yashoda.

And so it came to be that for all of spring, a playful little boy and a plaintive young woman spent their mornings by the riverbed.

'Why do you always have black rings around your eyes?' he would ask, circling them with curious fingertips.

'Because I cannot sleep,' Radha would answer gravely.

'And why not?' he would demand, puffing out his chest and crossing his arms over them. When in response Radha only smiled, he would climb on top of a wayside boulder to put his podgy arms around her. Sometimes she laid her head in his lap while he rocked her back and forth, like his mother rocked him to sleep at night. 'Sleep, sleep,' he would whisper, agitated when she could not.

'Perhaps I need your flute,' she finally said one day, taking his unhappy little face in her palms.

At that, his eyes lit up. Lifting his flute to his lips and closing his eyes, he began to play. As the smooth, honeyed notes trilled forth, the sky rippled and trees danced in joy. Rabbits cocked their ears, birds paused mid-flight and tigers halted their chase to sit demurely by the little boy's side. Even the Yamuna slowed down, enchanted. And Radha, for once, rested her throbbing head and slept for hours.

When she woke up, she saw Kanha staring at her. 'What is it?' she asked, rubbing her eyes. 'Struck speechless by my beauty? Have you never seen a woman before?' she teased, rolling her eyes.

Kanha scowled. 'You too will be left speechless by my beauty one day!' he shouted, before pinching her hard and running away.

As the verdant greens of vasant began to give way to the arid browns of an inevitable *grishma*, it was time for Radha to return to her husband's home.

'Who will I play with after you are gone?' Kanha asked, his kohl-lined eyes glinting.

'Why, there are so many pretty *gopis* in the village. Go play with them.'

'But you're the prettiest of them all,' he sobbed, while she burst into laughter.

'Then you'll just have to wait for me to come back,' she said, smiling at the boy who had crept into her room the previous evening to hide all her clothes just so she could not leave.

'We'll see who waits for whom,' he said, before running away in tears. When she followed him to his house, he went into the pantry and locked himself in. 'Go away,' he shouted.

The summer worsened after Radha left. The sun raged across the sky, scalding skins and fraying tempers. Cows lay listless in their sheds, their liquid eyes drooping. Sweat trickled down in slow rivulets and babies cried. The earth broke out in angry blisters and the Yamuna threatened to dry up.

'Why is it so hot this year?' children asked their mothers.

'Don't worry,' came the reply. '*Varsha* will soon be here.'

Days slipped into months and months into years, till many more fertile springs and famished summers had passed. Then, suddenly, without warning, came yet another varsha—the rains. Nights became inky blotches shot with streaks of light and sound. The sun was a shallow puddle and the skies dribbled endlessly through the day. The smell of wet earth perfumed the air. And news travelled from near and far that Radha was back.

'Do you remember Yashoda's naughty little boy who became speechless when he saw you and clung to his mother? That Kanha who used to trail noiselessly behind you on the banks of the Yamuna? He is now a strapping young man, and all the gopis fancy themselves in love with him! He only needs to play his flute and the girls swoon,' laughed one of the village women.

Radha was thoughtful. 'I remember him. But many seasons have gone by. Perhaps he does not remember me.'

That night it rained ceaselessly. When morning came, the sky was swollen and moody. 'The river is in spate. Stay away from its banks,' everyone warned. But Radha had to go. Somehow, she knew. Her tread was as light as her heart was heavy. *Turn back,* something in her kept saying. Yet she walked and walked, till she reached the muddy banks of the Yamuna. It was nothing like the Yamuna of her memories. That river of her past had flowed light and clear, it had sparkled with water lilies and lotuses, its green banks had been dotted with egrets and its flowery blossoms had held love. But this Yamuna of the present was an angry violet, and it curled and frothed and hissed. This river was as alive as it was dead. For a moment, her heart sank. And, then, just as she was turning back, a dark shape caught the corner of her eye. It was Krishna! Oh, this Krishna looked nothing like the child Kanha who had held her hand, yet Radha would have recognized him anywhere. He stood against a rock in the river, almost birdlike in his quiet grace. In yellow silk, a garland of wild flowers around his neck and with a peacock feather adorning his head, his dark form glowed. Radha stared at him, spellbound. *One day, I too will be beautiful. One day, you too will stare at me.*

The clouds gathered again. As the rain started falling thickly, Krishna turned to smile at the beautiful woman whose clothes were plastered wetly to her body, whose hair was a waterfall and whose eyelashes shone with a million silvery drops.

'You have come,' he said softly.

Radha nodded, unable to speak. He held out his arms. She walked into the river in a trance. He held her at arm's length and traced the outline of her face with his flute.

'I hear you play the flute even more beautifully now,' she said. He nodded.

'Will you not play it for me again?'

'Not now,' he replied. 'You will have to wait for the rains to end.'

'Oh, but I have to go back in autumn.'

Krishna smiled and traced her cheek with his finger, the way he had as a child many moons ago. But this time, he was no more a little boy. She closed her eyes, not trusting herself to speak. When she opened them, his gaze held hers.

'Stay,' he said.

It was, and always will be, impossible to grasp the true nature of love. Is love that which causes a pain so intense it splits open the heart into a hundred fragments, or that which gently soothes away all pain to make the heart whole again? Is it love only when it battles the world to declare itself, or even when it fills up the countless stretch of days and months with an easy, unspoken familiarity? And what of hate? The seething anger when one's beloved forgets, or even the absolute rage at one's own vulnerability. If there is no hate, can there be love?

These thoughts haunted Radha again and again in the months of *sharad*, when her days and nights were filled in equal measure with the agony and the ecstasy of Krishna's love. The agony was that he did not love her at all. The ecstasy was that he loved her too much and like none other. The agony was that there were women so numerous that she often lost count . . . Beautiful women, with many beautiful gifts to offer. Women young and old, who sucked in their breaths and waited for Krishna's magic flute to ring out through moonlit nights. And they would leave their homes and hearths far behind and trail out breathlessly, eyes alight and hips swaying in abandon to dance the rasa with him under the starry autumn skies. Afterwards, he would love them, scorching their skin and searing himself on their minds forever.

Later, they would remember and rejoice. And he, of course, would forget and move on. 'I am the wind,' he once whispered to her. 'I am doomed to be timeless, formless . . . I cannot be still. Then how can I be captured by one heart? For that which binds is not love . . .'

When Radha complained that it was she who was doomed because she loved him, who knew not what love was, he just laughed and gathered her close into the night.

'Sometimes I think I am like your flute,' she said, drawing away teary-eyed. 'Your flute—a dull, lifeless object that must lie in its dark corner and ask you for nothing. Yet when you pick it up and touch it to your lips, it bursts forth in a fresh spate of music. But I am not your flute, I am alive, I feel, I want, I cry . . .' Radha's large eyes spilled over.

With the tip of his finger, he lifted a solitary teardrop off her wet cheek and gazed at it in wonder. Then he ran his hands over her forehead until she felt the tight knot of her grief ease.

'I am yours, my Krishna, forever,' she said, laying her throbbing head on his chest.

'Radha, Radha,' he murmured, against the quivering arch of her neck.

He never says I am yours forever, warned a small voice inside her head. But still she went willingly into his arms, knowing that she had to make memories to warm her through a string of empty nights. Nights when she would know him to be with the others. Yet, when she met Krishna again, after an agonizing wait, she would once again burn in urgent, infernal ecstasy. The desire that had smouldered on the banks of the Yamuna since they met as man and woman, or perhaps even earlier, from the first heady days of vasant, was endless, infinite, all-consuming.

But when did desire turn to love? Was it on their first night together, when having nowhere else to go, she had turned to him and he had cradled her in his arms and kept all her sorrows safe from the world? Or was it when he had understood, without judgement or condemnation, and let light into her monsoon days—was that when she began to love him? Or was it when they finally made love and he whispered into her ears: 'I miss your hair when I'm not tangled in it'? That night, he had held her close while she slept. At the crack of dawn, she crept back home, hugging her secret to herself. She, who was often too much in turmoil to even sleep at night, slept like a child in the din of day. Only when the sun was high up in the sky did she wake up, light and free and with a song on her lips. She smiled. She lived. When the sun dipped low and the skies started turning crimson, she waited for the magic flute to play. And then she went once again, into the dancing shadows of night. He brought her necklaces of ivory and conch shells, and sulked till she laughingly let him put them around her neck. He ran his fingers through her long, long hair and adorned her thick braids with fragrant strands of champa. He fed her little morsels of food with his own hands and refused to eat on the days that she fasted. And when, unable to suffer any more his closeness with others, she held back from him, he suffered too. Those were the times when Krishna, lover, God incarnate and ruler of the world, broke down and wept.

'No, he feels no remorse,' Radha would say to those of her friends who carried the message of Krishna's grief. 'He does not understand love. Go tell him he can be with any woman he wants. You don't know me till you know my pride. I neither love nor want him any more.'

But they shook their heads in disbelief, knowing how warmly he coursed through her. And sure enough, she would be with him again, long before the Yamuna spilled over with either of their tears.

They say love is a song of seasons, a song whose rhythm slows down with time. Through all of autumn, Radha drank her fill of Krishna. And then came winter with its bands of chilling wind. Of course it did not happen in a day. As varsha gives way to sharad in snatches of colour, and then sharad slowly bleaches white to *hemant*, so did their love give way slowly and intermittently. In the beginning, Radha did not even notice when Krishna no longer lingered on to fasten her girdle or braid her hair after they made love. And if something seemed slightly amiss in the night and he held her briefly and then said that he must go, she tried not to dwell upon it. But it became impossible for her to pretend any longer the day she began to excitedly narrate to him how one of her pots had broken into six perfectly symmetrical shards, and he stared emptily at her, almost as if there was something larger looming beyond her which held his gaze. Her words stumbled into each other and she stopped in confusion, a sudden chill settling upon her heart.

'Krishna,' she whispered.

He snapped out of his reverie and gave her a pat on her shoulder. And then his perfect bee-stung lips mouthed that now-familiar refrain, 'I must go.'

As winter wore on, a dark shadow settled upon Krishna. 'What is the matter,' she would repeatedly ask, haunted by his silences. In response, he would bury his head in her bosom.

'Radha, Radha,' he would murmur while she cradled him, tears in her own eyes. In these moments, little bits of tales once heard would waft back through time to trouble her—tales of the infant Gopal being carried through a turbulent Yamuna by Vasudeva and being sheltered from the rains by none other than the serpent king Sheshnaag himself, tales of him conquering the mighty demons Vatsasura, Bakasura and Aghasura, tales of miracles big and small that the gopis would often swear to . . . And Radha would wonder who Krishna really was. But she did not ask him. Instead, each time shadows flitted across his handsome face, she would cup it with her palms and kiss his tired eyes, willing for sleep to come to him, just as he had once willed it for her.

And then one night—a night so black no stars peeped out from behind the curtain of clouds, a night so cold it froze the Yamuna into a sheet of ice—he uttered, once again, his old words, 'I must go.' And Radha knew that this time he spoke of greater distances, and of never coming back.

What else remains of the story to tell? Only that a few days later—some say it was when hemant turned to *shishir* and some say it was not—a chariot came from Mathura to take Krishna away. As word began to spread, a huge crowd gathered in Nanda and Yashoda's courtyard. Every heart was skipping, each eye fastened to the door of the puja room where Krishna was offering his prayers. The crowd was waiting to scold, berate, cajole—somehow convince the beloved son of Gokul that he belonged here, with and only with them. And when he emerged, resplendent in yellow silk but without his flute, they looked into his hard, hard eyes and realized that he had already left them for Mathura. Fathers were silent and mothers cried. A dozen gopis swarmed around him like angry bees.

Krishna smiled at everyone, hugging the children to his heart and touching the feet of elders to seek blessings for what he knew was to be a long war. Then he prostrated before Nanda and Yashoda, asking for forgiveness.

Tears streamed down Yashoda's cheeks as she looked at the future king of Mathura, regal in the robes of a raja, and saw instead an impish little boy who stole butter from the neighbours' kitchens. Images from his childhood flashed before her eyes, of Kanhaiya tugging at her aanchal when he was hungry, of him laughingly wagging a podgy little finger at her to mimic her own actions of scolding him, of him running to her to be scooped up in her arms so he could touch the sky. Once he reached Mathura and was reunited with Queen Devaki and King Vasudeva, his biological parents whom the evil King Kamsa had kept imprisoned in the palace's dungeons for many years, would he remember Yashoda and Nanda's humble hut in faraway Gokul? Yashoda, blinded by the past and frightened of the future, hugged Krishna and wept silently. *You will always be my son, won't you?* her sobs seemed to ask.

Krishna looked tenderly into her eyes and nodded. As he walked to the chariot, his eyes quickly skimmed the crowd. *You don't know me till you know my pride.* 'I will go to her one last time and then no more,' he promised himself, motioning his charioteer to wait. Then he began to walk through the groves to reach the sandy banks of the Yamuna. She was nowhere. For a moment, his heart sank. And then, just as he was about to turn back, a dark shape caught the corner of his eye. It was Radha! She stood against a rock in the river, almost birdlike in her quiet grace. Krishna stared at her, once again. In the meantime, a smattering of winter clouds had gathered and the skies had begun to rumble. As rain started falling thickly, an almost familiar scene began to unfold. Krishna smiled at the beautiful woman whose clothes were plastered wetly to her body, whose hair was a waterfall and whose eyelashes shone with a million silver drops.

'You have come,' she said.

He nodded. She held out his arms. Slowly, he walked into the river. She held him at arm's length and traced the outline of his face with her finger.

'Where is your flute?' she asked.

Her question jerked him back into the present.

'My flute, yes . . . I don't know. Did I drop it somewhere?'

She smiled sadly. *The flute's time is over,* she wanted to say. Instead, she asked him when he was leaving.

'My chariot is waiting. I have already bid farewell to everyone.'

She nodded, raising her face to his. 'I am yours forever, my Krishna,' she said softly.

'And I yours, my Radha,' he said then.

She closed her eyes. 'Stay. Please stay,' she pleaded with him at last, her heart pounding, her pride spent.

There was silence. Suddenly afraid, she opened her eyes. He was gone. And she threw back her head and laughed and laughed.

Radha, old woman, madwoman, crouches on the banks of the Yamuna. If she lays her ears against its shifting sands, she can hear whispers from many years ago. *Look at her. Kulta, adulteress. Throw her out. Shame. Shame. Shame!* She squints, and sees ghosts from yesterday. Her shrunken husband shuffles past. The women at the well turn away from her. The neighbour's child hurls a stone at her. Sometimes Radha is young and she cannot understand why they think her crime is greater than his, how they can hate her while still loving him so. And sometimes Radha is old and she understands too much, understands that in the dark histories of humanity the woman's crime is always greater than the man's.

Some say it is her fault because he was unattached while she belonged to another. But she knows they would have blamed her even if the roles had been reversed. Some say it is her fault because he was just a young boy and she older and wiser. But she knows it would have been the same even if she had been a young girl, and he older and wiser. The woman's crime is always greater than the man's. That is why Krishna could forget, while she was forever condemned to remembering. That is why Krishna never returned to Vrindavana. That is why he could move on to conquer kingdoms and become king, be hailed as the virtuous killer of Kamsa, and take a hundred, a thousand, no, 16,000 wives. (Of course, she knows it all. Word travels.) He is a man, and they say men are destined for great things, so they worship him. Tomorrow they might forgive her and worship her too, but what good would such worship do? What would change? Men would still love and leave. And women would still be women, and forgive the men while piously condemning each other.

Suddenly, Radha wants to shout louder than all of them—*Shame, not on me but on you. Shame, shame, shame!* Now Radha is tired of being a woman and wants to be a man. Cackling with laughter, she shrugs off her upper garments under the starlit skies.

The following morning, they find her sprawled on the banks of the river.

'It's that madwoman,' they whisper, embarrassed by her nakedness. One of the women hurriedly covers her up.

'What's this?' another woman exclaims, pointing to what looks like a broken flute in Radha's fist. They try to pry her fingers open, but the chill of death has already set in. Radha clutches the lifeless reed to her breast. Radha no longer has black rings around her eyes. Radha sleeps.

endures. As his childhood friend and soulmate, Radha is enchanted by the beauty of Krishna, who plays the flute to court the village *gopi*s, dallies with them and mischievously waylays them at the well or the river, playfully stealing their clothes as they bathe in the water. Her all-consuming love overpowers societal disapproval.

On growing up, however, Krishna falls under the competing demands of the state, and the call of duty takes him away from his home town, Vrindavana. He later marries Rukmini. A bereft Radha dedicates the rest of her life longing for her lover. Thus, she is effectively a female Devdas (with a twist), and the Radha–Krishna duo a Hindu version of the Romeo–Juliet or the Heer–Ranjha coupling; their legend dramatizes the inability of family, community and individual desire to align with each other.

The medium that has mobilized this legend of Radha more than any other is India's Bollywood cinema. It makes more allusions to Radha than Sita or any other goddess. What is fascinating is that Radha defies the tropes of the *sati-savitri naari*, the dominant view of women in Hindi cinema for the longest time. She is a married woman in love with another man and is quite unabashed about it. She openly expresses her feelings of sexual attraction for Krishna and is not afraid of the repercussions. There might be a subtle hint here at the rapture of 'forbidden' love—more so because popular lore has it that Radha was in fact Krishna's *maami* (maternal aunt)—so this narrative is not only about an extramarital affair but also a suggestion of incest. Then, there's the reciprocal, exciting and erotic nature of the relationship between Radha and Krishna, as contrasted with her dull marriage, which has no romantic connotations. Radha remains an alluring character for developing screenplay because of her unrequited love as well as her transgression of societal norms.

If the Mahabharata and the Ramayana are seen as the progenitors of the essential narrative form and ideological foundation of Indian cinema delineating its formal circularity and ethical compulsion of dharma and societal order (Mishra 1985), then it is my contention that Radha's relationship with Krishna offers the central narrative framework for romantic love in Indian cinematic discourse. The tragic love story of a devoted Radha and a playful Krishna caught in a triangle of desire and unfulfilment makes for potent and melodramatic film plots. This 'unfulfilment' is characterized by the stance of 'waiting', a recurrent theme in Hindi cinema, and especially in the romances of the 1960s, where the heroine was portrayed in the mould of Radha, patient, forlorn and faithful, waiting for her love to come back to her. Many songs referring to Radha's love equate the heroine's feelings with hers. Several popular lyrics that deal with a woman wistfully lingering cast the heroine, at least momentarily, in the role of Radha, waiting for or abandoned by Krishna.

The story of Radha and Krishna satisfies the need for romance in the Bollywood format, which was deemed to be essential to a film's commercial survival in postcolonial India, where cinema was not patronized by the state (Gopal: 15). Their legend constitutes the perfect text offering the challenges, impediments and the dramatic conflict that was necessary for the 'heterosexual couple formation' in film. Unlike in Hollywood films, in classic Hindi cinema, the romantic couple's declaration of the 'right to be' independent, self-determined individuals in itself triggered a narrative drama (Gopal: 2). Given the intersection between family, marriage, reproduction and population composition, one may surmise that individual emotions and couple formation were contingent upon the larger concerns of the family, community and the nation state (Gopal: 15, 17). Furthermore, owing to its socio-religio-cultural sanction, the legend of Radha–Krishna offers a legitimate framework within which to locate Bollywood's filmic romantic duo.

Radha's story is remembered and recalled in film after film. The ubiquity of this key mythological tale has ensured its familiarity among the audience that derives cinematic pleasure not from an accurate re-enactment of the original tale but through its variation, eagerly anticipating how the story will be reimagined and retold.

Radha's character in Hindi cinema is mostly implied, and the heroine's love is compared with Radha's devotion to her dark Lord. Many films show the couple near the river, the ocean, at a hill or in a forest. According to Heidi Pauwels, such landscapes are the 'later-day equivalent of the woods of Braj and Yamuna's banks', and the Raas Leela using several energetic dancers is a way of suggesting 'Krishna multiplicating and dancing with gopis' (Pauwels 2014: 190). The personae are introduced often through a song. While the Hindi film song has frequently been derided as an unrealistic, hyperbolic, extra-diegetic intrusion in film, it permits 'popular Hindi cinema to capture the particular stakes of couple-formation in India', says Gopal in her extended analysis of 'transgressive conjugality' which demonstrates how 'the song sequences allow us to sensually experience the stakes of such coupling' (Gopal: 25–26). Rather than replaying any one version of the Radha–Krishna story, filmic iterations invoke the pain of Radha's unrequited love to convey the transcendent beauty of an infinite romance which scores over the predictability of a domesticated marriage.

'The greatest showman of Indian cinema'—Raj Kapoor—has made some of the most well-known adaptations of the Radha–Krishna legend. His 1964 magnum opus *Sangam* has Radha's character caught between two lovers, a predicament resolved through death. The well-to-do Radha (Vyjayanthimala) and Gopal (Krishna's namesake, played by Rajendra Kumar) love each other but a working-class Sunder (Raj Kapoor) pines for Radha. The famous song 'Bol Radha Bol, Sangam Hoga Ki Nahi', where we see Sunder, imagining himself as the mythic Krishna, stealing Radha's clothes by the riverside (the key motif of many a Radha–Krishna song), and having her agree to 'unite' with him, becomes a premonition of things to come. On Gopal's advice, Radha marries Sunder, now a soldier in the Indian army, sacrificing her romance at the altar of the nation (Gopal: 17). In the process she exchanges innate love for mundane domesticity. There is further drama in the film. Confronted by a narcissistic, fatalistic and jealous Sunder, Gopal takes his own life to protect Radha's honour. But more importantly, given the film industry's intersection with the nation-building project, Gopal's sacrifice needs to be read as his commitment to ensure the married couple's continued service to the nation. The demands of the nation supersede. In this sense, she is akin to the mythological Radha whose personal desire for Krishna will forever be sacrificed. The mythical Radha, an ordinary milkmaid, is already married and will never be able to marry Krishna the prince without upsetting the social order.

And if at all there is the possibility of the two lovers coming together, it will only happen once the patriarchy is able to overcome the odds stacked against it. In Raj Kapoor's 1978 film *Satyam Shivam Sundaram*, Rajeev (Shashi Kapoor) falls in love with the village belle Roopa (Zeenat Aman), who, unbeknownst to him, has a facial scar that she keeps concealed behind her veil. Horrified at seeing her scar for the first time on their wedding night, he thinks he has been tricked into marrying the wrong woman. Rajeev goes back to his veiled Roopa, little realizing that she is in fact his wife. Buried in his decision to finally offer social respectability to Roopa as his legally wedded wife is Rajeev's defeat at being seduced by Roopa. In a song sung earlier in the film 'Yashomati Maiya Se Bole Nandlal', he had playfully reproached the erotic beauty's kohl-lined eyes for ensnaring him down the path of lust. It will take the androgynous and vulnerable hero an incredible moral courage to 'confront the choices: truth versus falsehood, rural life versus city, love versus lust, innocence versus knowledge . . .' (Ahmed 1992: 301) before he accepts Roopa back into his life. Radha/Roopa therefore has to be shamed, humiliated and dragged through a natural disaster before Krishna would come to her rescue.

The same fate awaits Radha in Raj Kapoor's 1985 end-of-the-career film *Ram Teri Ganga Maili*. Radha (Divya Rana) is promised to Narendra (Rajeev Kapoor) who falls in love with Ganga (Mandakini), who in turn overcomes familial, communal and social disgrace and physical obstacles to take Narendra away. In the song, 'Ek Radha, Ek Meera', Ganga publicly seals Radha's destiny by identifying herself as Krishna's other lover Meera, the famous mystic poet who had abandoned her marriage in search of Krishna, whom she believes is her true husband. In a series of interlocking episodes Ganga deflects the mythical Radha by instituting herself as Meera. In a film such as this, the characters are given names that resonate with traditional meaning and hence the drama of conflict becomes even more terse.

In *Mughal-e-Azam* (1960, directed by K. Asif) it is class and societal censure, and not a triangulated relationship, that comes in the way of the two lovers. Prince Salim (Dilip Kumar) falls in love with the court dancer Nadira/Anarkali (Madhubala). During the palace's Janmashtami celebrations, under the gaze of the Muslim king Akbar (Prithviraj Kapoor), his Hindu queen Jodha Bai (Durga Khote) and a full royal court, Anarkali openly insinuates her love to the prince, using the Radha–Krishna song 'Mohe Panghat Pe Nandlal'. Her dance brims over with innuendoes but remains completely unnoticed by the king who is mesmerized by Anarkali's rendition of the lyric. However, the young couple's love, articulated under the guise of the socially sanctioned Radha–Krishna song, is thwarted by the demands of the state that supersede individual emotions. Akbar will never allow his son's desire for conjugality with a slave girl, Anarkali, and sentences her to death.

In Sanjay Leela Bhansali's epic 2015 historical romance *Bajirao Mastani*, romantic and sexual indiscretion comes at the price of social disgrace and death. Feeling humiliated at losing her husband to Mastani (Deepika Padukone), Bajirao's (Ranbir Singh) wife Kashibai (Priyanka Chopra) compares her fate to that of Krishna's wife, Rukmini. Bajirao brings Mastani home as his second wife but cannot escape the pressure of his family and kinship groups. As he goes to battle, his own mother, Radhabai, imprisons Mastani. Towards the end of the film, as an injured Bajirao lay on his deathbed, despite Kashibai's pleas, Radhabai refuses to release Mastani, at the cost of letting her son succumb to his wounds. In many ways, Radhabai's character is reminiscent of Radha in Mehboob Khan's 1957 blockbuster drama *Mother India*. The two men that Radha (Nargis) is linked to are named after Krishna: her husband, Shamu, who abandons her after losing his arms in an accident, and her flirtatious and rebellious son Birju, who teases village girls, stealing their clothes, and whom she kills to maintain social order. She is both Radha and the wilful Kunti. In Bhansali's film, therefore, the audience recognizes the mother's violent decision as déjà vu, bearing in mind the changed set of circumstances under which she acts. Both films bring together two of the central mythological narratives structured around the Mahabharata and Radha.

Radha's portrayal in some of the post-2000s Hindi films has undergone a significant shift. *Dev.D*, Anurag Kashyap's 2009 remake of *Devdas*, for example, is a powerful illustration of this change. As the most frequently adapted literary piece, *Devdas* constitutes another of Indian cinema's enduring myths that resonates with the Radha–Krishna's love. Devdas's story reiterates the 'underlying model of the impossible triangle' (Creekmur: 181) where the lovers' union is thwarted by a competing set of forces located outside of the couple's control. In this popular legend of unrequited love, the upper-class parents of Devdas (played by a number of actors but most famously by Dilip Kumar in 1955 and Shahrukh Khan in 2002) prevent his marriage to his childhood sweetheart, Paro (Suchitra Sen, 1955, and Aishwarya Rai, 2002), who, in their eyes, is socially unequal to their family's prestige. Feeling snubbed by this rejection, Paro's parents retaliate by immediately marrying their daughter off to a rich widower, leaving a distraught Devdas to seek comfort with the demimonde Chandramukhi (Vyjayanthimala, 1955, and Madhuri Dixit, 2002) and drown his misery in alcohol, eventually seeking death at Paro's doorstep. Kashyap's 2009 adaptation has the hero (Abhay Deol) pull himself together and take his chances with the prostitute Chandramukhi (Kalki Koechlin) instead of taking to the bottle and pining for Paro (Mahi Gill). This adaptation that signals a departure from its earlier iterations embodies a powerful intersection between the new and old order in post-1990s neo-liberal India, which has triggered a new cultural movement by boldly challenging traditional mores (Kurian 2017: 21).

Karan Johar's 2012 film *Student of the Year* is the furthest removed from the original Radha–Krishna legend. The love triangle between Shayana (Alia Bhatt), Abhi (Siddhartha Malhotra) and Rohan (Varun Dhawan) is resolved with the two men settling their professional and romantic differences with each other and becoming friends, comfortable as they are with the ambiguity and agency that comes with modernity.[1] Embodying Indian millennials' socio-economic and cultural mores, the film is part of New Bollywood that began where classic Hindi cinema left off. If the central narrative drama in classic cinema was structured around the challenges of the couple coming together due to competing forces—family, community, state—then New Bollywood cinema sees the appearance of a 'post-nuptial couple-form . . . as private, nuclear, [that is] typically located in urban space with weak links to family and community' (Gopal: 2, 24). If in 'Radha Kaise Na Jale' (*Lagaan*, directed by Ashutosh Gowarikar, 2001) an indignant Gauri (Gracey Singh) gets upset at her fiancé, Bhuvan (Amir Khan, sporting Krishna's signature flute and peacock feather) for dallying with the white Englishwoman Elizabeth (Rachel Shelly), Johar's *Student of the Year*'s Shayana has a radically different reaction to her boyfriend, Rohan. In the song 'Radha on the Dance Floor' she first discards her billowing veil (worn Ganga-style by *Ram Teri Ganga Maili*'s Mandakini in the song 'Ek Radha, Ek Meera') before launching into an energetic dance. She then proceeds to ridicule Rohan's flirtatious behaviour and hypocrisy in blaming her for his failures and, in a role reversal, proceeds to make romantic overtures to Abhi instead. This open declaration of her sexual power represents New Bollywood's discomfort with the traditional 'Radha–Krishna' motif in Hindi cinema. It also promotes the shifting terrain in modern India with young Indian women refusing patriarchal demands and living life on their own terms.

The Radha–Krishna duo is no longer culturally relevant for couple-formation in New Bollywood. A sexualized Shayana derides patriarchal privilege, asserts the need for unconditional freedom and demands social acceptance. The articulation of this new form of sexual politics represents, as I have theorized elsewhere (2017, 2018), fourth-wave feminism in India.

In the film *Tevar* the triangulated relationship between the central character Ghanshyam (Krishna's namesake, played by Arjun Kapoor) and villain Gajendar Singh (Manoj Bajpai) is resolved by the hero and heroine's (Sonakshi Sinha) union. It is interesting to note that here it is the mafia and not tradition or culture that prevent the couple from coming together, making Radha's character all the more superfluous.

Radha, therefore, has come full circle: from providing the essential melodramatic context for the challenges of the couple formation in classic Hindi cinema to becoming irrelevant in New Bollywood, which does not need the Radha framework any more since the couple's right to come together is no longer threatened by external competing forces. In addition, Radha becoming an item number as a profit-generating strategy, as in some films, is of no cultural resonance. Given this, has Radha's time passed? Will she disappear from Bollywood cinema? Or will scriptwriters find new ways of intersecting Indian modernity with the myth of Radha?

number as a profit-generating strategy, as in some films, is of no

21

SITA AND RADHA: FROM HUMAN TO DIVINE

MANDAKRANTA BOSE

SITA AND RADHA were born mortals but were later elevated
into the list of goddesses. Both are seen as incarnations of Lakshmi,
while their partners, Sita's husband, Rama, and Radha's divine
lover, Krishna, are regarded as avatars or incarnations of Vishnu, as
emphasized in epic and Puranic texts. Given the background of both
Sita and Radha as women whose lives revolved exclusively around
their male partners, they are understandably held up as role models
for Indian women. For most devout Hindus Sita remains the epitome
of Indian womanhood as a totally voiceless, selfless, submissive and
devoted wife. This may not entirely agree with the original version
of her legend, as her portrayal by *adikavi* (First Poet) Valmiki in his
Ramayana shows, but that is the image in which she is revered by the
vast majority of Hindus and the reason for her apotheosis. In light
of the ideological pressures of a patriarchal society the adoration of
Sita is not hard to understand. On the contrary, Radha's deification
is most puzzling, as her conduct as a married woman taking a lover
violates every norm of the social order. However, in the bhakti mode
of defining the relationship between the deity and humankind,
the highest human joy—and duty—is to give oneself to one's god,

176

social obligations notwithstanding. That is, of course, what Radha does, transgressing against marital and family duties in the face of social censure. She is thus transformed from an erring wife into a role model of devotion and submission. These models call for a closer look because of their abiding influence on women's lives from medieval to modern times.

SITA

Sita is perhaps the most popular heroine of Hindu mythology. As Rama's ever-devoted wife she sets the pattern for wifely behaviour by remaining uncomplainingly loyal to her husband despite suffering injustice at his hand. In fact, in the original story by Valmiki she is not quite so meek, as several recent studies have demonstrated,[1] but it is by meek dependency that later tellers of the Ramayana came to define her, excising her self-asserting dignity from her legend. It is useful to note that the name Sita predates the character in the Ramayana. A goddess of that name appears in Vedic literature as a fertility figure, which is consistent with the meaning of the term *sita*, or furrow.[2] She is also attached to various gods during this early period. But Sita as a fully developed character blossoms in the epic Ramayana and forever remains the faithful and devoted wife of Rama. Although in the Valmiki Ramayana she is recognized as an incarnation of Lakhsmi,[3] the emphasis is on her human identity, not a goddess on earth. Her deification was a late development that occurred through regional versions of the Ramayana. Interestingly, though Sita was turned into a devi, her countless devotees do not think of her as an embodiment of power,[4] but rather as a submissive and docile wife.[5] In today's India, especially in northern India, Tulsidas's *Ramcharitmanas* has become the most influential Rama story, and public perception of the narrative and its characters is now dominated by the TV version produced by Ramanand Sagar in 1987 following Tulsidas, further reinforcing the submissive role of Sita.[6] In this north Indian version, Sita blames her fate on herself, saying that she must have done something wrong in either this or her previous life which brings her suffering. She never blames Rama but herself. In this version, Sita has a secondary role as a devotee who acts as an intermediary between Rama the god and his followers. In this role, although she is a goddess, she does not hold as high a position as Rama does and remains in a subordinate position in relation to God Rama.

It is worth pointing out that contrary to popular belief, Sita is a woman of great strength in the original source. It is possible to view her tragedy as a series of sacrifices she makes for the common good. It is her own decision to accompany Rama into exile in the forest (Valmiki Ramayana, ii.26) right at the beginning of the story. The decision to go through the fire-ordeal Rama requires after her rescue as proof of her chastity is again her own, voicing an impassioned protest at her humiliation (Valmiki Ramayana, vi.117–119). Finally, at the end of the story, after her final banishment, as it is told in the Valmiki Ramayana, it is she who decides to end her life by turning away from Rama to seek sanctuary with her mother, Goddess Earth. Throughout her life Sita never accepts injustice without protest, even registering her scorn for what she calls Rama's *praakrit* (ignoble) conduct in doubting her chastity and advising her to attach herself to another male.[7] Against this original representation of Sita as a powerful personality, she has come to comfort the hearts of devout Hindus as the voiceless and submissive wife and the epitome of Indian womanhood and remains so.[8] This ideal was constructed by post-Valmiki authors, whose manipulation of the story advances a particular view of women's place in society. Such is the potency of that ideal that it has traditionally succeeded in securing women's willing consent to subjugation.

RADHA

In contrast to Sita, Radha is a surprising nominee for apotheosis. She has not the faintest claim to divinity at the beginning of her legend, for she is no more than a human heroine in an adulterous relationship (she is *parakiya*, married to another man) with a man half her age, who is socially related to her. Her deification despite this otherwise censurable situation paradoxically elevates her to divinity because the object of her love is the god Krishna. This transmutes her offence into the highest virtue, that of desiring union with the Godhead. Interpreted not socially but metaphysically, her yearning for Krishna makes her a symbol of humanity's total, unconditional and selfless surrender to the ultimate Godhead.

The Radha–Krishna love story began as a human romance but in the Puranic era that story developed into an allegory of the human–divine relationship. The *Vayu*, *Matsya* and *Varaha Puranas* mention Radha but it is in the *Devi Bhagavata*, *Brahma Vaivarta* and *Padma Purana* that she is described at length. These texts reveal Radha as the complement to Krishna and therefore a divine being. Early legends accord her little importance beyond counting her merely as one of the *gopi*s, or cow-girls, but the later Puranas, such as the *Brahma Vaivarta Purana*, acknowledge her as an aspect of Devi, more specifically as Krishna's shakti. Her elevation is complete when at one point she is identified with Lakshmi.

Radha's deification has been problematic for some devotees who find it difficult to come to terms with an unsanctioned relationship. The Vallabha sampradaya, for instance, portrays her as Krishna's wife in order to justify their relationship. Vaishnavas, on their part, think of Krishna as the only male in the cosmos because he is the Creator. As a result of this belief, Vaishnavas, both male and female, see themselves as Radha in relation to Krishna. An example of this transforming devotion was Shri Chaitanyadeva, the 15th-century spiritual leader of the Vaishnavas, who aspired to union with Krishna as Radha. Today, most devotees accept Radha and Krishna as transcendental lovers and not as a married couple.[9] On the social plane Vaishnavas understand Radha's love as the ultimate type of selfless attachment because she sacrifices her reputation by rejecting social norms. On the metaphysical register, Vaishnavas, particularly those of the Bengali tradition, take her love as a potent metaphor of the human yearning for the divine.

Because Radha's love is at once intense and illicit, it has been a magnet for poets and artists. Her pining for Krishna appears in early writings by Hala (early Common Era), Bhatta Narayana (prior to 8th century AD), Vakpati (7th–8th century), Anandavardhana (mid 9th century), Abhinavagupta (10th century), Rajashekhara (9th–10th century), Kshemendra (11th century) and Hemachandra (11th–12th century).[10] But perhaps the most brilliant celebration of the Radha–Krishna theme appears in the 12th-century poet Jayadeva's *Gita Govinda*. This long poem in several parts portrays the culmination of their love in the romantic idiom of love poetry but views it allegorically as the human soul's spiritual union with the ultimate being. Jayadeva identifies her with Shri (i.2; i.23) and Lakshmi (xi.22), and Krishna as an incarnation of Vishnu. Jayadeva's Radha is tormented by *viraha*, or love-in-separation. Her world-forsaking urge to be with him compels her to follow him as an *abhisarika* (a woman who goes to meet her lover, ignoring social censure), travelling along hazardous forest paths at night, oblivious to reproaches by her husband's family. Vidyapati and Chandidas (both from around the 14th to 15th centuries) commemorate Radha's illicit love as the apex of romantic passion, exalting her unflinching resolve to stand up against the entire world. That despite this revolutionary character of her love Radha is passionately adored suggests the feminization of spirituality, which centralizes the female as the locus of mystic energy. This might seem like another strand in the spread of goddess worship under tantrism, except that here the perception of female divinity occurs not through occultism but by idealizing the man–woman relationship as allegorical truth.

How may one compare Radha with Sita? How could two such different women be adored as goddesses? Most of those who know the Ramayana regard Sita as the perfect example of the uncomplaining wife whose sole purpose in life is to follow her husband's every wish and to put his interests above her own. Clearly, Sita places her allegiance to duty above personal interest.[11] Undoubtedly, her love for Rama is a deep, emotional feeling but that is not an issue in the foreground of her fame. Her society and ours regard her love as her duty, and approve the fact that in fulfilling that duty she plays the role of wife exactly as expected by society. She is praised for her sustained *tyaga*, that is, renunciation of personal benefit and comfort for duty's sake.

A degree of irony enters into our comparison when we talk about renunciation: Radha too is a renunciate, but in quite the opposite sense. While Sita renounces her personal interests in favour of social and familial duties, it is precisely those duties that Radha renounces in pursuit of her personal choice. Radha throws aside exactly the bonds that Sita accepts and receives no blame for what would be an unthinkable transgression in any other woman, including Sita. Sita bows to a life of suffering entirely because she puts public good above the private. Yet, both are equally selfless, equally ready to sacrifice all in the service of a higher goal, except that Sita's goal is determined by social expectations and Radha's by their rejection.

Sita and Radha are very different characters and follow very different paths in forging links with their divine partners. But to their devotees they tower above common mortals by virtue of the force of their resolve, which demands the adoration due to the goddess persona characterized in Hindu thought by an inalienable ownership of primal energy. Under that condition, the deification of neither human heroine should be surprising. What is undoubtedly surprising is that both Sita and Radha are worshipped with their male consorts and never alone, no matter that they are goddesses. There is no temple that I know of dedicated to either of them where they are worshipped in their own right. Female dependency holds as true for goddesses as for ordinary women.

22

SONGS OF RADHA

i. VIDYA

'If early dates for Vidya are correct—around the seventh century—then this would be one of the first moments Radha steps from shadowy origins into poetry,' says Andrew Schelling.

And What of Those Arbors[*]

And what of those
arbors of vines
that grow where the river
drops away from Kalinda Mountain?
They conspired in the love
games of herding girls
and watched over the veiled
affairs of Radha.
Now that the days
are gone when I cut their
tendrils, and laid them
down for couches of love,

---

[*] *Bright as an Autumn Moon: Fifty Poems from the Sanskrit*, translated from the Sanskrit by Andrew Schelling, *Manoa*, General Editor, Frank Stewart.

I wonder if they've
grown brittle and if
their splendid blue flowers
have dried up.

ii. ANDAL

Mid-8th-century mystic Andal was the only woman among the twelve *alvar*s of south India. During her brief life of sixteen years she composed passionate songs to Narayana/Krishna: 'Thiruppavai' (The Path to Krishna) and 'Nacciyar Thirumoli' (The Sacred Songs of the Lady). Andal is regarded as an emanation of goddess Bhu Devi.

Nacciyar Thirumoli*

(Kannan, My Lord, My Love [*Kannan Ennum*, verse 8])

Anguish floods my body and will sweep
it away unlike the land he rescued by yanking

the mountain from earth's bosom to hold
as umbrella over devotees. Yet for me, no glance.

If I see that thief who's savaged me I'll savage
my breasts. Uproot their round mounds from

my body's earth, uproot my love to throw at him.
If he won't caress me, what use is this howling tenderness?

---

* Translated from the Tamil by Priya Sarukkai Chabria. Credit: *The Autobiography of a Goddess*, Zubaan, New Delhi, 2015, University of Chicago Press, 2016.

iii. IN PRAISE OF KRISHNA: TRANSLATION OF *GITA GOVINDA* OF JAYADEVA

The *Gita Govinda*, composed by Jayadeva in the 12th century in Odisha, is an evocative description of the love of Krishna and Radha set against the pastoral background of Vrindavana and the play of seasons. This lyrical poem is organized as twelve *sargas*, or cantos, and offers twenty-four songs rendered in various ragas. The poetic form is the *ashtapadi*, or couplets grouped into eights.

Canto 1*

Delightful Krishna

'The sky is dark with clouds
Tamala trees darken the forest
The night frightens him!
Radha you take him home!'
They leave at Nanda's order
passing through the trees in the forest
and the love-play of Radha and Krishna
triumphs on the bank of the river Yamuna.

Jayadeva, whose heart is adorned
by the grace of Saraswati, Goddess of Learning
and who is deeply devoted to Lakshmi,
Goddess of Prosperity,
Composed this long poem
of the passionate love-play of Sri Krishna.

If your mind is delighted
by contemplation of Hari's glories

---

* *In Praise of Krishna: Translation of Gita Govinda of Jayadeva*,
  edited and translated from the Sanskrit by Durgadas Mukhopadhyay,
  BR Publishing Corporation, 1990.

if you enquire into the art of love
listen then, to this series
of sweet, tender and lyrical
verses by Jayadeva.

Umapatidhara makes his words blossom.
Sarana is renowned for his subtle flowing sounds,
Acharya Govardhana is indeed peerless
in the dexterous handling of erotic emotions.
Dhyoi the sovereign poet
holds his listeners spellbound with his cadences.
But Jayadeva alone excels
in the art of pure and perfect composition.

Canto II

Careless Krishna

Hari was making love to any maiden
without distinction, in the woodland.
Radha's pride was shattered.
Thinking herself to be humiliated
she, with broken pride and jealousy
hides in her bower
with its swarm of humming bees.
She sat depressed
and told her friend the secret.

Song 5
(To the Raga Gurjari and Tala Yati)

The nectar of his lips
flows through the notes
of his melodious flute.
When glancing sideways
his crown sways

and his earrings dangle
on his cheeks.
My heart recalls Hari
here in his love dance
playing seductively, laughing, mocking me.

The curls of his forehead are encircled
by a coronet of peacock plumes,
each of half-moon eyes.
The gems of his dress
make his cloud-dark body glitter
with the colours of the rainbow.

He is eager to kiss
the *gopi*s of shapely hips.
His lips are red;
he smiles enchantingly
like blooming bandhujiva flowers.

His tendril-tender arms still thrill
with the embrace of a thousand gopis
The ornaments on his arms, ankles and breast
glisten, removing the surrounding darkness.

The sandal spot on his forehead
is a moon in a mass of rain-clouds.
His heart is a door
that is firm and cruel
in crushing the swelling breasts.

His dolphin-shaped jewelled earrings
adorn his beautiful cheeks.
The sages, men, the gods, and the demons
show allegiance to Hari,
majestic in yellow garments.

He, who allays the fear of sin
Of the aeon of *kali*,
made love to me
beneath the blooming *kadamba* tree
pleasing me in earnest
with quivering looks
as of bodiless Love embodied.

Sri Jayadeva sings
of the exquisite, charming beauty
of the slayer of the demon Madhu.
Surely this shall induce recollections
of the feet of Hari
in the mind of the blessed devotee.

Sakhi, Krishna is sporting
With other gopis now, deserting me.
Yet I desire him.
I forgive his guilt.
I feel no anger, not even accidentally.
Instead, I contemplate on his majestic grace.
Seeing only the good in him
I am blissful thinking of him.
My mind seems not under my control.
Tell me, sakhi, what can I do?

Song 6
(To the Raga Malava and Tala Ektali)

When in the night
I reach the lonely forest,
he hides himself.
Seeing me looking around
anxiously wandering
he laughs heartily
in a mood of passion.

Sakhi, bring him here to sport with me,
the magnanimous destroyer of Keshi,
that my longing for enjoyment
may increase his desire.

When I hesitate in my first
tryst of love
he skilfully coaxes me
with flattering words
and shatters my coyness.
I smile at him tenderly
As he unfastens my garment.

When I lie on the bed
of tender sprouts,
he lies on my breast, for long.
When I embrace and kiss him,
he returns the embrace
and drinks the honey of my lips.

When in love-play
my eyes close languidly,
his cheeks glisten in rapture.
When I sweat and moisten
all over with love's exertion,
he is restless in his brimming desire.

When in love-play,
I murmur like a cuckoo
he proclaims victor
in the true tradition of the art of love.
My hair gets tumbled
its flowers fluttering to the ground;
my breasts bear his nail-marks.

His sport of love
finds fulfilment
when my jewel anklets
vibrate, sounding sweet
and my loosened girdle tinkles.
And so he kisses me
drawing me close to himself.

When I am filled
with the taste of ecstasy,
his lotus eyes open a little
and watching my vine-like body collapse
Madhu's foe delights in my love.

May this song
of the endless loves of Krishna,
told by anxious Radha,
and sung by Sri Jayadeva
bring bliss to the devotees.

When the gopis glance passionately
to arouse him,
he sees me and becomes pale.
His cheeks moisten with sweat
and his enchanting flute fallen
he blushes amorously.
I see him surrounded by the women of Vraja
and I feel the joy of desire.
Sakhi, even the sight of the clustering buds
of the *ashoka* tree distresses me.
Even the wind from the lakeside garden
brings anguish with it.
The opening buds of the mango tree
alive with the humming of hovering bees
even that brings no comfort to me.

May our glorious Krishna remove your sufferings.
He who was followed by the yearning smile
and wistful glances of the gopis
as they want to only raise their arms
pretending to tuck back a loose strand of hair
so as to reveal the lower curve of their breasts.
This Krishna was reminded of the magnanimity
of his beloved Radha and fell into sweet reverie
dwelling on her charms.

Canto III
Bewildered Krishna

Krishna, the enemy of Kamsa
placed Radha in his heart;
submitted willingly to be chained
by the longings of worldly attachment
and so abandoned
the beautiful moment of Vraja.

Pierced by the shafts
of the god of love
he searched for Radha
everywhere in vain, and so dejected,
sought out the woods
on the banks of Yamuna
and thus lamented:

Song 7
(To the Raga Gurjari and Tala Yati)

Radha saw me surrounded
by gopis and went away,
I, too, in fear of guilt,
embarrassed, did not stop her!
Alas, alas, she is gone in anger
feeling that she is neglected.

What will she do,
what will she say to me
for this long separation from me?
What need is there
of wealth, kin, home
and life itself, without her?

I brood on her face
wrathful, eyebrows crooked,
a crimson lotus clouded by the bees
hovering eagerly over it.

I am delighted always
by her ethereal union in my heart.
Then why this wandering in the forest
why mourn in vain and lament?

O my slender one,
envy and anger wastes your hearts.
But how can I conciliate you
when I don't know where you are gone!

I feel you moving
about me, in front of me.
Then why not embrace me ardently
as you used to?

Forgive me now,
never again will I offend thee,
O beautiful Radha, come before me!
I burn with the passion of love.

This lamentation of Hari
sung so humbly by Jayadeva
who arose from the ocean,
a moon, from the village of
Kendubilva, his birthplace.

Lotus stalks garland my heart
not a necklace of serpents!
Blue lily-petals around my neck
Is not the streak of poison!
This sandal paste on my body
is not the crematory ash.
Mistake me not for Shiva
O love god, assail not me,
Pounce not on me in rage.

O love god,
Why make the mango sprout your bow?
There is no need to string it.
You vanquish the whole world in play.
What valour is there then
in wounding someone almost dead.
My heart waits to revive
from the pains of those other arrows of love,
the fluttering passionate glances of doe-eyed Radha.

Radha's tendril, arched eyebrows are the bow;
her sidelong glances are the arrows;
her long eyes stretching upwards to her ear
the bowstring.
The god of love it seems,
after conquering the world,
returned his arsenal to Radha.

O my slender one,
it is but natural
that the glancing arrows
released from your eyebrow-bow
cause pain in me.
Your wavy black tresses
are ready to slash me.
Your luscious crimson lips
like ripe *bimba* fruit

may spread a strange delirium in me;
this is natural.
But why does your breast, so perfect and chaste
ravage my life in play?

May those bewitching glances
of Krishna ensure your prosperity;
the earrings dangling on his cheeks,
the sweet notes of his flute
that makes the gopis absent-minded,
as he stealthily looks
at the moon face of Radha.

iv. *GITA GOVINDA*: LOVE SONGS OF RADHA AND KRISHNA, BY JAYADEVA*

Canto 4, Song 9

Krishna, without you Radha,
    Diminished to so frail a state,
    Finds her necklace weight too great.

Krishna, without you Radha,
    Feels poisoned by the sandal balm,
    The soothing unguent meant to calm.

Krishna, without you Radha,
    Is scorched by love, a flame that burns
    As, with every sighing breath, she yearns.

Krishna, without you Radha,
    With lotus eyes, is looking all around for you,
    Eyes like flowers plucked, streaming tears of dew.

---

* Translated from the Sanskrit by Lee Siegel: *Gita Govinda: Love Songs of Radha and Krishna, by Jayadeva* (Clay Sanskrit Library and New York University Press: New York, 2009).

Krishna, without you Radha,
    Rests cheek in hand, cradled there tight,
    A new moon steady in the dark of night.

Krishna, without you Radha,
    Imagines her bed of leaves a pyre—
    What should be cool is on fire.

Krishna, without you Radha,
    Anxiously chants, 'Oh my God, oh God above,'
    As if eager to die for the sake of your love.

Krishna, without you Radha,
    May Jaya-deva's song make joy complete
    For those bowed down at Krishna's feet.

~

'She bristles, moans, groans, laments, and gasps,
    blinks, sinks, rises, falls, and finally faints.
Should you not, like a heavenly healer, cure this lovely girl
    of passion's flagrant fever with the potion of your love?
    There is no other helping hand.'

'You are most dear to the doctors divine,
    And yet you do not heal Radha's afflictions;
She, so sick with love, can only be cured by the balm of your touch.
    You are more cruel than a thunderbolt, Indra's brother!'

'It's surprising how long she's suffered love's ardent fevers,
    her heart aching with reveries of sandal, the moon, and lotuses;
Although she's weary, she imagines that you, so dear to her,
    your body cool,
    are alone and waiting in hiding for her.
Only thus has she, though so weak, been able to survive
    from moment to moment.

v. VIDYAPATI

Vidyapati Thakur (1352–1448), known for his erudite Sanskrit works, was also the first writer to use Maithili as a literary language. His poems on the love of Radha and Krishna show delicate sentiments and emotions, specially exploring the female imagination.

Signs of Youth[*]

Radha's glances dart from side to side.
Her restless body and clothes are heavy with dust.
Her glistening smile shines again and again.
Shy, she raises her skirt to her lips.
Startled, she stirs and once again is calm,
As now she enters the ways of love.
Sometimes she gazes at her blossoming breasts
Hiding them quickly, then forgetting they are there.
Childhood and girlhood melt in one
And new and old are both forgotten.

Says Vidyapati: O Lord of life,
Do you not know the signs of youth?

First Joy

Away with childish thoughts.
Come to the bed.
Give up your shyness.
Lift your face.
Why waste time
Scratching lines on the earth.

---

[*] Translated from the Maithili by Deben Bhattacharya: *Love Songs of Vidyapati*, ed. W.G. Archer (Grove Press, 1970; 1st Indian edition, Motilal Banarsidass, 1987).

O beautiful Radha,
Stay with your lover.
Brush aside your fear.
For the first time
Join with him in love.

Your first joy
May soon become
Love's own great play
Of the lotus and the bee . . .

vi. NARSINH MEHTA

Narsinh Mehta (1414–81) is revered as the *adikavi* (First Poet) of
Gujarat. An ardent devotee of Radha and Krishna, Shiva and other
deities, he sought out traditional tales from saints and travellers and
composed numerous bhajans. 'Vaishnava Jana To Tene Re Kahiye'
was Mahatma Gandhi's favourite bhajan.

Artless Milkmaid*

Goes the guileless milkmaid
to retail the Lord
the beloved of sixteen thousand maids
filled in a pot.

Sells the Ahir girl
the Saviour of the lost
shouts as she walks the lanes
'Buy the Lord, O buy some Lord!'

Down she puts the pot
and inside a flute plays

_____

* Translated from the Gujarati by Pradip Khandwalla: *Beyond the Beaten Track: Offbeat Poems from Gujarat* (Gujarat Sahitya Parishad, 2008).

the maid of Vraja swoons
when the face inside she sees.

Watch the wondrous sight
Brahma, Indra and other gods
behold in the milk pot
the Master of fourteen worlds.

Such was her fortune
for her manifested the Lord;
how the divine Liege of Narsinh
pampers His serving folk!

vii. CHANDIDAS

Chandidas (born 1408 AD) is the sobriquet of a prominent
Bengali poet, or it possibly belongs to four poets bearing the
same name in this period. Over a thousand poems, several on
Radha and Krishna, allude to the parallels between human and
divine love and endorse relationships that cross hierarchical
boundaries. Chandidas's poetry forms the core of the
Vaishnava–Sahajiya movement.

O LOVE, what more shall I, shall Radha speak,
    Since mortal words are weak?
        In life, in death,
    In being and in breath
No other lord but thee can Radha seek.

About thy feet the mighty net is wound
    Wherein my soul they bound;
        Myself resigned
    To servitude my mind;
My heart than thine no sweeter slavery found.

I, Radha, thought; through the three worlds my gaze

I sent in wild amaze;
    I was alone.
None called me 'Radha!', none;
I saw no hand to clasp, no friendly face.

I sought my father's house; my father's sight
    Was empty of delight;
        No tender friend
    Her loving voice would lend;
My cry came back unanswered from the night.*

viii. SURDAS

Surdas (said to be born between 1478 and 1483, and died between 1561 and 1584) was famously a blind devotional poet and singer. Most of his work is in Braj Bhasha. Coming under the influence of Vallabha Acharya, Surdas became one of the renowned Aṣṭachāp *kavi*s of the Vallabha sampradaya. The work *Sursagar*, a magnificent collection of poems, is attributed to him. Speaking of Radha and Krishna's tender affections, Surdas excels in bringing attention to the minutiae of romantic experience.

Radha is lost to the onslaught of love.
She weeps from tree to tree and finally succumbs,
    searching through the forests and groves.
Her braid—a peacock grasps it, thinking it a snake;
    her lotus feet attract the bees;
The honey of her voice makes the crow in the *kadamb* tree
    caw, caw to mimic its cuckoo;
Her hands—the tender leaves of blossom-bringing Spring:
    the parrot, when he sees, comes near to taste;
And the full moon in her face inspires the cakor bird
    to drink the water washing from her eyes.

---

* *Collected Works of Sri Aurobindo*, pp. 86–87, https://bit.ly/2Jgxruk.

Her despair, her desperation—the Joy of the Yadus sees it
    and appears at her side just in time;
Surdas's Lord takes that seedbud of new birth
    and cradles it, a newborn in his arms.*

ix. RUPA GOSWAMI

Rupa Goswami (1489–1564) was a devotional teacher of the Gaudiya
Vaishnava tradition, closely associated with spreading the message
of Shri Chaitanya Mahaprabhu. His repertoire of poetic writing sees
Radha as the path to understanding the grace and divinity of Krishna.

Pleased with any person who, abandoning all hope of material
happiness and overwhelmed with love, reads this sweet *Shri
Radhastaka* with a pure heart, the prince of Vraja of His own accord
places him among Shri Radha's personal associates.†

x. BIHARI

Bihari (1595–1663) is best known for writing the *Satsai* (Seven
Hundred Verses). The poems on Radha and Krishna are mostly
about amorous and playful acts of joy. The poetic virtuosity of the
intricate and visual language has caused the text to be rendered in
several art forms.

Hungry for Krishna's love, she hides his flute,
Haven't got it, says she, her brows arching to her smile,
She offers to return it, then gestures 'no',
Wanting Him in eternal Play.‡

---

*   Translated from the Braj Bhasha by John Stratton Hawley.
†   Translation (from the Sanskrit) used by ISKCON; contributed by Shubha
    Vilas.
‡   Translated from the Hindi by Malashri Lal.

xi. SUBRAHMANYA BHARATHIYAR

Bharathiyar (1882–1921) was a popular writer, poet and journalist who is considered a pioneer of modern Tamil poetry. A social reformer and a fiery speaker, Bharathiyar believed in principles of equity and justice that looked beyond class and caste divisions. His works include songs that kindled patriotism during the national movement in India. His literary interests ranged widely and covered political, social and spiritual themes.

On the island of love O! Radhe Radhe
O! pearl of women I happened to see O! Radhe Radhe
In the garden of love O! Radhe Radhe
Are you a diamond or flowering tree O! Radhe Radhe
O! great queen! O! golden woman O! Radhe Radhe
O! life-breath of heavenly love O! Radhe, Radhe[*]

xii. RABINDRANATH TAGORE,
BHANUSINGHER PADAVALI

Rabindranath Tagore (1861–1941) started publishing the Padavali poems under the pseudonym Bhanusingh at the age of sixteen. Written in imitation of Vaishnava lyrics, he built up a literary hoax about a lost manuscript in the obscure language Brajabuli. The poems gathered praise and, at some point, the subterfuge was discovered, to everyone's amusement. The songs, however, remained popular for the Radha–Krishna lore and the musicality of the verses.

Vasant Aaval Re (Spring is Here)[†]

Spring is here!
Humming black bees
woods covered with

---

[*]   Translated from the Tamil by H.S. Shiva Prakash.
[†]   Translated from the Bengali by Lalit Kumar.

flower-laden mango trees.
Listen to me, friend,
my joyous heart goes restless . . .
Decked with the beauty of spring
mocks the universe
'O lovelorn Radha, where is your beloved, Madhav?'

xiii. KAZI NAZRUL ISLAM

Kazi Nazrul Islam (1899–1976), who became the national poet
of Bangladesh, was a writer, musician and revolutionary. Prolific
in his creative output, Nazrul wrote fiction and essays but is best
remembered for his poetry and songs. Brought up in a composite
culture, he created the first Bengali-language ghazals and inscribed
several songs to Radha.

Shyam! If only you were Radha
Like me, you would have chanted, day and night, the name of Shyam
The burning anguish left by Krishna's scandals
Would then appear as *malati* garlands
And yearning for Krishna's love would
Make you pray, life after life, for a return to Brajdham
How devoid of compassion is the music of your flute
How cruel is your failure to understand the women of Braj!
Like the tears you have reduced me to
Could I but make you weep too!
Only then would you realize
The endless heartburn born of a guru's neglect.*

* Translated from the Bengali by Reba Som.

23

SRI RADHA

RAMAKANTA RATH

17

Let's be clear about this:
If all is an illusion
and you construct every illusion,
why then do you rush into my arms,
try to pull away my clothes,
and join your lips to mine?

If you imagine every object is
a mere container of yourself,
and if every person is a fulfilment
of some desire of yours,
then go sleep on a waterless ocean
for as many epochs as you please.
An unending tempest rages here
and every fragment of being is blown away
in the gale of indiscreet love.

I forget myself
when our bodies touch.
I therefore manoeuvre my body
to touch yours as often as I can.
You do not comprehend
why I would forget myself or why
I seek to preserve you like a treasure
in the soul that exists beyond
all forgetting.

I would like to forget
all my futile years before I knew you
and the compulsory living after you have left.

25

It was a bad day yesterday.
My husband dragged me by the hair
and knocked my head against the wall
several times, and insisted
I came out with the true account
of where I spent the previous night.
It pained for some time,
but when he began an inspection
of my body, I could not
hold my laughter.

God, I said to myself,
what an imbecile I have
for a husband!
He is looking for proof
of my infidelity
in the body
and in the daytime too!

32

Who would believe
we neither touched
nor spoke to each other
throughout last night?
You ceased to be
what I knew you to be.
You, I found, had no body
and yet you were
my tireless companion
who always became
something he never was.
He was some time
my bonded slave
and, some other time,
my destroyer.

You are a dagger
of the colour of the blue water-lily
that tears me but when
I recover and look,
the one who is bleeding
is you, not me.
Before I can cry
because you are wounded,
you stand before me, smile,
and confound me.
When I close my eyes
so that I do not see you
you move about in my heart
that suddenly acquires eyes.

When I close my ears
so that I do not hear you,
You change into an aspiration that inflicts

perpetual restlessness.

I did not touch you
in the night, for I feared
I would become the air
and the water
that you were.
I feared my destiny
of seeking you
in life after life
would end, and I feared
my mind would never know
something of what you were.

The way to living is through dying.
I cannot do without
this losing through gaining,
or this gaining
through losing.

36

I knew there would be a day
when you would stop speaking,
stop smiling,
stop recognizing us,
stop finding your way about
towns and villages
you had lived in for years,
stop remembering
our fearless transgressions of history.

Those were the days
when, though we did not speak a word,
we chattered endlessly
with the world, with peacocks,

and with heaps of sand.
We opened the night's eyes
to hope
and to roads extinct long ago.

Those were the days
when, it seemed, the air
would be less heavy, and the road to death
less infested with terror
after a little rebellion,
a little reordering of the world,
a little spilling of blood.

Such days pass.
Look, I traverse my hollow days
like a sleepwalker
and, while sleeping, grope
for what I know I will never get.

Look, I paint my burnt future blue,
put sandalwood paste on it,
and sleep with it.
Look, I smile, I weep,
I am wild at its infidelity,
and I close my eyes
when its arms that do not exist
embrace me.

You, however, would stop speaking,
would consider all things including yourself
unreal, would create,
yet another evening,
would cast away all life history
into its darkness, would stifle all sound,
and would inhabit, all alone,
a territory that is neither death

nor life.

I have a different fate.
The day I die I will die
absolutely.
But till death comes, I do not have
a single free moment.
Even if you are an illusion,
it no longer matters.
I have come out of my house,
dressed for our night of love.
I have left my last breath so far behind
I can't go back to it.

58

You are the fragrance of rocks,
the lamentation of each flower,
the unbearable heat of the moon,
the icy coolness of the blazing sun,
the language of my letters to myself,
the smile with which all despair is borne,
the millenniums of waiting without a wink of sleep,
the ultimate futility of all rebellion,
the exquisite idol made of aspirations,
the green yesterdays of deserts,
the monsoon in an apparel of leaves and flowers,
the illuminated pathway from the clay to the farthest planet,
the fantastic time that's half-day and half-night,
the eternity of the sea's brief silence,
the solace-filled conclusion of incomplete dreams,
the dishevelled moment of waking up with a start,
the reluctant star in the sky brightening at dawn,
the unspoken sentences at farewell,
the restless wind sentenced to solitary confinement,
the body of fog seated on a throne,

the reflection asleep on the river's abysmal bed,
the undiscovered mine of the most precious jewels,
the outlines of lunacy engraved on space, and
the untold story of lightning.
You have, my dearest, always suffered
all my inadequacies with a smile.
I know I am not destined to bring you back once you've left.
All I can do hereafter, till the last day of my life,
is to collect the fragments of what you are
and try to piece them together.

60

Reports of your grievous injury
have reached us here.

You surely had
prior knowledge.
You hear the storm's first breath
before it breaks,
you know each single flower
before it becomes a bud,
and you have foreknowledge
of the river's murmur, of the shape
of every passing cloud.
You surely knew, before the sun rose today,
what the day would bring.
Like all other days and all other events,
this day and its events
were your own handiwork,
but you delude people into believing
it was all an accident.

I sometimes wish I had,
unknown to you, become
your accomplice. But a

moment later, I give up this
thought
and apologize to this body
for my years of neglect.
I beg it to give me
tears and pain
that do not occur in your scheme,
a second gift of youth
that will bewilder you,
and years will pass
before you recover your wits
and resume the frolic
of dying.

Those will be the years
when, while you looked at the blue river,
you will forget who you are;
when flowers will frighten you
with their mutiny of colour;
when you will forget that your will was the law
governing all objects in space;
when you will writhe in pain;
when, like a patient writhing in pain,
you will look at me;
and when your eyes will ask me
like the eyes of a patient writhing in pain,
to stay,
to hold you in my arms.

I wish I had wings
and reached you where your body
writhes like a thunder robbed of its voice,
or like a leaf imprisoned
in a whirlwind's unending moment
of futile movement.
I would then install

everywhere in your body
a longing more ancient than your play
engrossing men, women, and
all universe.

I would fill your veins
with wayward blood,
and lead your body tenderly
to the riverbanks,
to nights of small mischiefs
and of joys larger than ourselves,
to knowledge wet with tears,
to my arms, breasts and thighs,
where the blue marks you made
shone with greater splendour
than the whole solar system
created by you.

You belong to none.
Everyone who comes to you
is extinguished in your ruthless game
of non-discrimination.
I wish I could give you
a true body, a body with ears
that heard the voice of all my years
of sorrow, envy and hope,
a body with hands
that wandered all over my body.
Perhaps then you would understand
the smallness of all your universe,
and the art of waiting for people
either far away or dead.
I would then instruct you
in weeping for days for ever past,
and in slipping away
from life's drab days and nights.

All you have to do
is to first hold a warm hand,
its shadow thereafter,
and begin walking.
You will thus pass
this life,
and many others.

61

Reports of your passing away
have reached us here.

Don't count me
among your widows,
or among those who carry your body
in procession.

Your body, mercifully,
is far, far away.

In the parting of my hair,
the vermilion mark
is brighter than ever.
Now stop joking,
become the bridegroom,
 and come.

I wear
the bride's heavy silk
and gold.
My bangles
tinkle and snub
all scandals.

You no longer are

anyone's father, son, husband.
You are the pure naughtiness
of our last night together,
the voice,
that teases me,
and the touch that breaks
the virginity of my loneliness.
Just when I'd start crying,

you arrive and tickle
my lifeless longing
into unrestrained laughter.

When they deposit your body
on the pyre,
all that you ever meant to them
will be consumed by the flames.
They would return home
and, a few days later,
would fill your absence
with thoughts of you
and a thousand other things.

My joy today
is uncontrollable.
If you had not died for them,
you would not have become
entirely mine.

Since everyone believes you are dead,
my journeys to the riverbank
will now be without fear.
They will forget me,
or sleep like the dead
when I hold you in my arms,
when your hands traverse

my body,
when I renounce all power
to resist, or to speak, and when it is utterly impossible
for me to die,
or to live.

24

KANUPRIYA

DHARAMVIR BHARATI

TRANSLATED FROM THE HINDI BY ALOK BHALLA

Under the Mango Tree

You stood under this mango tree
and called to me.
    Even now
        when I come here
        I find peace.

No,
I think of nothing
    recall nothing at all.

Words: Meaningless

But, Kanu,
how will you explain to me
the meaning of all this?

Words, words, words . . .
For me, they are meaningless
If I don't hear them
from your trembling lips when you sit by me,
your fingers entangled in my dry hair.

They are meaningless . . .
Words, words, words . . .
Karma, *swadharma*, judgement, obligation . . .
I've heard these words in every lane.
Arjuna may have found in them
something of value.

But, my love,
when I hear them
I understand nothing.
I stand on the wayside and
dream only of your lips
when they must have
uttered these words
for the first time . . .

I imagine myself
in place of Arjuna
And my heart fills with desire
And I don't know which war it is
And whose side I am on
And what the problem is
And what the fight is about
but my heart is filled with desire
because I dearly love the way
you explain it to me . . .
and the warring armies are motionless
and history stands still
and you are explaining to me . . .
Karma, swadharma, judgement, obligation . . .

But by the time they reach me
their meaning has changed
and I only hear
Radha, Radha, Radha . . .

Words, words, words . . .
Your words are countless, Kanu—infinite
But they only have one sign, one meaning
     me
     me
     me
     only Me!

Then how will you explain
history to me
with those words?

NOTES

Introduction: The Dream of the Awakened by Namita Gokhale

1. Binodini, *The Maharaja's Household: A Daughter's Memories of Her Father* (New Delhi: Zubaan Books, 2015).

Chapter 2: In Search of the Historical Radha by Jawhar Sircar

1. Pierre Amiet et al., *Arts Asiatiques*, Tome XXVI, Parcourir Les Collections, 1973.
2. P. Banerjee, *The Life of Krishna in Indian Art* (New Delhi: National Museum, 1978), p. xvi.
3. Sumanta Banerjee, *Appropriation of a Folk Heroine: Radha in Medieval Bengali Vaishnava Culture* (Shimla: Indian Institute of Advanced Study, 1993), p. 9.
4. Ibid.
5. Banerjee, *Appropriation of a Folk Heroine*, p. 225.

Chapter 3: Radha and the Completion of Krishna by Meghnad Desai

1. Barbara Stoler Miller in her scholarly translation of the *Gita Govinda* mentions an ambiguous reference in the *Bhagavata*. '[T]he mention of a favoured cowherdess who is "worshipped" or "desired" (arid hits) by Krishna in the tenth book of the *Bhagavata Purana* . . .' See Barbara Stoler Miller, *The Gitagovinda*

217

of Jayadeva: Love Song of the Dark Lord (New Delhi: Motilal Banarsidass, 1984), p. 28.

2. Miller's work mentioned directly above quotes a citation in the Atharva Veda that Radha occurs in the reference to the *nakshatra* Vishakha, which is a dual-starred constellation. Indra is in the Vedic literature called a *gopa* (cowherd) and is paired with the two stars of Vishakha described as *adhipatni* (half wives). Radha is translated as 'perfection, wealth or success'. Indra is called *radhaspati*: Miller, *The Gitagovinda of Jayadeva*, pp. 26–27.

3. Miller, *The Gitagovinda of Jayadeva*, p. 29.

4. Chapters 19 and 23 in Volume 1 of *Mohak Vansali* (Seductive Flute) in K.M. Munshi's *Krishnavatar* (New Delhi: Bharatiya Vidya Bhavan, 1963).

Chapter 4: *Gita Govinda*: Illustrated Manuscripts from Rajasthan by Kapila Vatsyayan

1. M.R. Mazmudar, 'A fifteenth-century *Gita-Govinda* manuscript with Gujarati painting', *Journal of the University of Bombay*, vol. VI, part VI (May 1938): pp. 128–36.

2. Karl Khandalavala, '*Gita Govinda* in the Prince of Wales Museum', *Prince of Wales Museum Bulletin*, 1953–54. Also see *New Documents of Indian Painting*, p. 85. Karl Khandalavala ascribes the set to 1525–75 AD.

3. M.R. Mazmudar, 'A fifteenth-century *Gita-Govinda*', *University of Bombay Journal*, vol. X, part 2 (September 1941): pp. 119–31. Original manuscripts are at the B.J. Institute of Indology, Ahmedabad.

4. The paintings of the Kankaroli *Gita Govinda* have been rarely published. U.P. Shah had a few folios in his personal collection. Others are presumably still in the Kankaroli Palace.

5. Unpublished manuscript. Original in the Jodhpur Library.

6. U.P. Shah, *New Documents of Jaina Paintings*, L.P. Institute, Ahmedabad. Illustrations of the *Laghu Samgrahani Sutra*.

7. N.C. Mehta, 'A New Document of Gujarat Paintings', *Journal of the Indian Society for Indian Art*, vol. XIII (1945): pp. 36–48.

8. Ibid.

9. Kapila Vatsyayan, 'Miniatures of the *Gita-Govinda*'—17th-century manuscript of north Gujarat, Jaipur, Maharaja Sawai Man Singh II Museum, 1980.

10. Karl Khandalavala, 'Leaves from Rajasthan', *Marg*, vol. IV, no. 3 (1950): pp. 8–9 ff.

11. Kapila Vatsyayan, 'The Jaur *Gita-Govinda*', National Museum, New Delhi, 1982.

12. Ibid.

13. Andrew Topsfield, 'Sahibidin's *Gita-Govinda*', *Chhavi*, II Golden Jubilee Volume (1981): pp. 231–36 (Bharat Kala Bhavan, Varanasi).

13a. Pramodchandra: Article on Indian painting in *Encyclopedia Britannica*, see *Gita Govinda* illustrations as Plate 6.

14. Kapila Vatsyayan, *The Mewari Gita-Govinda* (New Delhi: National Museum, 1987), and *An Illustrated Manuscript of the Gita-Govinda from Mewar*, Dr Moti Chandra Commemoration Volume (Calcutta: JISOA, 1978), pp. 36–60.

15. Kapila Vatsyayan, *The Bundi Gita-Govinda* (Varanasi: Bharat Kala Bhavan, 1981).

Chapter 5: Integrating the Natural, the Divine and the Erotic in the *Gita Govinda* and *Shir Ha-Shirim* by Yudit K. Greenberg

1. For an English translation of the *Gita Govinda*, see Barbara Stoler Miller, ed. and trans. *Love Song of the Dark Lord: Jayadeva's Gitagovinda* (New York: Columbia University Press, 1977).

2. For an English translation of Song of Songs, see Ariel Bloch and Chana Bloch, *The Song of Songs: A New Translation* (Berkeley and Los Angeles: University of California Press, 1995). *Song of Songs* is also known as *Canticles* and as *The Song of Solomon*.

3. For an earlier version of this comparative study, see Yudit K. Greenberg, 'The Languages of Love and Desire in the *Gitagovinda* and the Song of Songs', *Journal of Vaishnava Studies* 22.1 (2013): pp. 69–78. For a comprehensive reference book

on love and religion see, Yudit K. Greenberg, ed. *Encyclopedia of Love in World Religions* (Santa Barbara: ABC-CLIO, 2008).

4. Masterpieces of erotic poetry and prose include the troubadours Shakespeare, Dante, Rumi and Teresa of Avila.

5. See Sir Edwin Arnold, *Light of Asia and the Indian Song of Songs* (New Delhi: Crest Publishing House, 1994). He explains that his title 'The Indian Song of Songs' is justified insofar as both the *Gita Govinda* and *Shir Ha-Shirim* are mystical allegory. See also Lee Siegel, *Sacred and Profane Dimensions of Love in Indian Traditions, as Exemplified in the Gītāgovinda of Jayadeva* (New Delhi: Oxford University Press, 1978).

6. See, for instance, Renita Weems, 'Song of Songs', in *The Women's Bible Commentary*, ed. Carol A. Newsome and Sharon A. Ringe (Louisville: Westminster/John Know Press, 1992), p. 157.

7. Phyllis Trible, *God and the Rhetoric of Sexuality* (Minneapolis: Fortress Press, 1978), pp. 144–66.

8. On the theme of love-in-separation, see Maurice Jacques Valency, *In Praise of Love: Introduction to the Love Poetry of the Renaissance* (New York City: Macmillan, 1961); Denis de Rougemont, *Love in the Western World* (Princeton: Princeton University Press, 1983); Edward C. Dimock, *The Place of the Hidden Moon: Erotic Mysticism in the Vaisnava-Sahajiya Cult of Bengal* (Chicago: University of Chicago Press, 1989).

Chapter 8: Enjoying God: The Divine Paramour by Makarand R. Paranjape

1. An earlier version of this paper was presented at the workshop on 'Radha: Transformation from Gopi to Goddess', organized by Professor Harsha V. Dehejia (Carleton University, Ottawa), at the School of Arts and Aesthetics, Jawaharlal Nehru University, New Delhi, 29–30 January 2010. My special thanks to Harshabhai and Sudhatai, his wife, for nurturing these words and for their affection.

Several scholars attest to the importance of the feminine aspect of God in Hindu traditions. In his introduction to *Hindu Goddesses:*

Visions of the Divine Feminine in the Hindu Religious Tradition (Berkeley: University of California Press, 1986), David Kinsley compares this feature of Hinduism with other religions (1–5); see also John Stratton Hawley's *Prologue to Devi: Goddesses of India* (1–3). In the opening lines of *The Divine Feminine in the Theology of Krishna*, Graham M. Schweig declares: 'Nowhere in the panorama of world religious traditions, from ancient times to the present, do we find such a strong presence of the feminine voice within the divinity as we do in the Hindu complex of religion' (441). But of all these manifestations of the divine feminine, none is as charming, attractive or romantic as Radha.

2. By the late 16th century, however, there would be a reversal. For instance, the Radhavallabha sect would accord a higher status to Radha than Krishna, so much so that in the 19th century, a member of the sect, Vamsi Ali, would compose a poem called 'Sri-Radhika-maharasa' 'to avenge the wrong that had been done to their deity [Radha] by the author of the Bhagavata in not mentioning her name in his work' (B. Mazumdar, *Krishna in History and Legend*, cited in Siegel 122). In this poem 'the name Krishna does not find any place at all. In it we find Radha playing on the flute and calling her female friends to the forest . . .'

3. For an indigenous study of *Gita Govinda*, see Vidya Nivas Mishra's *Radha Madhav Rang Rangi* (2004).

4. Nimbarka (c. 13th century AD) initiated the worship of Radha–Krishna long before Chaitanya. According to the *Sri Navadwipadham Mahatmya*, a later Chaitanyite text, he saw Sri Gauranga, the combined form of Radha and Krishna, who would later incarnate as Chaitanya, in a vision. Later practitioners of Radha–Krishna worship, through such back projection and invention, tried to create continuity in the tradition.

5. See Ramakanta Rath's *Sri Radha* (1996). Rath, speaking of how he came to write the poem, reminisces, 'The anticipation of death, the thought that all this beauty would be beyond my reach some day was the theme [. . .] I reflected on who else could have experienced this kind of emotion—love and terror in equal

measure. I decided that it could be only one person, Radha'
(Hariharan Balakrishnan, *Hindu Literary Review*, 2 April
2006). Rath's Radha is not simply Krishna's beloved, but is
endowed with a subjectivity that is independent and strong,
not merely relational. For instance, in one of the stanzas,
translated by Rath himself into English, Radha considers her
own bygone years:

As I bathed that morning, I looked through the water
at my legs and thought these legs are not mine, nothing
is mine, this body is not mine, the history of all my
hopes and despairs is not mine. And my husband, my
house, my herds of livestock—they too are not mine.
Neither this life nor the death that shall surely come
some day are mine. I am forever a beggar woman, a
disturbed void enclosed between these two arms that
reach into outer space.

Interestingly, Rath's next major work, *Palataka*, featuring
Krishna, was simply not as well-received or significant.

6. It was Harshabhai's suggestion that I include an analysis of the
opening *doha*, the traditional *mangalacharan* of Bihari's *Satsai*,
in this paper. Also see H.S. Shiva Prakash's essay in this volume
for more reflections on the modern Radha.

7. I owe thanks to Dr Imre Bangha of the faculty of Oriental Studies,
Oxford University, for his help in explaining this couplet to me.

8. Verse 1.3.28 of the Bhagavata extols the greatness of Krishna
over all other incarnations: 'These [other incarnations] are
amsha, or *kala*, partial incarnations, but *krishnas tu bhagavan
svayam*, 'Krishna is Bhagavan, God, himself' (Bryant 114).
Most Krishna theologians resort to this verse, regarding it the
mahavakya, or 'pivotal statement', of their theology. A similar
strategy has been used by other sects to exalt their master over
others; for instance, commenting on Sri Aurobindo, the Mother
said, 'What Sri Aurobindo represents in the history of the earth's

spiritual progress is not a teaching, not even a revelation. It is a mighty action straight from the Supreme.'

9. This is a variation of a metaphor used by Rabindranath Tagore in his celebrated essay 'Viswa-Sahitya', the sun being an allusion to himself (Rabi means sun) (222; 225).

10. Scholars like Jessica Frazier, however, offer insightful and alternative readings, invoking Zizek and Kristeva. Frazier argues that Radha, the *gopi*-turned-goddess, trades in her subjection for passionate commitment, incorporating both her divine lover and the audience into her purposive agency. For Frazier, she is a model of a strong—rather than weak—woman. Frazier, thus, makes a persuasive case against the conventional view that 'even in *sringara*, the erotic mode, there is no notion of equality between devotee and deity. The function of this rasa is primarily to spiritualize and aestheticize male dominance of gender relations. In the numerous legends about Krishna's sexual adventures among the milkmaids (gopis) of Braj, the initiative is always his to seduce, dally with and desert his female partners [. . .] This implies, among other things, the passivity of the female. Bhakti actually prescribes such passivity by depicting the gopis as women who have no sexual passion (*prakrta-kama*) of their own, but are merely conducive to Krishna's pleasure' (Guha 48–49).

11. *Nyasa* literally means 'placing', 'touching', 'applying' or 'founding', as when a worshipper touches himself in certain places and in certain ways to consecrate himself before commencing the puja, or ritual of worship. Gavin Flood describes *pranapratisha* as 'A ritual of consecration in which the consciousness or power of the deity is brought into the image awakens the icon in a temple' (7).

12. From the *Krishna Charnamritam* of Bilvamangal, translated by Frances Wilson, quoted in Bryant (462).

13. From the Dimock and Levertov translation, quoted in Bryant 464–65.

14. From the Dimock and Levertov translation, quoted in Bryant 466.

Chapter 9: Radha: The Play and Perfection of Rasa by Shrivatsa Goswami

1. Prabodhananda Sarasvati, *Sri Radha-rasa-sudha-nidhi*, ed. Puridasa (Vrindavana: Haridasa Sarma, 1953), verse 26, p. 3.
2. Jiva Goswami, *Bhakti Sandharba*, ed. Puridasa (Vrindavana: Haridasa Sarma, 1951), *anu.* 310, pp. 157–79.
3. Cf. Jiva Goswami, *Priti Sandharba*, *anu.* 110ff., pp. 65ff.
4. Ibid., p. 67, 110–11.
5. Rupa Goswami, *Ujjvala Nilamani*, ed., with two commentaries by Puridasa (Vrindavana: Haridasa Sarma, 1954), 4.6–7, p. 24.
6. Raghunatha Dasa Goswami, *Stavavali*, ed. Puridasa (Mymensingh: Sacinatha Rayachaudhuri, 1947), 15.1-10, p. 40.
7. Rupa Goswami, *Ujjvala Nilamani*, 14.1-237, pp. 124–56.
8. Ibid., 14.219, p. 155.
9. *Bhagavata Purana*, 9.4.63; *Priti Sandharba*, *anu.* 41, p. 34.
10. Jiva Goswami, *Krsna Sandarbha*, ed. Puridasa (Vrindavana: Haridasa Sarma, 1951), *anu.* 189, p. 117.
11. *Aphorisms on the Gospel of Divine Love or Narada Bhakti Sutras*, ed. and trans. Swami Tyagisananda (Madras: Sri Ramakrishna Math, 1967), no. 52, p. 15.

Chapter 11: The Heart-throb of Chaitanya by Harsha V. Dehejia

1. Edward C. Dimock, *The Place of the Hidden Moon: Erotic Mysticism in the Vaisnava-Sahajiya Cult of Bengal* (Chicago: University of Chicago Press, 1966), p. 32.

Chapter 14: Krishna: The Playful Divine by Pavan K. Varma

1. Keshav Das, *Rasikapriya*, in M.S. Randhawa, *Kangra Paintings on Love* (New Delhi: National Museum, 1962), pp. 46–60.
2. Ibid., p. 59.
3. Id., p. 62.

Chapter 15: Radha in Nazrul Geeti by Reba Som

1. 'Tumi Jodi Radha Hotey Shyam', translation mine.
2. See Nitish Sengupta, *History of the Bengali-Speaking People* (New Delhi: UBSPD Publishers, 2001), p. 96.
3. Harsha V. Dehejia, 'The Heart-throb of Chaitanya', in *Radha: From Gopi to Goddess*, ed. Harsha V. Dehejia (New Delhi: Niyogi Books, 2014), p. 173.
4. See Priti Kumar Mitra, *The Dissent of Nazrul Islam: Poetry and History* (New Delhi: OUP, 2007).
5. Krishna-Muhammad (died in infancy); Arindam-Khaled, also called Bulbul, died of smallpox at age three; Kazi Sabyasachi and Kazi Aniruddha.
6. Rabindranath Tagore, 'Sahitye Nobyota', in *Rabindra Rachanabali*, vol. 14 (Government of West Bengal, 1961), p. 332 et seq.
7. 'Aami Jaar Nupurer Chhondo Benukaar Shur', translation mine.
8. 'Bodhu Ami Chhinu Bujhi Brindabaner Radhikar Aakhi Jauley', translation mine, from the enclosed booklet in my CD album *Love Songs of Kazi Nazrul Islam*, Times Music, 2016. The album can be heard on YouTube and www.timesmusic.com.
9. 'More Ghumo Ghorey Eley Manohar', translation mine, from the enclosed booklet in my CD album *Love Songs of Kazi Nazrul Islam*, Times Music, 2016.
10. 'Tumi Haath Khani Jaubey Rakho More Hather Paurey', translation mine, from the enclosed booklet in my CD album *Love Songs of Kazi Nazrul Islam*, Times Music, 2016.

Chapter 16: Lovelorn Radha, Forlorn God: Tagore's *Bhanusingher Padavali* by Lalit Kumar

1. The two poems in the epigraph are excerpts from Tagore's *Bhanusingher Padavali*, poem number one and nineteen respectively. For the transliteration of these two complete poems in Devanagari, see *Rabindra Rachnavali, Kavita*, vol. 1.

2. The role of Kadambari Devi as Tagore's muse, writes Malashri Lal, has been endlessly speculated upon. She further argues that 'for young Robi, Kadambari was a secret love that became apotheosized as poetry or image'. See *Tagore and the Feminine*, Introduction, p. xxi.

3. For the English translation of the biography *The Life of Bhanusimha Thakura*, see Appendix to *The Lover of God*, pp. 113–20.

4. Ibid., p. 120.

5. Thomas Chatterton (1752–70) was a precocious English poet who managed to pass off his work as a fictional 15th-century poet called Thomas Rowley. Tagore intended to be the second Chatterton.

6. George Abraham Grierson had claimed that Vidyapati was the 'first of the old Vaishnava master-singers who spoke and wrote in the language of the people', that is, Maithili. See *Chrestomathy*, p. 84.

7. For the early English translation of Tagore's autobiography, *Jiban Smriti*, see *My Reminiscences*. For a more recent translation, see *The Picture of My Early Life*. For the chapter on Bhanusingh see pp. 135–38 and 92–94, respectively. Tagore also claimed in this section that while Bhanusingh's songs were being published in *Bharati* magazine, one Nishikanta Chattopadhyaya earned his doctorate on them by comparing the traditional lyric poetry of India with that of Europe: see *My Reminiscences*, p. 137. However, subsequent efforts to locate such a thesis submitted in all the major German universities around that time bore no fruit: see *The Lover of God*, p. 106.

8. Rosinka Chaudhuri calls the language of these poems 'Maithili dialect (a mixture of old Hindi and Bengali prevalent in eastern India)'. This seems to be a case of misrepresentation of a language as dialect, for Maithili was neither a dialect, nor a mixture of old Hindi and Bengali. Ironically, a language that Tagore was enamoured with had to contest with Hindi and Bengali in order to debunk the myth that Maithili is a dialect. For Chaudhuri's discussion of *Bhanusingher Padavali*, see 'The Rustle of Language'.

9. See Sisir Kumar Das, *A History of Indian Literature 1800–1910*. Das argues that the hybridization, or mixing, of languages is an essential feature of not only everyday linguistic activity in India, it is also an interesting feature of Indian literary activity, p. 346.

10. For Grierson's analysis of Vidyapati's imitators in Bengal and his coinage 'bastard language', see *Chrestomathy*, pp. 34–36.

11. *The Picture of My Early Life (Jivansmriti)*, p. 92.

12. Though there is no direct mention of Radha in the *Bhagavata Purana*, the tenth book of this text mentions a cowherdess who is favoured and desired by Krishna. See Das, *A History of Indian Literature 500–1399*, p. 186.

13. Ibid.

14. Barbara Stoler Miller, in the introduction to her translation of *Gita Govinda*, argues that Radha is one of the most obscure figures in early Indian literature. Before Jayadeva made her the heroine of his poem, she appeared only in some verses scattered through Puranas, anthologies of Sanskrit and Prakrit poetry, grammar, drama and a few inscriptions. See Barbara Stoler, *The Gitagovinda of Jayadeva: Love Song of the Dark Lord* (New Delhi: Motilal Banarsidass, 1984), p. 26.

15. Ibid.

16. For the commentary section on Tagore's songs, if not mentioned otherwise, I have used Tony K. Stewart and Chase Twichell's translation of *Bhanusingher Padavali*, titled as *The Lover of God*. The book contains all the twenty-two poems of *Padavali* in English translation along with their original in Bengali script.

17. For a discussion on Rupa Goswami's text *Ujjvala Nilamani*, see *Early History of Vaisnava Faith and Movement in Bengal*, pp. 126–70.

18. *The Lover of God*, p. 103.

19. Ibid., p. 109.

20. Ahirs and Yadavs are often used interchangeably. They refer to a caste, which was conventionally known for cow-herding and agriculture.

21. Since Vidyapati was inspired by Jayadeva, and he attempted to achieve in Maithili what the latter had achieved in Sanskrit, he

is also called 'New (Abhinav) Jayadeva'. See publisher's note to *Vidyapati Ki Padavali*.

22. See Miller's translation of *Gita Govinda*, 90.

Chapter 20: 'Radha' in Bollywood Cinema by Alka Kurian

1. In a further distancing from the Radha song, Shayana, the source of sexual indiscretion, ceases to exist and disappears from the scene and the film ends in a happy, hyper-masculine space of unalloyed male friendship.

Chapter 21: Sita and Radha: From Human to Divine by Mandakranta Bose

1. A detailed discussion about Sita as a role model for Indian women appears in Heidi R.M. Pauwels, *The Goddess as Role Model: Sita and Radha in Scripture and on Screen* (Oxford and New York: Oxford University Press, 2008), pp. 8–12. Madhu Kishwar's interviews with women in modern India question Sita's submissiveness (*Manushi* 98 [1997]: pp. 21–34).

2. Sir Monier Monier-Williams, *A Sanskrit–Hindi Dictionary* (Oxford: Clarendon Press, 1964), p. 1218.

3. Sita Lakshmi, *VR*.vi.117.27.

4. Except in some little-known retellings of the epic from the *sakta* angle, such as the 18th-century Bengali language *Jagadrami-Ramprasadi Ramayana*.

5. Thomas Coburn, *Manushi* 90 (September–October 1955).

6. In February 2008 there was a serious controversy at Delhi University over teaching an essay by A.K. Ramanujan, 'Three Hundred *Rāmāyaṇas*', which discusses regional versions of the Ramayana, in some of which Sita has a prominent role with a voice of her own.

7. *VR*.vi.119.5.

8. An example of this ideological orientation appears in Jacqueline Suthren Hirst's *Sita's Story*, written for Indian girl children in the United Kingdom.

9. David Kinsley, *Hindu Goddesses: Visions of the Divine Feminine in the Hindu Religious Tradition* (Berkeley, CA: University of California Press, 1986), pp. 85–92. For a fuller understanding of Radha's love for Krishna, see Barbara Stoler Miller, *Love Song of the Dark Lord: Jayadeva's Gitagovinda* (New York: Columbia University Press, 1977).

10. See Kinsley, *Hindu Goddesses*, pp. 82–83; Miller, *Love Song of the Dark Lord*, pp. 29–30.

11. For a more modern interpretation of Sita and Radha based on recent films as well as scriptures, see Pauwels, *The Goddess as Role Model*.

BIBLIOGRAPHY

Chapter 6: Becoming Radha by Alka Pande

Beck, G.L. 'Krishna as Loving Husband of God: The Alternative Krishnology of the Radhavallabha Sampradaya'. In *Alternative Krishnas: Regional and Vernacular Variations on a Hindu Deity*, edited by G.L. Beck (pp. 65–90). Albany: State University of New York Press, 2005.

Brown, Mackenzie. 'The Theology of Radha in the Puranas'. In *The Divine Consort Radha and the Goddesses of India*. Edited by John Stratton Hawley and Donna Marie Wulff (pp. 57–72). Berkeley: University of California Press, 1982.

Bussagli, Mario. *5000 Years of the Art of India*. New York: Harry N. Abrams, 1990.

Craven, Roy. *Indian Art: A Concise History*. London: Thames and Hudson, 1997.

Daljeet, and Jain P.C. *Indian Miniature Paintings: Manifestation of a Creative Mind*. New Delhi: Brijbasi Art Press, 2007.

Dehejia, Vidya. *Indian Art*. London: Phaidon Press, 1997.

Desai, Devangana. *Erotic Sculpture of India*. New Delhi: Tata McGraw-Hill, 1975.

Desai, Vishakha et al. *Contemporary Art in India: Traditions/Tensions*. New York: Harry N. Abrams, 1996.

Dimock, Edward, and Levertov, Denise. *In Praise of Krishna: Songs from the Bengali*. Chicago: University of Chicago Press, 1967.

Goswami, Shrivatsa. 'The Play and Perfection of Rasa'. In *The Divine Consort: Radha and the Goddesses of India*, edited by John Stratton Hawley and Donna Marie Wulff (pp. 72–89). Berkeley: University of California Press, 1982.

Hawley, John Stratton, and Wulff, Donna Marie, eds. *The Divine Consort: Radha and the Goddesses of India*. Berkeley: Graduate Theological Union, 1982.

Lerner, Martin. *The Flame and the Lotus*. New York: Harry N. Abrams, 1984.

Maharaja, Srila Bhaktivedanta Narayana, trans. *Jayadeva Gita Govindam*. New Delhi: Gaudiya Vedanta Publications, 2005.

Menon, Usha. 'Making Śakti: Controlling (Natural) Impurity for Female (Cultural) Power. *Ethos* 30(1/2) (2002): pp. 140–57.

Miller, Barbara Stoler. 'The Divine Duality of Radha and Krishna'. In *The Divine Consort Radha and the Goddesses of India*, edited by John Stratton Hawley and Donna Marie Wulff (pp. 13–27). Berkeley: University of California Press, 1982.

Mukhoradhyay, Durgadas. *In Praise of Krishna*. Delhi: B.R. Publishing Corporation, 1990.

Nanda, Serena. *Neither Man nor Woman: The Hijras of India*. California: Wadsworth, 1990, p. 9.

O'Flaherty, Wendy Doniger. *Women, Androgynes, and Other Mythical Beasts*. Chicago: University of Chicago Press, 1980.

Pande, Alka, and Dane, Lance. *Indian Erotica*. New Delhi: Roli Books, 2001.

Pande, Alka. *Ardhanarishvara: The Androgyne*. New Delhi: Rupa and Co., 2004.

——Pande, Alka. *Indian Art: The New International Sensation: A Collector's Handbook*. Bhopal: Manjul Publishing House, 2008.

——Pande, Alka. *Shringara: The Many Faces of Indian Beauty*. New Delhi: Rupa Publications, 2011.

Pattanaik, Devdutt. 'Krishna: The Girl'. Available on https://bit.ly/2RgMDKY.

Paturi, Nagaraj. Personal interview with the author. 2 June 2018.

Randhawa, M.S. *Kangra Paintings on Love*. New Delhi: Patiala House, 1994.

Rawson, Philip. *The Art of Tantra*. London: Thames and Hudson, 1973.

Rosenstein, L. 'The Radhavallabha and the Haridasi Sampradayas: A Comparison'. *Journal of Vaisnava Studies* 7(1) (1998): pp. 5–18.

Uma, Shankar. Personal interview with the author. 7 June 2018.

Vanita, Ruth, and Kidwai, Saleem. *Same-Sex Love in India*. New York: St Martin's Press, 2000.

Vaudeville, Charlotte. 'Krishna Gopala, Radha, and the Great Goddess'. In *The Divine Consort Radha and the Goddesses of India*, edited by John Stratton Hawley and Donna Marie Wulff (pp. 1–13). Berkeley: University of California Press, 1982.

Watts, Alan. *Erotic Spirituality*. London: Collier-Macmillan, 1971.

Zimmer, Heinrich. *Myths and Symbols in Indian Art and Civilization*. Princeton: Princeton University Press, 1946.

Chapter 8: Enjoying God: The Divine Paramour by Makarand R. Paranjape

Bahadur, Krishna P., trans. *The Satasai*. New Delhi: Penguin Books, 1992.

Balakrishnan, Hariharan. 'Ode to Beauty'. *Hindu Literary Review*, 2 April 2006. https://bit.ly/2ELePUO.

Beck, Guy L. 'Krishna as Loving Husband of God: The Alternative Krishnology of the Radhavallabha Sampradaya'. In *Alternative Krishnas: Regional and Vernacular Variations on a Hindu Deity*, edited by Guy L. Beck (pp. 65–90). Albany, NY: SUNY Press, 2005.

Bryant, Edwin F. 'Krishna in the Tenth Book of the Bhagavata Purana'. In *Krishna: A Sourcebook*, edited by Edwin F. Bryant (pp. 111–36). New York: Oxford University Press, 2007.

Dube, Shyamsunder, trans. *Bihari Satsai*. New Delhi: Publications Division.

Flood, Gavin. *The Blackwell Companion to Hinduism*. Oxford: Blackwell Publishers, 2003.

Frazier, Jessica. *Becoming the Goddess: Female Subjectivity and the Passion of the Goddess Radha. New Topics in Feminist Philosophy of Religjon: Contestations and Transcendence Incarnate*, edited by Pamela Sue Anderson (pp. 199–216). London: Springer, 2010.

Guha, Ranajit. *Dominance without Hegemony: History and Power in Colonial India*. Cambridge: Harvard University Press, 1997.

Hawley, John Stratton, and Wulff, Donna Marie. *The Divine Consort: Radha and the Goddesses of India*. Berkeley, CA: Graduate Theological Union, 1982.

Jha, Amar Nath, and Mathura, Girija Kumara. *The Veiled Moon: English Translations of Bihari Satsai*. New Delhi: Indian Council for Cultural Relations, 1973.

Kinsley, David. *Hindu Goddesses: Visions of the Divine Feminine in the Hindu Religious Tradition*. Berkeley: University of California Press, 1986.

Mishra, Vidya Nivas. *Radha Madhav Rang Rangi*. New Delhi: Bharatiya Jnanpith, 2004.

Ritter, Valerie. 'Epiphany in Radha's Arbor: Nature and the Reform of Bhakti in Hariaudh's Priyapravas'. In *Alternative Krishnas: Regional and Vernacular Variations on a Hindu Deity*, edited by Guy L. Beck (pp. 177–208). Albany, NY: SUNY Press, 2005.

Schweig, Graham M. 'The Divine Feminine in the Theology of Krishna'. In *Krishna: A Sourcebook*, edited by Edwin F. Bryant (pp. 441–74). New York: Oxford University Press, 2007.

Siegel, Lee. *Sacred and Profane: Dimensions of Love in Indian Traditions as Exemplified in the Gita Govinda of Jayadeva*. New Delhi: Oxford University Press, 1978.

Tagore, Rabindranath. *Viswa-Sahitya*. 1907; Das, Rijula, and Paranjape, Makarand R. 'Punctuated Renewals: Rabindranath Tagore in the 21st Century'. *Journal of Contemporary Thought* (Winter 2011): pp. 213–25.

Tharu, Susie J., and Lalita, K., eds. *Women Writing in India: 600 B.C. to the Present*, vol. 1. New York: Feminist Press at the City University of New York, 1991.

Vaudeville, Charlotte. 'Krishna Gopala, Radha, and the Great Goddess'. In *The Divine Consort: Radha and the Goddesses of India*, edited by John Stratton Hawley and Donna Marie Wulff (pp. 1–12). Berkeley, CA: Graduate Theological Union, 1982.

Chapter 16: Lovelorn Radha, Forlorn God: Tagore's *Bhanusingher Padavali* by Lalit Kumar

Bharati, Dharamvir. *Kanupriya*. New Delhi: Bharatiya Jnanpith, 1984.

Chaudhuri, Rosinka. 'The Rustle of Language'. In *Rabindranath Tagore in the 21st Century Theoretical Renewals. Sophia Studies in Cross-cultural Philosophy of Traditions and Cultures*, vol. 7, edited by Debashish Banerji. New Delhi: Springer, 2015.

Choudhury, Indranath, ed. *Rabindranath Tagore Rachnavali*. New Delhi: Sasta Sahitya Mandal, 2014, pp. 55–67.

Das, Sisir Kumar. *A History of Indian Literature 500–1399: From the Courtly to the Popular*. New Delhi: Sahitya Akademi, 2005.

———*A History of Indian Literature 1800–1910 Western Impact: Indian Response*. New Delhi: Sahitya Akademi, 1991.

De, Sushil Kumar. *Early History of Vaisnava Faith and Movement in Bengal*. Calcutta: General Printers and Publishers Limited, 1942.

Grierson, George Abraham. *Maithili Chrestomathy and Vocabulary*. Edited by Hetukar Jha and Vedanatha Jha. Darbhanga: Kalyani Foundation, 2009.

Kapur, Shubhkar. *Vidyapati Ki Padavali*. Lucknow: Ganga Pustakmala Karyalaya, 1968.

Lal, Malashri, ed. *Tagore and the Feminine: A Journey in Translations*. New Delhi: Sage, 2015.

Miller, Barbara Stoler, ed. and trans. *The Gitagovinda of Jayadeva: Love Song of the Dark Lord*. New Delhi: Motilal Banarsidass, 1984.

Tagore, Rabindranath. *Bhanusingher Padavali: The Lover of God*. Translated by Tony K. Stewart and Chase Twichell. Washington: Copper Canyon Press, 2003.

———*Gitanjali. (Song Offerings)*. Introduction by W.B. Yeats. New York: Macmillan Company, 1920, pp. 59–60.

——*Jibansmriti. My Reminiscences.* Translated by Surendranath Tagore. New York: Macmillan Company, 1917.

——*Jibansmriti. The Picture of My Early Life.* Translated by Prasenjit Saha. Kolkata: Frontpage, 2013.

Chapter 20: 'Radha' In Bollywood Cinema by Alka Kurian

Ahmed, S. Akbar. 'Bombay Film: The Cinema as Metaphor for Indian Society and Politics'. *Modern Asian Studies.* 26(:2) (1992): pp. 289–320.

Creekmur, Corey. 'Remembering, Repeating, and Working Through *Devdas*'. In *Indian Literature and Popular Cinema: Recasting Classics*, edited by Heidi Pauwels. London and New York: Routledge, 2007.

Gopal, Sangita. *Conjugations: Marriage and Form in Bollywood Cinema.* Chicago and London: University of Chicago Press, 2011.

Kurian, Alka. '#MeToo Campaign Brings the Rise of Fourth Wave Feminism in India'. *Wire*, 2 February 2018, https://bit.ly/2JeVOsz.

——*New Feminisms in South Asian Social Media, Film, and Literature: Disrupting the Discourse.* (Co-edited with Sonora Jha). New York: Routledge, 2017.

Mishra, Vijay. 'Towards a Theoretical Critique of Bombay Cinema'. *Screen* 26 (3–4) (1985): pp. 133–46.

Mukherjee, M. *Realism and Reality: The Novel and Society in India.* New Delhi: Oxford University Press, 1985.

Pauwels, Heidi. '"The Woman Waylaid at the Well", or Paṇaghaṭa-līlā: An Indian Folk Theme Appropriated in Myth and Movies'. *Asian Ethnology*, 69(1) (2010): pp. 1–33.

——'From Vrindavan to Bollywood'. In Harsha V. Dehejia, *Radha: From Gopi to Goddess.* New Delhi: Niyogi Books, 2014.

LIST OF CONTRIBUTORS

Alka Kurian
'Radha' in Bollywood Cinema

Alka Kurian is faculty at the University of Washington Bothell, where she teaches postcolonial film and literature, gender studies and human rights. Alka has a single-author book entitled *Narratives of Gendered Dissent in South Asian Cinemas* (Routledge 2012, 2014). She is co-editor of *New Feminisms in South Asia: Disrupting the Discourse through Social Media, Film and Literature* (Routledge 2017). Alka has published various book chapters on South Asian film and was the founder-co-editor of the peer-reviewed journal *Studies in South Asian Film and Media*. She is currently working on a new book project on global fourth-wave feminism. Alka is a board member of Tasveer, a South Asian film and art non-profit, for which she helps organize film and literature festivals.

Alka Pande
Becoming Radha

Alka Pande is an art historian who taught Indian arts and aesthetics at Panjab University for more than ten years. She has been felicitated with various honours for distinguished contribution to art including the Knight of the Order of Arts and Letters by the French government, the Australia–India Council Special Award, the L'Oreal Paris Femina

Women under Design and the Amrita Sher-Gil Samman, to name a few. Currently, Dr Pande is a consultant art adviser and curator of the Visual Arts Gallery, India Habitat Centre, in New Delhi.

Alok Bhalla
Translation of *Kanupriya* by Dharamvir Bharati

Alok Bhalla obtained his master's in English from Delhi University and his PhD from Kent State University, USA. As a writer he has published extensively on the Partition of India and Latin American literature. Amongst his recent books are *Stories about the Partition of India* (three volumes). He is the author of two books on the gothic novel. He has translated Dharamvir Bharati's *Andha Yug* into English verse, as well as the stories of Intizar Husain, Ram Kumar, Manto, Gulzar, and others.

Andrew Schelling
Translation of Vidya

Andrew Schelling is a poet, eco activist and translator from Sanskrit. He teaches at Naropa University in Colorado, USA. Among his twenty books, his most recent is *Tracks Along the Left Coast: Jaime de Angulo & Pacific Coast Culture*, a folkloric account of Western wilderness encounters, linguistics, poetry, medicine power and creation tales. His Sanskrit translations are widely anthologized.

Aruna Chakravarti
Translation of 'Raikamal' by Tarashankar Bandyopadhyay

Aruna Chakravarti has been the principal of a prestigious women's college of Delhi University for ten years. She is also a well-known academic, creative writer and translator. Her first novel, *The Inheritors*, was shortlisted for the Commonwealth Writers' Prize and her third, *Jorasanko*, received critical acclaim and also became a bestseller. Her seven translated works include an anthology of songs from Rabindranath Tagore's *Gitabitaan*, Saratchandra Chattopadhyay's

Srikanta and Sunil Gangopadhyay's *Those Days, First Light* and *Primal Woman: Stories*. She also has two academic works to her credit. Her latest novel *Daughters of Jorasanko* is a sequel to *Jorasanko*. Among the various awards she has received are the Vaitalik Award, a Sahitya Akademi Award and the Sarat Puraskar.

Bulbul Sharma
Radha: Beloved of the Blue God

Bulbul Sharma is an artist and author based in New Delhi. She has published twenty-two books, several of which have been translated into French, Italian, Spanish and Chinese. She has worked as an art educator for children with special needs for fifteen years and conducts 'story-painting' workshops as part of literacy projects in informal schools.

Deben Bhattacharya
Translation of Vidyapati

Deben Bhattacharya (1921–2001) was a Bengali radio producer, record producer, ethnomusicologist, anthropologist, documentary film-maker, photographer, translator, poet, writer, broadcaster, lecturer and folk-music consultant. He produced over 100 records, twenty-three films and published more than a dozen books in his lifetime; much of his work was carried out under the auspices of UNESCO.

Debotri Dhar
A Flute Called Radha

Dr Debotri Dhar is a creative writer, educator, editor and columnist. Dhar teaches women's studies at the University of Michigan, Ann Arbor. Her books worldwide, published or forthcoming, include *Maya of Michigan: A Novel of Linked Stories* (New York, 2019); *The Courtesans of Karim Street* (New Delhi, 2016); *Education and Gender* (London, New York, 2014, Bloomsbury); and *The Best Asian Short Stories* (Singapore, 2018), among others.

Devdutt Pattanaik
A Milkmaid Called Radha

Devdutt Pattanaik writes on the relevance of mythology in modern times, especially in areas of management, governance and leadership. He is the author of thirty books and 600 columns, with bestsellers such as *Jaya*, *Sita* and *Shyam*. He was a speaker at TEDIndia 2009. His TV shows include *Business Sutra* on CNBC-TV18 and *Devlok* on Epic TV. He consults with organizations on culture, diversity and leadership, as well as with various television channels and film-makers on storytelling.

Dharamvir Bharati
Kanupriya

Dharamvir Bharati, journalist, novelist, playwright and poet in Hindi, was honoured with a Padma Shri for literature in 1972 and the Sangeet Natak Akademi Award in playwriting (Hindi) in 1988. He was the chief editor of the popular magazine *Dharmayug* for several years. His best-known works include *Suraj Ka Satwan Ghoda* and *Gunaho Ka Devta*, both experiments in narrative form, and *Andha Yug*, a play based on the Mahabharata.

Durgadas Mukhopadhyay
Durgadas Mukhopadhyay is the editor and translator of *In Praise of Krishna: Translation of Gita Govinda of Jayadeva*.

Gayatri Bhattacharya
Translation of 'The Blue-necked God' by Indira Goswami

Gayatri Bhattacharya is a retired professor of English at the University of Guwahati. She has translated ten books from Assamese to English, including the classic *Jivanar Batot* by Birinchi Kumar Barua.

H.S. Shivaprakash
Translation of Subrahmanya Bharathiyar

H.S. Shivaprakash is a poet and playwright writing in Kannada. In 2012, he received the Sahitya Akademi Award. He is professor at the School of Arts and Aesthetics, Jawaharlal Nehru University, New Delhi, and was the Director of the Tagore Centre at Berlin, administered by the Indian Council for Cultural Relations, Government of India. He has seven anthologies of poems, twelve plays and several other books to his credit.

Harsha V. Dehejia
The Heart-throb of Chaitanya

Harsha V. Dehejia has a double doctorate, one in medicine and the other in ancient Indian culture, both from Mumbai University, India. He teaches Hinduism and has a special interest in Hindu aesthetics. He is a doctor of medicine and a professor of Indian studies at Ottawa, Canada. His special interest is in Krishna *shringara*. He has twenty-five books, two films and six curated exhibitions to his credit.

Indira Goswami
The Blue-necked God

Indira Goswami was a pre-eminent Assamese writer, known for her fresh and original style with novel themes. When taking on the tough social issues of urban life, the harsh lives of labourers and the plight of widows in Vrindavana and Assam, Goswami displayed great empathy and compassion. Considered an expert on Ramayana literature, Goswami's voluminous works on the Assamese and Hindi Ramayanas won her many laurels. She won the Sahitya Akademi Award in 1983 for her novel *Mamore Dhora Torowal*. In July 2001 Goswami was awarded the Jnanpith, India's highest literary award.

Jawhar Sircar
In Search of the Historical Radha

Jawhar Sircar was culture secretary from 2008–12 and then the chief executive officer of Prasar Bharati, India's public service broadcaster that runs All India Radio and Doordarshan. He has published several articles and research papers on history, culture and society. His focus is on specific aspects of Hindu myths and beliefs, in an attempt to decipher the underlying societal conflicts and their dynamics.

John S. Hawley
Translation of Surdas

John Stratton Hawley—informally, Jack—is Claire Tow Professor of Religion at Barnard College, Columbia University. He has written or edited over twenty books on Hinduism, India's bhakti traditions and the comparative study of religion. Hawley has directed Columbia University's South Asia Institute, has been a Guggenheim Fellow and Fulbright–Nehru Fellow and has been elected to the American Academy of Arts and Sciences.

Kapila Vatsyayan
Gita Govinda: Illustrated Manuscripts from Rajasthan

Kapila Vatsyayan is an internationally recognized scholar of Indian arts and literature, dance, drama, etc. She has written over twenty publications and nearly 200 articles. She has been awarded the fellowship of the Sangeet Natak Akademi and the Lalit Kala Akademi and many other institutions. She is a recipient of the Padma Vibhushan. She was formerly secretary, Department of Arts, Ministry of HRD; academic director, Indira Gandhi National Centre for the Arts; member, UNESCO Executive Board; and member of Parliament (Rajya Sabha–nominated).

Lalit Kumar
Lovelorn Radha, Forlorn God: Tagore's *Bhanusingher Padavali*

Lalit Kumar teaches English at Deen Dayal Upadhyaya College, University of Delhi. He has extensively translated and back-translated from the Hindi and the Maithili into English. He has also contributed to the editorial page of national dailies like the *Times of India* and the *Pioneer*. His research interests include translation and translation studies, Indian and European classical literature, 18th-century British literature and reforms in the education sector.

Lee Siegel
Translation of Jayadeva

Lee A. Siegel is a novelist and emeritus professor of religion at the University of Hawaii at Manoa. Siegel studied comparative literature at the University of California, Berkeley, and fine arts at Columbia University. His many books include: *Love in a Dead Language*, *Love and Other Games of Chance*, *Love and the Incredibly Old Man* and, most recently, *Trance-Migrations: Stories of India, Tales of Hypnosis*.

Madhureeta Anand
Radhe Radhe

Madhureeta Anand is an Indian independent film director, writer and producer. She has directed two feature films, written five, directed many documentary films and series, spanning an array of genres. Many of her films have won national and international awards. She writes for various publications and has been featured in several books and magazines. She is also an activist for women's rights and the rights of other minorities.

Makarand R. Paranjape
Enjoying God: The Divine Paramour

Makarand R. Paranjape is currently director, Indian Institute of Advanced Study, Shimla. Professor of English at Jawaharlal Nehru University, New Delhi, he has published over forty-five books, 170 academic papers and 500 articles in newspapers and periodicals. His books include *Decolonization and Development: Hind Swaraj Revisited*, *Nativism: Essays in Literary Criticism* (ed.), *Another Canon: Indian Texts and Traditions in English* and *Altered Destinations: Self, Society, and*

Nation in India. His poetry collections include *Playing the Dark God* and *Confluence.* He has also published short stories and a novel.

Mandakranta Bose
Sita and Radha: From Human to Divine

Mandakranta Bose is Professor Emerita and till recently Director of the Centre for India and South Asia Research at the University of British Columbia, Vancouver. Her research interests comprise performing arts texts in Sanskrit, the Ramayana, the Hindu tradition and gender studies. Her two most recent books are *The Ramayana in Bengali Paṭas* (New Delhi: Niyogi Books, 2017) and *The Goddess* (an edited volume, Oxford: Oxford University Press, 2018). Dr Bose has been a visiting professor at many universities, including Calcutta and Oxford.

Meghnad Desai
Radha and the Completion of Krishna

Lord Meghnad Desai is Emeritus Professor of Economics at the London School of Economics. He has written or edited nearly thirty-eight books. His latest two books are *Politic Shock: Trump, Modi, Brexit and the Prospects for Liberal Democracy* and *The Raisina Model: Indian Democracy at Seventy.* He is a life peer at the British House of Lords.

Pavan K. Varma
Krishna: The Playful Divine

Pavan K. Varma is a writer-diplomat, and is now in the field of politics, where he was till recently an MP in the Rajya Sabha and, earlier, adviser to the Chief Minister of Bihar, with a rank of cabinet minister. The author of over a dozen bestselling books, he has served as the Indian ambassador to several countries; was director of the Nehru Centre in London; was official spokesperson of the Ministry of External Affairs; and was press secretary to the President of India.

He is currently the national general secretary and national spokesman of the Janata Dal (United).

Pradip Khandwalla
Translation of Narsinh Mehta

Pradip Khandwalla is a translator and researcher on creative thinking who has published several books, including *Fourth Eye: Excellence through Creativity*. Khandwalla is a professor at IIM Ahmedabad, an organization theorist and management scholar.

Priya Sarukkai Chabria
Translation of Andal

Priya Sarukkai Chabria is an award-winning translator, poet and writer acclaimed for her radical aesthetics. Her books include speculative fiction, literary non-fiction, two poetry collections, a novel and translations from classical Tamil of the mystic Andal. Her anthology publications include *Another English: Anglophone Poems from Around the World*, *The HarperCollins Book of English Poetry*, *South Asian Review*, *PEN International*. Her forthcoming books include the anthology (ed.) *Fafnir's Heart World Poetry* (translation, Bombaykala Books, 2018) and speculative fiction, *Clone* (Zubaan, 2018, University of Chicago Press, 2019). She edits poetry at Sangam.

Ramakanta Rath
Sri Radha

Ramakanta Rath is a renowned modernist poet in Odia literature. He received the Sahitya Akademi Award in 1977, the Bishuva Samman in 1990, the Saraswathi Samman in 1992 and the prestigious Padma Bhushan in 2006. He was the president of the Sahitya Akademi of India from 1998–2003, and received the Sahitya Akademi Fellowship a few years later. Along with an illustrious career as a civil servant, Ramakanta Rath published his poetry to great acclaim, *Sri*

Radha in particular being a path-breaker in creative form. A number of his poems have been translated into English and other Indian languages.

Reba Som
Radha in Nazrul Geeti

Reba Som is a doctorate from Calcutta University and the recipient of the prestigious Jawaharlal Nehru Fellowship in 2000–02. She has served as director of ICCR, Kolkata (2008–13). Her publications include *Gandhi, Nehru and Bose: The Making of the Modern Indian Mind* (Penguin Books, New Delhi, 2004), *Rabindranath Tagore: The Singer and His Song* (Penguin Books, New Delhi, 2009) and *Margot: Sister Nivedita of Vivekananda* (Penguin Random House, New Delhi, 2017). A trained singer of Rabindra Sangeet and Nazrul Geeti, Reba Som's compact-disc albums *Selected Songs of Rabindranath Tagore* (Saregama) and *Love Songs of Kazi Nazrul Islam* (Times Music, 2016) include her English translations of the Bengali lyrics.

Renuka Narayanan
Radha: The Unfading Mystic Blossom in Our Midst

Renuka Narayanan is a commentator and columnist on religion and culture. She presently writes for the *Times of India*. Her published books include *The Book of Prayer, Faith: Filling the God-sized Hole, The Little Book of Indian Wisdom, A Madrasi Memoir, The Path of Light: Tales from the Upanishads, Jatakas and Indic Lore* and *Hindu Fables from the Vedas to Vivekananda*. She is presently working on a book on Shiva.

Shrivatsa Goswami
Radha: The Play and Perfection of Rasa

Acharya Shrivatsa Goswami is a member of an eminent family of spiritual leaders and scholars at Sri Radha Raman Temple, Vrindavana. His writings have been published by the university presses of Princeton, Berkeley, Oxford and others. Goswami is the director of Vraja Prakalpa, a multidisciplinary research project jointly sponsored by Sri Chaitanya Prema Samsthana and the Indira Gandhi National Centre for the Arts. Several volumes on the various facets of Vraja culture are already published.

Shubha Vilas
Understanding Radha's Symbolic Love

Shubha Vilas is a TEDx speaker, lifestyle coach, storyteller and author. He studied patent law after completing his engineering degree. But, finally, he chose the path of a spiritual seeker. He is the author of the bestselling books *Open-eyed Meditations* and Ramayana: The Game of Life series. The focus of his work is the application of scriptural wisdom in day-to-day living and addressing the needs of corporates and youth through thought-provoking seminars. He has delivered more than 4000 lectures across the globe. He has also been a visiting speaker at the Indian Institute of Management Ranchi, the Massachusetts Institute of Technology (MIT) and other institutions.

Sri Aurobindo
Translation of Chandidas

Sri Aurobindo, born Aurobindo Ghose (1872–1950) was an Indian philosopher, yogi, guru, poet and nationalist. He joined the Indian movement for independence from British rule for some years and was an influential leader. After being jailed for his political activities and realizing that his path lay elsewhere, he became a spiritual reformer. From his ashram in Pondicherry he spoke and wrote extensively about his vision of human progress and spiritual evolution.

Tarashankar Bandopadhyay
Raikamal

Tarashankar Bandyopadhyay was a leading Bengali novelist. He was awarded the Rabindra Puraskar, the Sahitya Akademi Award, the Jnanpith Award, the Padma Shri and the Padma Bhushan.

Yudit K. Greenberg
Integrating the Natural, the Divine and the Erotic in the *Gita Govinda* and *Shir Ha-Shirim*

Yudit Kornberg Greenberg is the Cornell Endowed Chair of Religion and founding director of the Jewish Studies Program at Rollins College, Florida. She lectures internationally on topics in modern and contemporary Jewish thought, comparative religion and women and religion. Her recent books include *The Body in Religion: Crosscultural Perspectives* and *Dharma and Halacha: Comparative Studies in Hindu–Jewish Philosophy and Religion*. Dr Greenberg is the recipient of numerous awards including the Fulbright–Nehru Scholar Award at the University of Mumbai in 2019.

COPYRIGHT ACKNOWLEDGEMENTS

Grateful acknowledgement is made to the following for permission to reprint copyright material:

Amal Shankar Bandopadhyay for permission to use Tarashankar Bandopadhyay's original story 'Raikamal' in a new English translation.

BR Publishing for the use of Canto I and Canto II (extracts from English), originally published in *In Praise of Krishna: Translation of Gita Govinda of Jayadeva*, edited and translated by Durgadas Mukhopadhyay.

Clay Sanskrit Library for the use of Canto 4, Song 9, originally published in *Gita-govinda: Love Songs of Radha and Krishna, by Jayadeva*, translated by Lee Siegel.

Devdutt Pattanaik for the use of the essay 'A Milkmaid Called Radha', from his website http://devdutt.com/articles/indian-mythology/a-milkmaid-called-radha.html.

Harsha V. Dehejia for the use of the essay 'The Heart-throb of Chaitanya', originally published in *Radha: From Gopi to Goddess*, ed. Harsha V. Dehejia, 2014.

H.S. Shivaprakash for the use of his translation of a poem by Subrahmanya Bharathiyar, beginning, 'On the island of love O! Radhe Radhe . . .'

John Stratton Hawley for the use of his translation of the poem by Surdas titled 'Radha Is Lost.'

Kapila Vatsyayan for the use of the selected section '*Gita Govinda*: Illustrated Manuscripts from Rajasthan', originally published as an 'Introduction' to *The Darbhanga Gita-Govinda*, 2011.

Lalit Kumar for the translation of a poem by Tagore, 'Vasant Aaval Re' (Spring Is Here), from his essay 'Lovelorn Radha, Forlorn God: Tagore's *Bhanusingher Padavali*'.

Makarand R. Paranjape for the use of the essay 'Enjoying God: The Divine Paramour', originally published in *Radha: From Gopi to Goddess*, ed. Harsha V. Dehejia, 2014.

Malashri Lal for the use of her translation of the verse from Bihari, beginning 'Hungry for Krishna's love, she hides his flute.'

Mandakranta Bose for the use of the section 'Sita and Radha: From Human to Divine', originally published in *Women in the Hindu Tradition: Rules, Roles and Exceptions*, Routledge, 2010.

Manoa journal and Andrew Schelling for the use of the poem 'And What of Those Arbors', originally published in *Bright as the Autumn Moon: Fifty Poems from Sanskrit*.

Motilal Banarsidass for the use of the two poems 'Signs of Youth' and 'First Joy', from *Love Songs of Vidyapati*, translated by Deben Bhattacharya and edited by W.G. Archer.

Pavan K. Varma for the use of an extract from the chapter 'Lover', originally published in *Krishna: The Playful Divine*, Viking, Penguin Books India, 1993.

Priya Sarukkai Chabria for one song, 'The Sacred Songs of the Lady', originally in *Andal: The Autobiography of a Goddess*, published by Zubaan.

Pushpa Bharati for permission to translate two poems 'Under the Mango Tree' and 'Words: Meaningless', originally in *Kanupriya* by Dharamvir Bharati.

Rajendra Patel and Pradip Khandwalla for the use of the poem 'Artless Milkmaid', originally published in *Beyond the Beaten Track: Offbeat Poems from Gujarat.*

Ramakanta Rath for the use of extracts from 'Sri Radha', translated by the author from the original *Sri Radha.*

Sabita Sarma for permitting the reprint of a translation by Gayatri Bhattacharya of Indira Goswami's novel *Nilakantha Braja*—in English, *The Blue-necked God*, Chapter 2, published by Zubaan, 2014.

Shrivatsa Goswami and the Graduate Theological Union, University of California, Berkeley, for the use of a selection from the essay 'Radha: The Play and Perfection of Rasa', originally published in *The Divine Consort: Radha and the Goddesses of India*, eds. John Stratton Hawley and D.M. Wulff, 1982.

Shubha Vilas Das for contributing a text by Rupa Goswami, used in ISKCON: 'Pleased with any person . . . Shri Radha's personal associates.'

Vikas Bamba for the use of a translation of a poem by Chandidas, 'O Love, what more shall I, shall Radha speak', from the website titled *Collected Works of Sri Aurobindo* (http://www.collectedworksofsriaurobindo.com).

While every effort has been made to trace copyright holders and obtain permission, this has not been possible in all cases; any omissions brought to our attention will be remedied in future editions.

INDEX

In Search of Sita: Revisiting Mythology
Namita Gokhale and Malashri Lal

Who was Sita, and what does she mean to contemporary India?

Sita is one of the defining figures of Indian womanhood, yet there is no single version of her story. Different accounts coexist in myth, literature and folktale. Canonical texts deify Sita while regional variations humanize her. Folk songs and ballads connect her timeless predicament to the daily lives of rural women. Modern-day women continue to see themselves reflected in films, serials and soap operas based on Sita's narrative. Sacrifice, self-denial and unquestioning loyalty are some of the ideals associated with popular perceptions of Sita. But the Janaki who symbolized strength, who could lift Shiva's mighty bow, who courageously chose to accompany Rama into exile and who refused to follow him back after a second trial, is often forgotten. However she is remembered, revered or written about, Sita continues to exert a powerful influence on the collective Indian psyche. In Search of Sita presents essays, conversations and commentaries that explore different aspects of her life. It revisits mythology, reopening the debate on her birth, her days in exile, her abduction, the test by fire, the birth of her sons and, finally, her return to the earth—offering fresh interpretations of this enigmatic figure and her indelible impact on our everyday lives.